D0713207

Brain-Behavior Relationships

Brain-Behavior Relationships

Edited by
James R. Merikangas
Yale University School of Medicine

LexingtonBooks
D.C. Heath and Company
Lexington, Massachusetts
Toronto

Library of Congress Cataloging in Publication Data

Main entry under title:
  Brain-behavior relationships.

  Includes index.
  1. Neuropsychiatry. 2. Neuropsychology. 3. Brain-Diseases. 4. Human
behavior. I. Merikangas, James R. [DNLM: 1. Brain—Physiology. 2. Brain
diseases—Physiopathology. 3. Mental disorders—Etiology. WL 348 B813]
RC343.B666   616.89'071   79-2075
ISBN 0-669-03082-1

Published simultaneously in Canada

Printed in the United States of America

International Standard Book Number: 0-669-03082-1

Library of Congress Catalog Card Number: 79-2075

To Vernon B. Mountcastle, M.D.,
scientist and teacher

Contents

Introduction

Regardless of the school of psychology to which one subscribes, there must be consensus on one point: diseases of the brain are accompanied by disordered behavior.

The dispute begins when certain symptoms or syndromes are discussed, that is, the thought disorder conventionally called schizophrenia, the poverty of thought and movement of some depressive syndromes, and the incredible energy and grandiose ideation of the manic. These prototypic psychiatric illnesses lack a known etiology, but the alterations in human functioning are no less profound than the hemiparesis of a cerebral vascular accident or the tremor and rigidity of Parkinson's disease. Huntington's chorea has symptoms of both a movement disorder and a thought disorder, yet it is classified as a neurologic disease rather than a psychiatric illness.

What then is the distinction between the subject matter of neurology and psychiatry? Are they to be divided along a behavioral axis of higher to lower brain functions, or autonomic to voluntary nervous systems, or disorders with detectable neuropathology from those without? Perhaps the distinction should be peripheral nervous system (neurology) versus central nervous system (psychiatry). The distinction by therapy has broken down: neurologists use drugs and somatic therapies, but in the past fifty years psychiatrists also have discovered effective pharmacologic and somatic therapies. Both specialities use some form of psychotherapy for patients who do not respond satisfactorily to drugs.

Neurologists touch the patient and do a physical examination, take a history, get laboratory tests, and prescribe medication. At least on inpatient services, psychiatric patients get a physical and laboratory tests. It is an amazing fact that outpatients can get drugs from some psychiatrists without having a physical or any laboratory determinations. Psychotherapy is of course available from professionals who are not medical doctors, without even a diagnostic workup or medical prescription.

My viewpoint is that such distinctions are artificial. The real basis of separation of psychiatry and neurology is operational. Neurology is what neurologists do; psychiatry is what psychiatrists do.

What then is behavioral neurology? Behavioral neurology seeks the neurological basis for disorders that affect the intellectual life of individuals. As Freud moved from neurology to psychoanalysis around the problem of hysteria and conversion, so modern psychiatrists and neurologists are converging on the problems of human behavior with the investigation of neurotransmitters and psychoactive drugs. Dopa, GABA, norepinephrine, prostaglandins, and endorphins only begin the list. Drugs like L-dopa and the phenothiazines have diverse and multiple actions on the same synapses. These drugs have profound effects on thought, mood, and behavior, and therefore anyone observing their actions is forced to reconsider psychological or sociological theories of mental disorder.

Even functional disorders have genetic and therefore metabolic factors in their etiologies. The definition of functional illness is becoming predicated on treatment modality. Psychotherapy becomes the common denominator for diseases of unknown etiology: functional disorders.

In this book, the contributors examine these questions from differing biochemical, physiological, anthropological, and clinical viewpoints, but with the common bias that the brain is the organ of behavior and that understanding its function will enrich the particularly human aspects of people's lives.

**Brain-Behavior
Relationships**

1 Cultural Programming of Brain-Behavior Relations: A Neuropsychiatric Emphasis

Horacio Fabrega, Jr.

Introduction

All of us are aware that people of different societies and in isolated parts of the globe behave differently. They speak different languages, endorse different values, follow different religious precepts, reflect different social conventions, and engage in different types and levels of physical and social activity during the daily cycle. That such behavioral differences exist is today a truism. Anthropologists explain these differences as the result of cultural factors. As participants in our own society, we are aware of great variability in the behavior of others, a fact which we explain as due to personality, social upbringing, or heredity. Any psychiatrist or neurologist is aware that patients who are diagnosed as having the same disease often behave very differently; in other words, that the manifestations of and responses to any one disease entity vary across individuals. In summary, the prevalence of behavioral differences in either a healthy or neurobiologically ill person is a basic assumption in the social, biologic, and clinical sciences.

In this chapter I present a way of looking at the problem of how cultural factors might affect the behavior of patients with psychiatric or neurologic illnesses. I also focus somewhat on behavior of individuals who are not ill. I approach this problem of culture and behavior by giving emphasis to neurobiologic factors. I begin by providing a set of definitions and defining aspects of the problem of culture and brain-behavior differences. I then review pertinent literature in psychiatry, neurology, and the social sciences which bear on the problem. I conclude by offering some speculations about how culture might influence the manifestations of behavioral neurology (or neuropsychiatric) syndromes.

Background and Definitions

Culture

Culture is a system of social symbols and their meanings. To a cultural anthropologist the object of analysis and description is the semiotic dimen-

1

sion of human affairs: the array of signs, symbols, and concepts a people use to communicate with each other and to interpret themselves and the world around them. Culture might also be defined as the historically derived patterns of thinking and feeling, including the programs for behaving that are shared in large part by all members of a particular society. It should be clear that the referent of this definition is somehow carried in the mind or in the head. Adopting the doctrine of psychoneuronal identity, it seems reasonable to posit the culture can be equated, at least analytically, with a pattern of neural organization.

Some questions which engage the cultural anthropologist can be surmised: what is the relationship of meaning to language? Meaning might refer to words in isolation, to whole sentences, or to the ways in which words and sentences are used in conversations. Similarly, what is the relationship of meaning to thought? How do meaning and thought relate to overt social behavior, including the way members of a society arrange themselves in space? And finally, what is the relationship between language and culture? At the level of the individual person, this question can be restated: what are the boundaries between linguistic and cultural knowledge and how are these types of knowledge used during communication and action? These issues were recently discussed by Keesing [1].

Implicit in my definition of culture is the notion that culture is learned. An individual is not born "showing culture," but rather with the capacity to learn the system of meanings endorsed by his family. Moreover, culture is learned as an individual grows and matures physically. The development, organization, and eventual functioning of the central nervous system (CNS) all take place as the individual learns his culture so that influences linked to culture come to affect and to be embodied in the CNS.

I defined culture as a special type of environmental factor or influence. A system of social symbols (meanings) refers to a people's understanding, something which they learn and which is somehow linked to language and thought. A cultural anthropologist is interested in examining the various ways in which culture operates in a given context or situation and he will in fact be seeking ways of understanding the reality to which the people subscribe. The logic, structure, and rationale of social activity viewed symbolically (symbolic behavior) and purely for its own sake—regardless of other determining factors—are what will claim his interest. If one were to find a mythical group whose members operated without brains, livers, or hearts, the cultural anthropologist's interest in culture would in no way weaken, for the relevance of these physical organs to his domain of interest is not critical.

However, we are interested in behavioral organizations construed as outputs of concrete persons with brains, livers, and hearts. As observers interested in separating out different types of influences operating on a given phenomenon (in this instance, behavior), we seem driven to distinguish among environmental influences, both physical (things like diet or altitude) and nonphysical (social, cultural, or symbolic), and also between environmental and nonenvironmental influences, specifically genetic factors. To the claim of the cultural anthropologist that behaviors of a certain type reflect culture, we often counter that they really reflect genetic influences or organic factors.

Exchanges such as these illustrate the nature-nurture quandary which is integral to the study of biologic phenomena, especially human social behavior. We have little problem in understanding that eye color or blood-group substances (a class of phenotypes) are mainly genetically determined. Even color blindness, we unproblematically accept, is largely genetic though we would be prepared to accept that the intrauterine environment of the fetus might possibly contribute some variance to this phenotype. The possible role of cultural factors as symbolic phenomena in affecting things such as these seems remote indeed if not nonsensical.

Yet there is a way in which "culture" as symbolic phenomena could be made relevant. If one could show that eating preferences and social living habits (symbolic phenomena) affected maternal nutritional status and health and that these in turn influenced dramatically the intrauterine environment of a pregnant mother, then a way would be open for a discussion of possible cultural influences in eye color or color vision. A seeming competition between culture and physical environmental factors, and indeed between environment and genes, can in fact be said to be inherent in analysis of most biologic phenomena whose form or structure varies across individuals. It is precisely because competitions of this type are so integral to explanations of phenomena like human social behavior that we are forced to give up the quest for either/or solutions of the problem of understanding their bases or causes. I hope to succeed in illustrating that for certain classes of human behavior problems it simply is not feasible or appropriate to reduce analysis to either/or perspectives, but rather to acknowledge an indeterminacy of sorts and indeed a complementarity. Because of the inseparability of biologic and cultural sources of variation in human behavior we use the term *biocultural*. We are left, nonetheless, with the need to understand how symbolic phenomena (culture) might affect brain organization: function and behavior.

Neuropsychiatric Disease and Illness

I define a neuropsychiatric disease as a physical change in the CNS which produces a disturbance in higher-cortical functions. A neuropsychiatric disease obviously varies in intensity and duration. When I speak of disease I refer to biomedical and physical phenomena. On the other hand, I define a neuropsychiatric illness as consisting of disturbances or alterations of psychologic and social behavior and functioning. Such behavioral phenomena are observable and rooted in a social context. Because I make a logical distinction between certain types of phenomena (the ontology of disease versus that of illness) it is possible to claim that someone could have a disease without an illness and vice versa. These stipulations are consistent with those discussed in other publications [2, 3].

A neuropsychiatric disease or illness has to be recognized (perceived, labeled, acted upon, and so on). The process of recognizing a neuro-psychiatric illness is social; that is, the process entails moral and jural considerations and involves the rights and responsibilities of people. Now a class of neuropsychiatric illnesses (severe and chronic) appear to be recognized unproblematically in all societies. This type of illness thus seems to be a universal in human groups. Societies have terms, nomenclatures, and theories about such illnesses. The remaining neuropsychiatric illnesses (those that are neither severe nor chronic) seem to be recognized problematically: this is to say that a social negotiation of some sort is involved, having political ramifications [4, 5, 6].

Psychologic and Social Behavior

In a very concrete sense one is led to posit the concept of culture as a way of explaining or at least accounting in some parsimonious way for differences in behavior. In other words, it is as a result of noting large group differences in the way people live and behave that scientists were led to invent the concept of culture. Thus culture and behavior are linked together in some significant way. For our purposes, behavior having cultural significance can be looked at from two distinct standpoints. By social behaviors one can refer to activities such as gestures, demeanor, facial displays, and simple or coordinated actions (including the performance aspects of language and speech) which are viewed in an interindividual context. The appropriate performance of a social role belongs in this category of behavior. As summarized in detail elsewhere, social behavior is a category that both social and biologic scientists have fruitfully applied to human and infrahuman groups. This category of behavior has been equated with the functioning of the frontal systems of the brain.

Behaviors which reflect internal discriminative processes and which are correlated with observable social behaviors are here termed *psychologic*. They often imply learning and, in humans, the internalizations of shared symbols and rules. Each category of behavior (social and psychologic) logically implies the other. Psychologic behaviors embrace such things as thinking, perceiving, interpretation of actions, rules for expressing actions, remembering, and problem solving. Although psychologic implies conscious or deliberate, it has to be acknowledged that many psychologic behaviors cannot easily be judged in this fashion. The problem of volition and awareness will not be tackled directly here, though facets of this are discussed later. An individual's capacity for and creativity of language will be viewed as a component of psychologic behavior.

Psychologic and social behaviors which are disvalued and which deviate from established norms are what make up illness [2, 3]. Adopting a semiotic perspective one could say that psychologic and social behavior changes of certain types are the signs of illness, where a sign is taken to mean a referent which is integral to or physically a part of that to which it refers. One could also say that psychologic and social behavior changes constitute symbols of disease. In semiotic theory a symbol is not integrally connected to that which it refers to but rather represents it on the basis of arbitrary conventions. Consequently, by convention certain behaviors are judged to symbolize or express an underlying disease process which is physically separate.

Signs of Disease

The word *disease* has been defined as referring to physical changes in the body. These changes are elicited or measured using biomedical criteria. Since a sign is integral to or a physical part of that to which it refers, we can speak of signs of disease and mean phenomena which physically indicate disease: such things as swellings, discolorations, lumps, and emanations from body orifices such as vomitus or diarrhea. Many signs of disease are not visible to the naked eye but rather hidden from view and observed or measured by instruments which in effect extend one's powers of observation; but the phenomena observed and recorded are equally physical and also constitute signs of disease.

Certain behaviors constitute signs of disease. We can term these *sensorimotor behaviors*. In this category are placed reflexes, postural changes, muscular tone, sensory changes, and the coordination of finely graded muscular contractions which are viewed purely as physical phenomena. Covert (hidden) vegetative responses involving the viscera, blood vessels, and organs are also sensorimotor behaviors. Such behaviors are ordinarily studied by neurobiologists and physical anthropologists. They are associated with (that is underlie or serve as substrates for) social and psychologic behaviors but can be studied independently of them.

**Three Types of Brain-Behavior
Relationships in Humans**

I would like now to briefly review three ways in which one can look at the
problem of brain-behavior relationships in humans. My aim is to summarize the ways in which different types of scientists conceptualize brain-
behavior relations and the relevance this has for behavioral neurology and
neuropsychiatry.

Intrasocial or Personality Domain

Persons of Pittsburgh of any well-demarcated age and social group when ill
due to a specific disease will display different behavioral changes and be
preoccupied with different types of concerns. They will, of course, appear
to share basic premises about reality and their way of thinking, perceiving,
and remembering could be said to be similar. But despite this, one could
point to differences in behavior. We explain this as due to personality or
psychosocial factors. Insofar as behavior is the output of a brain one can
properly speak of personality or psychosocial programming of the brain.
We can explain this programming in different ways; psychoanalysis and
behavior-reinforcing principles come to mind. It seems that most neuroscientists are referring to this particular type of brain-behavior relationship
when they speak of the mind-body problem. A recent exposition or theory
of this problem is presented by Mountcastle and Edelman [8].

Cultural-Linguistic Domain

Consider now two highly different societies which we will term society A and
society B. Members of A are literate, school-educated, and speak an Indo-
European language. Those of B live in the highlands of a remote continent,
are not literate or school-educated, and speak a non-Indo-European language
whose lexicon and grammar differ substantially from the language spoken by
the members of A. The life-styles of the two groups are sharply different. In
choosing to distinguish the groups on the basis of literateness, formal education, and language structure (as well as life-style differences that go with this),
I have maximized the likelihood of the existence of what anthropologists,
linguists, and psychologists speak of as cultural differences. Now in certain
respects members of A and B can be said to differ in their behavior; one could
say that differences appear to exist in such areas as use of color terminology,
memory, and thinking. Members of both groups all obviously perceive, re-

member, and think; and moreover behavioral variation obviously exists among members of group A and those of group B. But the point is that superimposed on intrasocietal differences are group differences. If there exists behavior differences across these two groups in the areas noted, then in some way the organization and functioning of the brains of members of the two groups differ. When psychiatrically or neurologically ill, members of A and B might be expected to show different patterns of illness. I am referring to this type of brain-behavior difference as a cultural one involving some form or level of brain organization and function. It is this type of brain-behavior relation that constitutes the subject of this chapter.

Phylogenetic Domain

Work in primatology reveals a high degree of social organization in infrahuman primates. Individual members of a foraging group are seen to engage in any number of behavioral activities. The cognitive abilities of chimpanzees and baboons are well known, and include a sense of self, ability to orient spatially (to represent the world and make discriminations about it), and ability to communicate emotionally and through symbols. Although there is great controversy about the nature of the differences in the cognitive activities of infrahuman primates versus those of man (are these differences qualitative or quantitative), the existence of some form of difference is accepted and includes speech, elaborate propositional thinking, and capacity to remove self from the now and project oneself forward or backward in time. These behavioral differences between humans and infrahuman primates, one intuitively believes, are associated with differences in brain organization and function. One can say that these differences reflect a phylogenetic type of brain-behavior relationship [7].

Some Clinical Psychiatric Problems

I would like to discuss now some clinical psychiatric issues which pointedly raise the question of brain-behavior relations in the cultural domain. My goal is to analyze briefly two types of clinical psychiatric issues in relation to the ideas of culture: so-called culture-bound or culture-specific disorders and major psychiatric disorders. My strategy in this discussion is to first present a very brief summary of what is known about the behavioral differences in these two classes of psychiatric problems and then to touch on the way the question of cultural programming of the brain seems to be handled if at all.

Culture-Bound or Culture-Specific Disorders

For well over the last half century anthropologists and then psychiatrists have been interested in the nature of certain behavior disturbances which were seen in specific cultures or regions of the world. Some of these disturbances (variously called culture-bound syndromes or disorders) are familiar and include Bena Bena, amok, koro, susto, Windigo psychosis, and arctic hysteria. Their properties appear to include (1) abrupt onset, (2) relatively short duration (days, seldom weeks, though information here is notoriously weak), and (3) absence of what psychiatrists term a *formal thought disturbance*. In some instances, persons afflicted show unusual mental content and hyperactivity, and though behavior can appear to us as bizarre, it must be judged as reasonably organized. In other words, the behavior in question makes sense to the group. In fact, it is the coherence and pattern inherent in the manifestations of these disturbances that render them interesting and important. Some of the disturbances are characterized by mental symptoms whose content is highly specific (koro, fear of the penis disappearing) and in some instances symbolic (Windigo, possession by a mythologically important spirit leading to a craving for human flesh, eventually cannibalism).

In general, culture-bound syndromes raise basic kinds of questions about the nature of psychiatric disease and illness. Thus, since the disturbances are so radically different in manifestations, their mere existence underlines the important role of culture in providing content and organization to behavior disturbances. The specificity of the content of the culture-bound syndromes has drawn attention to social and psychodynamic influences. Conversely, their neurobiologic basis has been all but neglected and the question of brain-behavior relations simply not raised. Since purely psychosocial emphases have until recently been prominent in psychiatry as a whole, this is hardly surprising.

One dominating opinion about the culture-bound syndromes seems to be that they are in some way reactive to sociocultural circumstances and that they are atypical variations of psychogenic disturbances which are felt to have a very wide distribution in human populations anyway. It scarcely needs mentioning that the words *reactive* and *psychogenic* raise problems for anyone trying to formulate an understanding of psychiatric disease and illness; the words, as it were, block out the nervous system. That the nervous system is grossly affected in some varieties and instances of culture-bound disturbances is very clear, for persons afflicted sometimes show features of a toxic or confusional psychosis with an impairment in the level of consciousness which is followed by amnesia. In other instances, a phobic or obsessive hyperalerted state without impaired consciousness is found. There is little more that can be said about the neurologic substrates of culture-bound syndromes. I want to emphasize the poverty of information which exists about the phenomenology and behavioral manifestations of the culture-bound disturbances; relatively few firsthand, in-depth, and clinically relevant descriptions of culture-bound syndromes exist. Moreover, discussions about neurologic substrates are almost totally lacking. A recent critical review of the literature dealing with the concept, supporting evidence for and validity of the so-called atypical psychoses, concluded that problems of methodology, sampling, and diagnosis preclude drawing firm generalizations about the nature of these psychoses. The reviewer included in his analysis so-called culture-bound syndromes [9].

In raising the topic of level of consciousness, confusion, amnesia, and attention in some persons with culture-bound disturbances, I mean to touch base with the subject of my discussion: brain-behavior relations and cultural programming. In reflecting on culture-bound syndromes one is left with two classes of phenomena which cannot be adequately bridged in contemporary behavioral neurology or in neuropsychiatry: a range of culturally interpretable behaviors varying in degree of organization and an altered state of brain function (which varies as to visibility). Thus persons showing culture-bound disturbances, like those showing many American culture-behavior disturbances, reflect concerns, preoccupations, and themes integral to the social milieu in which they live. Their behavior is patterned and channeled in ways which reflect prevailing values, conventions, and concerns. In some instances, one can indeed point to behavioral indicators of an underlying brain disorder, and in many other instances such evidence is not as yet available to us but we assume that there exists a correlated neurologic disturbance nonetheless. At present, we can say very little more than this. Obviously, the question of causation begs to be answered: what brought this syndrome on; is the primary cause a psychosocial one? Attempting to answer this question is beyond the scope of this chapter. Physical disease changes in certain lower centers of the brain (so-called limbic lobe, diencephalon, and brainstem) are currently held to underlie or produce psychiatric illness manifestations. These physical changes in the brain can be primary (originate there) or secondary (originate elsewhere), but in either case they will produce significant behavior changes in areas affected by the subcortical centers. Psychiatric illness behaviors may not as clearly reflect their physiologic structure as do neurologic illnesses, such as those consisting of motor weakness and paralysis (in the case of a stroke). However, there is unquestionably a physiologic-anatomic basis to them.

A factor that partly obscures the neuroanatomic and neurophysiologic patternings and bases of psychiatric illness behavior such as seen in culture-bound syndromes is worth making explicit at this juncture. This involves the fact that in these illnesses the lesion appears to be early or proximal in the chain eventuating in human behavior. This chain leading to behavior has many influences connecting to it, which is another way of saying that the neural system involved is relatively open. Moreover, the lesion does not involve a neural system whose anatomic features are like those of sensorimotor systems that is, systems containing fairly specific representations of activities structured neuroanatomically in terms of pathways with direct and differential accessibility to lower-neural centers which regulate action and sensation. Neural systems responsible for psychiatric illness appear to serve more generic activities, such as attention and motivation. The systems are not prepotent for discrete actions or movements or for elementary sensations, but for general mental functions which are realized in psychologic and social behaviors.

A paralysis, on the other hand, is based on a lesion somewhat late or distal in a linear chain eventuating in behavior. This is to say that the lesion affects a system whose anatomy gives it direct and differential access to motor neurons controlling movement and action. In this sense, the neural system eventuating in behavior is relatively closed. A paralysis also constitutes a physical constraint on behavior; the person's behavior clearly becomes disordered or impaired, and he suffers socially and psychologically from this. However, in a person with a stroke, basic elements of identity (conception of self, capacity to think, feel, relate socially, remember, plan, deploy attention) remain relatively unchanged. In certain ways in a stroke victim, his identity and self stand outside the illness and one can enlist his support to understand and deal with the illness. In psychiatric illness, on the other hand, basic elements of the self seem to be more directly affected by the illness. In this instance, then, culturally programmed social and psychologic behaviors which make up the self blend with general CNS disturbances in the production of illness behaviors, creating ambiguities not found in illness behaviors which are sharply separated from sociocultural influences, as in aphasias or convulsions.

Implicit in this discussion is the notion that when one looks at a culture-bound behavioral syndrome (and indeed any psychiatric illness) one finds bundled together a myriad of things like role expectations, attitudes, values, social conventions, style of emotional expression, and ideological concerns. More briefly stated, a psychiatric illness implies a whole behavioral "thing" which encompasses human experience, awareness, and identity, whose content and style are learned during socialization. It is a culturally organized psychosocial milieu which necessarily realizes or fills out higher-brain functions and when the neurologic substrates of these functions are physically disturbed, it is culturally organized psychosocial behaviors which will be altered. In other words, optimal brain function means that neurologic substrates and routines are contextualized such that the person functions in a culturally and socially adaptive manner. This generalization holds in both an ontogenetic and a phylogenetic sense. Human evolution has yielded a brain whose making was governed in a complementary fashion by biologic-organic and sociocultural influences. General disturbances of this brain will lead to culturally contextualized behaviors. The striking fact of the culture-bound syndromes is their apparent organization and specificity, a factor we cannot fully explain neurologically in analogous Western syndromes, such as atypical and psychogenic psychoses [9].

Cultural Aspects of Major Psychiatric Disorders

In discussing schizophrenia and depression one is dealing with psychiatric diseases and illnesses which are somewhat better understood than those classified as atypical or reactive. This is so whether one takes a psychologic, behavioral, or neurobiologic point of view. I will not attempt to summarize this information nor elaborate on the large number of unanswered questions about the major psychiatric disorders. In discussing the major psychiatric disturbances in relation to culture many topics could be covered; for example, epidemiology and cause. However, I will deal exclusively with the matter of the manifestations of these diseases in relation to culture for it is this which touches on the question which is the theme of my chapter, namely, cultural influences in brain-behavior relations.

Schizophrenia. There exists a large literature in anthropology and psychiatry dealing with the role of culture on the manifestations of the major psychiatric disorders. One traditional perspective has been that behaviors which in one culture are viewed as pathological may be viewed as entirely normal in another. This perspective seemed to totally deny the possibility that psychiatric disorders possessed any universal aspects. A related perspective was that cultural factors could mask the manifestations of psychosis and even protect certain individuals (such as shamans) suffering from specific psychiatric illnesses. While not denying possible universal aspects of psychosis, this perspective also argued for a relativistic emphasis regarding manifestations. In recent years these old relativistic perspectives have been severely undermined. Two lines of attack have been prominent: one stemming from an increasing appreciation of the neurobiologic aspects of psychosis (schizophrenia) and the other from a scrutiny of data from cross-cultural field studies dealing with social interpretations of psychiatric illness manifestations [5, 14].

Murphy's article in particular seems to suggest that the neurobiologic changes of schizophrenia produce changes in behavior which will inevitably be judged as illness and not as deviance, shamanism, or eccentricity. It is important to keep in mind that Murphy's argument is directed at the extremist claims of but a few labeling theorists (regarding the specious, fictive, and culture-boundedness of schizophrenia). Moreover, the material reviewed in her article is based largely on severe, chronic, and deteriorated forms of schizophrenia. In brief, as Edgerton implied [4], it is in no way inconsistent to judge that schizophrenia has a neurobiologic basis, that severe and chronic form of schizophrenia (and other forms of insanity-madness) are consistently judged as illness across societies and historical epochs, and that sociocultural factors are critically important in affecting both the manifestations of and social responses to psychiatric illness [2-7, 9]. This point requires further discussion.

I stated that cultural factors are somehow operative during socialization as individuals come to acquire adult behaviors. One could also say that cultural influences are operative during the period of brain maturation. Persons and selves are thus partly constructed in a cultural context and this construction process embraces all levels of the nervous system. Schizophrenia also is realized in (an alteration of) the nervous system and will be manifest in the different spheres of behavior which this system regulates. It may be that important loci are the neostriatum and limbic striatum, but given their roles in brain-behavior regulation, effects are likely to be general and widespread indeed. As an example, it is said that (limbic system) behaviors released during schizophrenia are relatively insensitive to ordinary neocortical regulation [14]. Yet, such behaviors do not simply occur as physical phenomena but are enacted and expressed in terms of prevailing ideas and cognitions. The important point is that, given the view of culture endorsed here, to some extent the physical changes of schizophrenia take place in different types of nervous systems. In other words, the neurophysiologic and neurochemical changes of schizophrenia affect behaviors whose neurologic substrates are themselves affected by culture.

One needs to focus on an important implication of the unique tie which neuropsychiatric diseases, like schizophrenia, have with cultural factors. Since these diseases, when fully played out in social and psychologic illness behaviors, are connected in special ways with cultural symbols, one is forced to ask: to what extent is the form and content of the neuropsychiatric entities, as we now undertand them, an outgrowth of our own natural language system and scientific culture? Or to what extent might we be promulgating a deviant or atypical view of what these diseases look like and have looked like in human history?

To develop and make this point clearly, one needs to keep separate two different aspects about science and the perspective of humans which it necessarily fosters. On the one hand, this perspective is instrumentally useful and moreover undoubtedly correct. Science occupies an obviously dominating position in contemporary society, and it will some day unquestionably become the main governing principle in the species. Science and the scientific perspective have allowed the species unparalleled success in its quest for persistence and maintenance in the planet. It has allowed people to control the environment, to make and verify predictions, and to achieve a greater understanding about nature, life, and human origins. From this standpoint, then, science constitutes a powerful method, procedure, and body of knowledge about the world.

Viewed from another standpoint, science also constitutes a cultural perspective that humans have about themselves and the world and in this sense it is simply one of many such perspectives which have existed in the species. In other words, science constitutes an ideology or perspective about the world which humans (as part of their culture) internalize and pass on to descendants. Moreover, this perspective importantly shapes human behavior. It is necessary to emphasize the comparative newness and indeed atypicality of this scientific perspective. It is associated with a view about people far different than those across millenia. People are now seen as having brains, composed of any number of structures such as speech centers and verbal memory centers. The individual is now said to have free will, to be his own agent, and to live in a world which houses only naturalistic forces or causes and not preternatural ones. This general scientific perspective is clear enough and need not be developed further. What must be emphasized is how different this perspective is from that of nonliterates and by implication from that held during by far the longest portion of human existence. Thus, when viewed across human history, the contemporary scientific cultural perspective contains any number of new and indeed atypical assumptions about people and behavior. These views are products of science and though undeniably correct and useful nonetheless are still simply cultural premises which shape how people behave and conceive of themselves.

It follows, then, that contemporary realizations of neuropsychiatric entities, like schizophrenia, reflect the peculiar cultural environment in which the individual himself gets shaped. One is thus forced to ask questions such as the following: to what extent are the descriptors of schizophrenia peculiar to our own cultural assumptions about the world and about ourselves. By descriptors I mean the set of social and psychologic behaviors which are believed to realize the "lesion" of schizophrenia.

To illustrate the importance of language and cultural factors in the definition of schizophrenia one can take the so-called first-rank symptoms of schizophrenia which many believe constitute sufficient conditions to diagnose the disease in Western nations. These symptoms include having audible thoughts; experiencing that one's thoughts are being withdrawn or inserted in one's mind by others; experiencing the diffusion or broadcasting of thoughts; experiencing one's feelings, impulses, or actual actions as somehow alien or externally controlled; and having a delusional mood or perception. These psychologic experiences, it is claimed, constitute the fundamental symptoms of schizophrenia. Level of social functioning is not an explicit component of these symptoms though it is implied that this is likely to be impaired. Koehler recently discussed first-rank symptoms as embracing three types of continua [15]. Specifically, he posits a delusional continuum, a passivity continuum, and a sense-deception continuum. Rather than constituting basic indications of schizophrenia per se, one can view these phenomena as implicating basic Western assumptions about human action and social reality. It may very well be the case that among Western people the neurobiologic changes of schizophrenia produce manifestations which include, phenomenologically, the eroding or blurring of these particular assumptions.

In other words, a working assumption can be that the first-rank symptoms of schizophrenia are partly based on our cultural conventions about the self. These symptoms imply that to a large extent persons are independent beings whose bodies and minds are separate entities and function autonomously. In particular, they imply that under ordinary conditions external influences do not operate on and influence an individual: that thoughts are recurring inner happenings that the self "has"; that thoughts, feelings, and actions are separable sorts of things which together account for self-identity; that thoughts and feelings are silent and exquisitely private; that one's body is independent of what one feels or thinks; and finally that one's body, feelings, and impulses have a purely naturalistic basis and cannot be modified by outside supernatural agents. In brief, contemporary Western psychology articulates a highly differentiated mentalistic self which is individuated and looks out on an objective, impersonal, and naturalistic world; and it is based on this psychology (a Western cultural perspective) that schizophrenic symptoms are articulated.

In summary, all the assumptions which underlie the first-rank symptoms (which provide a rationale for their pathological nature) seem linked to Western notions about human psychology and causality. Any careful ethnography of the way simpler people explain phenomena, account for human action, and delineate personal identity will point to ethnocentric components in these assumptions. Many simpler societies believe in the constant interconnection between the natural and preternatural, between the bodily and the mental, and between the various dimensions and contents of human awareness which are arbitrarily set apart in Western psychology. If in fact people already believe themselves affected by external influences, if they sense and experience these influences constantly and accommodate themselves in various ways to the necessary connection which holds between feeling, thinking, bodily activity, and external control, then how will the basic lesion of schizophrenia show itself behaviorally? In short, which of the behavioral descriptors of schizophrenia is one not likely to see; and which elements is one likely to see different versions of in the event that the assumptive world of the person with the basic lesion rests on highly different premises about self, behavior, and causality? It should be clear that the claim here is not that unusual psychologic experiences or social behaviors are not part of schizophrenia but rather the form and meaning which they take in modern European culture (enunciated by Schneider) are partly an outcome of the way selves are constructed there. Murphy pointed out that chronic and deteriorated forms of insanity are recognized cross-culturally and that they are labeled and dealt with similarly [5]. Hers is a social argument about the uniformities in social responses to psychiatric illness. My argument here stresses the role of culture in brain-behavior relations in individuals, particularly its role in manifestations. In brief, I have been concerned with the possible effects of culture on the organization and content of behavior changes which make up psychiatric illness.

Depression. A recent review of the literature on the manifestations of depression across cultures revealed that depression does not assume a universal form [16]. The review encompassed literature involving clinical observations, culture-specific disorders, symptoms among patients matched by diagnosis and sample, international surveys, and factor-analytic studies. Of special importance is that psychologic aspect of depression (depressed mood, guilt, feelings of self-deprecation, and purposelessness) seen in the Western world are often absent in non-Western societies. Somatic aspects were noted quite frequently, regardless of culture. Often it was only when non-Westerners became westernized that the anticipated psychologic aspects of depression emerged. Depressed somatic functioning (vegetative depression) thus appeared not to have the corresponding depressed mental experience seen in the West. Whether there exists a depression in the operation of psychologic processes was not reported. If the consequences and implications of depression for an individual are affected by the quality of mental experiences correlated with the depression, different types of social behaviors can be anticipated.

One could use the conclusions of this review of empirical studies to argue for a uniform disease entity termed *depression* which affects subcortical structures of the brain (the similarity in vegetative phenomena). On the other hand, differences in the psychologic and social behaviors of depressive illness would imply differences in the organization and function of cortical substrates which subserve language, thought, and experience.

Related to this question of the character of psychosocial behavior changes in depressive illness in different cultures is the study by Leff [17, 18]. He used reliable information collected (by means of the Present State Examination) on patients hospitalized in different psychiatric centers. Psychiatrists' ratings of patients' verbal reports and social behavior thus constituted the data base. Scores on three emotion variables were correl-

ated: anxiety and depression, depression and irritability, and anxiety and irritability. Leff compared the correlations of emotions across a number of
sociocultural groups of patients which he classified as belonging to
developed and developing nations. In using correlations between emotion
scores Leff posited that a correlation of $+1$ between two emotions
represented the least possible discrimination between the two emotions. A
correlation of -1 represented the greatest possible discrimination between
the two emotions. One could say that both types of emotions could in fact
be present, but implicit in Leff's reasoning is that a similar level of overlap
of symptoms probably existed in these centers and that the size of the correlations reflected the degree of discrimination of the subjects. His results
showed an interesting pattern of differences. For example, China and
Nigeria subjects showed the highest intercorrelations. As predicted, patients
from developing countries showed significantly higher correlations in all
three pairs of emotions when compared to patients from developed countries. Leff concluded that groups (cultures) differ in ease of differentiation
between emotional states and that this was due to the relative availability of
linguistic categories for the description of subjective states.

Explanation of the appearance of depression is facilitated if one
distinguishes between emotion as a basic category of human experience and
emotion as a symbolic domain which is lexically coded and which languages
capture in a direct and explicit way. All indications are that emotions are
probably universal and that the structure of affective experience also has
universal features [19]. However, the prevalence of linguistic labels for
emotions may vary in frequency across societies. By means of lexically encoded emotional terms, one can speak and think more precisely and
elaborately about internal subjective states. In a fundamental way the domain of emotion and that of the self impact on each other semantically.
Besides serving as a means for qualifying the state of the self, emotion words
can also be used to qualify other types of phenomena. In our culture we
often qualify social situations and bodily states using emotional terms.

If a semantic domain is richly encoded (that is, if words of a particular
category are prominent) in a group's language, one can assume that the domain is important in a sociocultural sense. The domain not only has been
clearly demarcated from related domains but has been differentiated as
well. This appears to be the case with emotion in our culture, with the effect
that social relations, bodily experience, and the self are linked semantically
and in an elaborate way through emotion and related mentalistic terms.

The points just discussed can be used to illustrate the connectedness
which exists between things we describe as biological as opposed to cultural,
or in epistemological terms to the biological as opposed to the sociocultural
side of medical problems. In Western populations, depression (the disease)
and conditions of social disarticulation produce behaviors which carry a

mentalistic and emotional emphasis. It is very likely that this is partly a consequence of what anthropologists term the *psychic unity* of humans. This is to say that all people, regardless of culture, are likely to feel down and bad when things go awry socially or physically. However, to a certain extent the similarity between depression and social disarticulation is partly a consequence of the fact that the psychic sphere, considered as a semantic domain, is richly encoded and symbolically important in Western cultures. The fact that our (lay, cultural) theories of illness and of personhood draw heavily on emotion and related mentalistic premises serves to further confuse the appearance of these conditions.

In summary, a review of the literature suggests cultural differences in the manifestations of depression. Psychologic and mental symptoms appear tot be less prominent (or less differentiated) in certain simpler societies. One way of explaining those differences is to point to the influence of our (culturally dominant) psychologic perspective which is heavily mentalistic and elaborates semantically on emotion as a descriptor of the self. In my view it is not strictly correct to say that depression is different in other cultures; one should say that depression is different in our culture. When thinking of the major psychiatric illnesses (schizophrenia and depression) we need to realize that at issue are psychologic and social (illness) behaviors which necessarily are colored by cultural factors. This means that our view of these illnesses is to an indeterminate extent ethnocentric.

Some Clinical Neurological Problems

Empirical Reports

Among the topics which most pointedly raise the question of brain-behavior relations, that involving human language has received much attention. In general, the neurology of language, like that of memory as an example, tends to be examined in a generic way; the universal or pancultural features of the way the brain is organized vis-à-vis language are emphasized. This topic has gained a great deal of momentum in clinical neurology in the recent past [7, 10, 11].

Bilingualism has attracted considerable interest and research in the social sciences (psychology and linguistics). Neurologists have been interested in bilingualism insofar as polyglots show different patterns of recovery from aphasia. However, though provocative case histories exist which challenge traditional views of how the brain is organized vis-à-vis language, there are few systematic studies which allow drawing clear-cut inferences about brain aspects of bilingualism [20]. Part of the problem lies in the different definitions of bilingualism, emphasis being given to passive competence (listening), productive competence (speaking, writing), degree of proficiency, age of second-language acquisition and the manner of learning, and usage patterns. One set of terms involves degree of proficiency: a balanced bilingual has native-language proficiency in both languages whereas a dominant bilingual is more fluent in one language than another. Another set of terms involves the alleged degree of independence in the way the languages are handled in the brain: a compound bilingual is assumed to have the two languages organized as a single system whereas a coordinate bilingual is judged to have each language organized as a separate system.

Albert and Obler recently wrote a monograph that summarizes the literature on bilingualism [21]. They reviewed studies in linguistics, psychology, and neuropsychology. They also present results of their empirical studies on bilingual Israeli subjects. Their main conclusion is that "Language is organized in the brain of a bilingual in a manner different from that which might have been predicted by studies of cerebral organization for language in monolinguals" [21, p. 243]. In particular, they indicate that in bilinguals there exists a major contribution from the right hemisphere in language. Even in adults the right hemisphere plays a major role in the learning of a second language. In their estimation, "the brain is seen to be a plastic, dynamically changing organ which may be modified by processes of learning . . .[it] does not have a rigid, predetermined neuropsychological destiny" [21, p. 243].

Proficiency in more than one language is thus a topic which has pointedly raised the question of cultural-linguistic influences in brain-behavior relations. The influence of cultural-linguistic factors in neurologic illness behaviors has been studied in monolinguals who nonetheless also command two writing systems. One example is provided by a central (or conduction) aphasia in a Japanese patient [22]. In writing and reading, Japanese can use a Kanji system which involves ideograms or the Kana system which is phonogrammatic. Thus a unit of linguistic meaning in Kanji can represent a whole word which includes a variable number of syllables whereas a linguistic unit of Kana represents only one syllable. In the case in point, the patient was a 66-year-old Japanese widow who showed evidence of an aphasia presumed to have a vascular basis. Clinical findings included a preservation of comprehension of spoken language and of spontaneous verbal expression. She comprehended well-written orders. Her defects included verbal repetition, naming of visually presented objects, reading aloud written words, and transcription of dictated words into Kanji and Kana. These tasks are held to involve the generation (via a stimulus) of a target word which has to be expressed verbally or in written form. The patient usually performed adequately when the target word had one or two syllables, but failed as the number of syllables increased. When she failed, she usually uttered the first syllable correctly, the number of syllables produced was roughly the same as that of the target word, and many constituent syllables of the target word appeared in her utterances. Significantly, she did much better in Kanji transcription (versus Kana transcription) where meaning is represented directly and exact syllabic sequencing is less critical for writing. However, in reading Kanji characters the acoustic features of a word cannot be bypassed, and she failed on this task. These findings reinforced the belief that conduction aphasia involves a defect in motor encoding of an acoustic image with receptive ability well preserved. It would seem that in the Japanese brain Kanji and Kana systems are represented in separate areas or networks which can be lesioned in a separate fashion.

A different report deals with a case of alexia with agraphia in a Japanese patient [23]. In this syndrome one finds difficulty in writing but preserved ability in copying; impaired reading, with letters being more affected than words; and a variety of other difficulties (such as aspects of the Gerstmann syndrome). By subjecting a Japanese patient with this syndrome to reading tests involving ideograms versus phonograms, the basis of the reading difficulties could be tested. Results indicated that the patient had extreme difficulty in reading Kana characters and words but did far better when responding to Kanji characters. Finally, the patient could write his name in Kanji but not in Kana. Generally, he had a severe writing deficit. The author concluded this report by discussing the close connection that exists between the visual and auditory-oral system in the generation of meaning. To phonographically encode or decode a unit of meaning, auditory-oral and visual systems must be integrated. Ideograms are less tied down to auditory-oral control and can be processed within the visual system even with poor auditory control. Thus whole words (in Americans, one's name or address) are perceived and read by direct impression with relatively less involvement of the neurolinguistic structures subserving the phonetic system. Apparently, differences in the way the brain processes the Kana and Kanji linguistic systems in Japanese subjects allow for this pattern of findings to emerge.

These reports deal with a relative impairment in the handling of Kana (phonetic) versus Kanji (nonphonetic) symbols. There are instances where the reverse is demonstrated: rare patients who show a selective impairment in the handling of Kanji versus Kana symbols [24, 25]. Even in patients with severe global aphasia there remains some ability to match high-frequency Kanji words to corresponding pictures. Analysis of errors suggest that the strategies used to decode these two types of symbols differ: visual (direct graph-meaning) processing for Kanji versus phonological (indirect graph-phoneme-meaning) for Kana. These reports pointing to a disassociation in linguistic functioning as a result of brain lesions have led to a series of studies conducted on normal Japanese subjects. They show that Kana and Kanji systems are processed differently in the cerebral hemispheres, with Kana symbols seeming to preferentially engage the left hemisphere whereas the opposite is the case with Kanji symbols [26, 27, 28]. In general, these studies raise the question of whether and how the right hemisphere participates in language. For a review of this see Zaidel [29, 30, 31].

From the standpoint of the theme of this chapter, the data about the neurolinguistic aspects of the Japanese language writing systems are important for two interrelated reasons. First, the data show clearly that differences in the conventions underlying the reading of Kana and Kanji symbols (a cultural trait) are associated with differences in neurologic circuits and functioning. To the extent that the Japanese people as a whole differ in their ability to read Kana and Kanji symbols, they show intrasocietal differences in neurolinguistic functioning. Second, as far as is generally known, the writing systems of most Western languages do not rest on differences in the way symbols and units are apprehended and then processed neurologically. This difference between Western and Japanese writing traditions can thus be expected to be reflected in cross-cultural differences in neurolinguistic functioning. However, it is important to realize that the posited neurolinguistic difference reflects a difference in the emphasis to which Western and Japanese brains are put. In other words, the special ability and neurolinguistic trait of the Japanese merely reflect their having utilized special potentials inherent in the right-cerebral hemisphere, a potential all humans have and no doubt to some extent apply to language as the work of Zaidel implies. The point that culture provides experiences that draw on potentials inherent in the human brain also applies to music.

Another neuropsychologic problem which has relevance to the question of cultural differences concerns national recognition and expression. One must recall that linguistically relevant sounds are processed in most normals in the left hemisphere. Nonlinguistic sound patterns and music seem to be processed on the right side, though there is some controversy about this. Amusia, as an example, appears to result from a dominant side lesion. Yet, there is also evidence that the organization of musical abilities differs depending upon the level of the person's skill. Skilled musicians appear to orient to music more analytically, relying heavily on the left dominant hemisphere [13]. In general, sequential or rhythmic material, including musical series, seem to be left-sided functions, though music ability considered as a cognitive system has a cortical representation that differs between persons.

Gardner et al. conducted a study which involved comparing how unilateral left- versus right-brain-damage subjects handled the denotative and connotative aspects of music [32]. An attempt was also made to investigate how the linguistic system interacted with the musical system by comparing aphasiacs versus nonaphasiacs on musical tasks. Because two culturally distinct groups of patients were tested, namely Americans and Italian patients, it was possible to determine whether musical competence breaks down comparably among people who share the same musical tone system. Though results of this study were complex, the following generalizations are possible. Sensitivity to both musical denotation and connotation is impaired by unilateral lesions. It appeared that both hemispheres participate in music appreciation. Left-hemisphere patients, especially those with anterior lesions, performed relatively better on songs as opposed to lyric recognition. Right-sided patients performed better than left-sided patients on the musical connotation test. And most central to our purposes, Americans and Italians performed comparably.

In a sense, this study is formally like those which concentrate on language disability, and whose results point to a discrete cortical localization of the language function regardless of the individual's background. In this case, a different cognitive or communicational system is being assessed, namely music. Any one interested in making a strong claim about the effect of cultural factors on brain-behavior relations would of course insist that the comparison groups show widely divergent musical systems or conventions as was the case in language among bilinguals and the Japanese. This is so largely because of the claims of Sapir and Whorf [55, 56 below]. Similarly, one expecting to find a compelling instance of a cultural influence in brain organization vis-à-vis music would look for brain-behavior differences among groups that pattern and structure their music differently. Speculating somewhat, one might anticipate that similar anatomic centers subserve music (regardless of its structure) or that there exists an anatomic dissociation such that different brain structures handle different types of music [13].

Theoretical Possibilities

It seems that a number of neuropsychiatric syndromes or diseases would serve as useful objects of study for someone hoping to clarify the kind of influences culture might have on brain-behavior relations.

Frontal-Lobe Syndrome. Despite its looseness and heterogeneity, it is worth giving attention to the frontal-lobe syndrome since it influences activities which are of interest to both neurologists and psychiatrists. An intriguing set of experiments on free-ranging monkeys underlined the important contributions which the frontal systems of the brain (the cortex of the tip of the temporal lobe and the prefrontal-orbitofrontal cortex) make to social behaviors and affect. Bilateral destruction of this system was associated with decreased frequencies and critical alterations of a number of behavior sequences classically termed social: for example, allogrooming, facial expressions, and maternal and sexual behavior [33]. In another experiment similar procedures were found to inhibit the sociality of monkeys who failed to rejoin their social group on release and remained solitary until their death. Increased levels of aimless pacing were also documented [34]. Interestingly, these deficits were not seen after prolonged observations of yearling and infant rhesus monkeys whose frontal systems were destroyed. The behavioral deficits appeared with increasing severity among 2-year-old and 3-year-old juveniles. Thus, it appears that a certain degree of prior maturation is required (during which social skills achieve some neural structuring) before the effects of destruction of this system are manifest [35]. Related to these experiments are the findings which show that this same neural system appears to regulate social preferences of monkeys [36]. Thus differences in gender-related social-preference patterns were noted between (frontal system) operated and control monkeys. The experimenters were unable to detect gross differences in behavior which might underlie social discriminations. Insofar as discriminations are involved, one must acknowledge that cognitive behaviors were also affected. Observations noted on eleven monkeys with bilateral lesions of the frontal system paralleled those reported above, with those operated being more withdrawn and showing less proximity and contact with stimulus animals [37]. Many other behavioral alterations can easily be brought under the rubric "social." At the same time, these animals also showed distress, disturbance behaviors, and differences in aggression that suggest malfunctioning of the limbic system with which the frontal system is known to be connected.

Although the function of the frontal lobes in humans has posed a longstanding puzzle to clinicians and researchers alike, there seems to be consensus now that this part of the brain is important for the overall regulation of action. The accomplishment of complex tasks requires an active state of the cortex and the frontal lobes are believed to control this. The intentional, elective, purposive, strategic, and organizational qualities of behavior are said to be importantly subserved by the frontal lobes. It seems that maintenance of complex programs of activity and matching effects with intentions are aspects of this overall regulation. The frontal system cannot be treated as a homogeneous unit and many researchers have emphasized this [38, 39, 40, 41, 42]. Some pointed to a mnemonic (memory), spatial, and an effective component of functions disturbed by frontal-lobe injury and related these to more-or-less distinctive regions (each of which is known to connect with other brain regions believed to subserve the functions in question) [43]. Others distinguish between the polar, medical, mediobasal parts (important for regulation of the state of overall cortical activation and selective functioning), and the convexity parts (more relevant to the complex organization of motor movements). Still others indicate that prefrontal-convexity lesions in humans produce a pseudodepression (indifference and slow apathetic and automaticlike responses which, however, are appropriate and intelligible) whereas orbital-area lesions seem to produce pseudopsychopathic behaviors (with loss of tact and social restraints, coarseness, impulsiveness, and antisocial activity) [44]. Teuber offered a general and theoretical account of how frontal-lobe functioning might be explained physiologically [45]. In this account, behavioral regulation always involves two streams of neural impulses: a set of command impulses to motor and effector systems, and a corollary discharge to sensory systems (which preset these for inputs generated by the expected actions and movements which follow the intended motor discharges).

How might attention to cultural factors broaden one's understanding of this area of brain-behavior relations? As traditionally conceptualized by social scientists, social behaviors seem to encompass at least the following: (1) subtle nonverbal, particularly facial cues, displays, mannerisms, and maskings all of which enunciate cultural norms of social intercourse; (2) mode of location, gesturing, and spatial distancing; (3) linguistic and paralinguistic features involving communications; (4) patterns of execution and restraints involving vegetative functions, such as alimentary, excretory, and sexual; (5) patterned forms of interactions with age, sex, and status-specific members of the group at large (role behaviors); and (6) style of emotional expression. Many other ingredients of social behavior can be suggested, such as the capacity to appreciate humor and to show it appropriately. One may posit that the style of each of these components of social behavior varies across cultural groups and that each component is fully understood only by cultural comembers. That is, the perfect execution and understanding of a style of social behavior is what is meant by culturally appropriate behavior. In this view all members of a culture are able to speak and understand a more-or-less distinctive social language.

Anthropologists tend to view style of social behavior as involving a whole: it is the system which encompasses social behavior that makes sense. This system is learned and programmed into the brain through the mediation of culture and language. Yet, whether this system can be defective in subtle ways in an adult who still retains full linguistic and cognitive competencies is not ordinarily asked. Indeed, the parts making up the whole and their degree of independence is not often an issue. Social psychologists whose interest is the coupling betwen verbal and nonverbal behavior are principally concerned with emotional expression, an important component of social behavior, in which one finds both pancultural and culture-specific influences. Little is known about other components of social behavior (and how these interrelate) and in particular about the possible role of culture in the neurologic mechanisms which subserve these behaviors.

The information drawn from primate studies suggests that frontal-lobe pathology will be correlated with behavior disturbances in humans that are pancultural. At the same time, ethnological science points to the rich subtleties in social-cognitive behavior associated with culture differences. To the claim that the frontal lobes help regulate an individual's social actions and choices and restrain appetitive functions, thereby accounting for his tendency to conform to the rules of his group, an ethnologist is obligated to counter that to a large extent social behavior reflects the distinguishing system of social symbols of the individual's group. Any number of subtle rules about propriety, order, restraint, and human conduct underlies a group's social behavior, and it is against such a distinctive cultural background that one must carefully evaluate the functions of the frontal lobes. Changes in motivation and social sensitivity may in fact be typical of frontal-lobe pathology, but this will only be established if putative frontal-lobe behaviors of different people are carefully analyzed. The following questions can be raised: to what extent are culturally appropriate social behaviors dependent on the integrity of the frontal lobes? Which elements of each component of social behavior are necessary for the preservation of style or how are the components themselves tied to the frontal system? Can persons with frontal pathology appropriately recognize subtle culture-specific social cues of comembers? Is there a specieswide style of social behavior to which cultures merely add trivial refinements or is human social behavior fully realized only in styles made possible by language and cultural symbols? Such questions immediately raise the issue of coherence, integration, and neural representation of the components of social behavior; their independence from behaviors regulated by different cortical centers; and the possible correlates of culture in all of this.

It may well be that many of the specific recorded behaviors of the frontal-lobe patient reflect the unusual valence which certain categories of socially appropriate behavior have in our culture. In other words, social appropriateness involves control of basic visceral and physiologic functions which are unequivocably universal in humans. However, how a people choose to regulate each behavioral sphere which implicates these functions varies and reflects their prevailing culture. Each viscerally and physiologically conditioned behavioral sphere may be assumed to carry a valence and to relate in a patterned way to that of other spheres. In short, one can hypothesize that putative frontal-lobe behaviors of Western patients merely reflect the differential restraints and weights which are placed on the regulation of aggression, sexuality, emotional expression, bodily excretion, pleasure, and humor in our culture and not merely the general release of specific behavioral tendencies considered independently. Basically, in pointing to impulsiveness, emotional fatuousness, or social indifferences one has simply indicated areas of behavior disturbed by frontal-lobe pathology. The mechanisms and subtleties of these behaviors implicate a person's system of social symbols. One may posit that only by carefully analyzing the form and content of many types or models of frontal-lobe behaviors in different cultural settings that a full understanding of what functions these areas subserve will be gained.

Temporal-Lobe Epilepsy. Another neuropsychiatric problem that can be considered involves temporal-lobe epilepsy [48]. A basic orientation is that in one sense this disorder involves relatively specific neuronal excitations in certain areas of the brain; however, these constitute areas in which are encoded basic routines that carry the experiential base of a people's way of life, and neuronal activation in them is likely to elicit behaviors which reflect this experience. It is very likely that much of the ictal behavior of the person with temporal-lobe epilepsy will display characteristics that are culturally invariant. Thus one anticipates little cross-cultural variability in such things as automatisms of the face and mouth, confused and dazed wanderings, epigastric and abdominal sensations, and unformed hallucinations, all of which are typically described as accompaniments of seizures. Such phenomena are thought of as reflexive and unmotivated, stereotyped and elementary in a visceral and sensorimotor sense.

Phenomena which reflect higher forms of cortical activation such as formed hallucinations, illusions, dyscognitive states, and affective experiences would seem to present intriguing material for the culture-oriented neurobiologist. In a trivial sense, cultural differences are likely to be manifest in the content of such mental phenomena; for example, what an individual hears, sees, or misperceives. Cultural differences are also likely to be manifest in the general interpretations which are given to those experiences, both by the person and comembers. Cultural differences are likely in these instances because content and interpretations are obviously based on native categories of meaning or world views. On the other hand, cultural differences may also be manifest in more subtle ways. Thus the structure or form of these mental experiences is likely to contain interesting clues; for example, in our culture formed-auditory hallucinations are often heard as voices speaking about the person; these reflect themes of general cultural significance (such as sex or violence); they often appear in the first or third person and may involve the actual name of the person. If similar types of formed-auditory hallucinations occur cross-culturally, in which grammatical form do they appear; where are they actually heard; what dimension of experience and self do they draw on; and do they involve actual naming? More generally, how are formed-auditory hallucinations structured among people who speak languages which are sharply different in a grammatical sense and among whom conceptions of personhood are also sharply different? A key point is that in one sense a hallucination of this type represents a limbic-seizure spread but in another, a reading of the way the brain codes experience structurally; that is, self, other, and a symbolic view of the world are fused in the hallucination. Assessments of how hallucinations are interpreted give one a surface view of culture whereas structural analysis of many such hallucinations provide deeper views. Such analysis might reveal the kinds of coordinates of experience which in an elementary sense are represented neurologically and the types of emotions associated with them. In a similar fashion one may inquire about the uniformities versus differences in structure of formed-visual hallucinations and in distortions of the sense of time (dèjá vu, jamais vu) which are frequently seen during ictal states. Is the form and content of these disturbances universal or might they differ among people who imply different conventions about time and space?

Electrical stimulation of the human hippocampal formation and amygdala evokes emotional phenomena. However, the category of phenomena appears to be independent of the exact site stimulated and instead to be related to the person being stimulated [49]. It is thus reasonable to posit that the type of emotional reactions (anxiety versus pleasure versus anger) found during ictal states may bear a relation to the modal patterns of emotional regulation and expression which are prevalent in a group. Of course, what is found pleasurable, frightening, or irritating will differ cross-culturally. However, one must inquire whether the manner in which these emotional experiences are structured and enacted will also differ (the psychophysiology of the emotion, the way in which self or others are incorporated in the emotion). Consider that whatever emotion *is* involves a subjective experience of some type which includes sensations about the body, a linguistic reading of this, and an enacted routine (emotional expression). Emotions bear the impact of specific types of situations and relations which a person has been involved in, and the categories of experience which a group conventionally endorses as appropriate to situations and relations are thus also important in how emotions are construed. The study of emotion cross-culturally is beset by methodological problems linked to the differential ways in which language and cognitive categories relate to subjective phenomena and bodily sensations [17, 18]. Comparative study of ictal emotional states may provide a way of better articulating the influence of these categories. Finally, an assumption in the study of emotion is that both pancultural and culture-specific influences play a role in the nonverbal expression of emotion [46, 47]. Cross-cultural studies of emotional expression during ictal states might also reveal clues as to how these two influences are neurologically encoded.

Of equal if not greater interest to the culture-oriented neurobiologist are the kinds of changes in interictal behavior which are observed in patients with temporal-lobe epilepsy. These patients are said to show personality and social behavioral traits which may very well be a consequence of repeated and more-or-less random limbic-system activation [50, 51, 52]. For example, they have been described as showing religiosity, hypergraphia, deepened affects, hypermoralism, changes in sexual interest and activity, and a humorless sobriety. Such behavior changes may be judged as the long-term (sociopsychological) effects of limbic system stimulation in brains whose functions already bear the influences of Western cultural conventions about emotion, thinking action, bodily experience, and worldly-other worldly governance. Such clinical descriptions inform one about the disorder and about the organization, mode of functioning, and transformation of the brain in which the disorder occurs. It is thus reasonable to inquire about the kinds of personality and behavior changes which might be observed among persons with temporal-lobe foci who operate in terms of different religious and moral conventions, whose patterns of discourse differ, who verbally and cognitively code emotions differently, who place altogether different values on self and aggression and who are unable to record in writing their unusual experiences. In this context, a personality change should be viewed as a shorthand way of describing the cultural logic which behavior takes on given that basic affective states underlying approach and avoidance are activated randomly and over a protracted period of time. In other words, the amygdala and related limbic structures emotionally tone and contextualize complex environmental stimuli which arise in conjunction with social relations and actions of various types [53]. However, the rationale, significance, and possibly organization of the resulting experiences will more than likely bear the influence of cultural conventions. Continued random stimulation of these areas can be expected to produce culture-specific emotional experiences which may in time come to transform (in an equally specific way) the behaviors and interests of the persons. The nature of this transformation should inform one about basic elements of emotional experience and of their social consequences; specifically, what profiles of emotions are encoded, the significance accorded to them, how these affect conceptions of self-other and social relations, and how culture normalizes or molds their expression over time.

Nonclinical Problem Areas

Studies in Linguistic Anthropology

Obviously, people of different cultures place different emphases on aspects of the world around them. If languages are molded by accidental properties of technology and culture, features of language will differ across groups. As Clark and Clark indicate [54], in certain groups, such as the Eskimos, snow is an important feature of the environment; similarly, in Southeast Asia varieties of rice are important. Because of the importance of these factors it follows that the respective languages of the people will code these domains more elaborately than will be the case in groups in which rice and snow are less important. Given these differences in language one could say that people think about and look at rice and snow differently. However, exactly how are the words *think* and *look* to be understood? Do they refer merely to a way of talking about the environment or do they actually refer to perceptual and cognitive functions? There has been much research attempting to correlate psychological differences with language differences.

Social and behavioral scientists have been strongly influenced by this linguistic relativity hypothesis which is associated with the names of Edward Sapir and Benjamin Lee Whorf [55, 56, 57]. This hypothesis has been and continues to be extremely controversial [58]. Its strongest interpretation involved the claim that language influenced the actual way in which people perceived and cognitively organized the world around them. If language does in fact shape perception and cognition, one might anticipate that it has some effect on the way the brain is organized and functions; implied by the linguistic relativity hypothesis, then, is that there might exist differences (at some level) in the way the brain is wired or programmed.

Differences in language immediately raise the question of possible universals in language. A group's language should be easily learned by children and should so promote an easy and efficient representation of ideas that it can be readily understood and spoken by all comembers. Because language constitutes a system for communication and operates in a social setting it serves basic sociobiologic functions which are common to humans [59]. These considerations plus the fact that nature contains constancies or uniform things reinforces one's intuition about possible universals in languages. Whereas earlier research (prompted by the Sapir-Whorf hypothesis) stressed differences, in recent years it is the universals of language which have received more emphasis [54, 60-62].

The way in which languages deal with the domain of color has received a great deal of attention [63-65]. With respect to color, the Sapir-Whorf hypothesis would suggest an arbitrary partitioning of the physical (color) spectrum, with the color terms of one group referring to different regions of the continuum. Yet comparative studies indicate that there is no arbitrary labeling of the spectrum. This extensive work can only be summarized briefly. First, the basic color terms of languages refer to similar regions of the spectrum. There are distinctive colors which are lexically encoded in all languages. In addition, it appears that basic color terms are added to languages in a systematic fashion such that one can speak of stages in the way languages acquire such terms [62, 65, 66]. For example, languages which are classified as belonging to stage one contain two basic color terms that roughly refer to dark and light. Actually the term for dark includes black and cool hues (blues and greens) and that for light includes white and most warm hues (yellow, red, and orange). The next stage involves encoding red as a separate color, followed by yellow or blue-green.

The existence of lexical universals for colors and the positing of a general pattern to the way languages acquire color terms point to universal biologic factors in the perceptual system and has represented a challenge to the Sapir-Whorf linguistic relativity hypothesis. This hypothesis claims that language and culture critically influence how phenomena are perceived. From a position which ascribed to culture-language factors (for example, color words or classifications) an important and influential role in perception, opinion has shifted to that which ascribes to perception an influential role on culture and language. Specifically, the position now is that basic neuroanatomic structures and physiochemical processes underlie color vision and these have a determining influence on how humans respond to color, code it through language, and retrieve it in memory. As an example, it has been shown that infants as young as 4 months old respond to two physically different wavelengths provided these wavelengths are selected from regions which mark adult hue categories [67]. The infants behaved in a habituation task that involved looking at colors as though they also perceived adult categories of hue. They thus show what is termed categorical perception of hue or color vision long before the acquisition of culture and language. The perception of color in humans is based on neurologic mechanisms very similar to those found to operate in infrahuman primates [68].

The pattern of distribution of basic color terms in all languages has allowed anthropological linguists to point to *implicational universals* in color terminology. An implicational universal is a statement which allows a person to claim that if he finds a particular color word in a language (one for yellow), this means he will also find one (or several) in that language for other colors (such as red) but not vice versa. A term for red in a language does not necessarily mean that a term for yellow will also be found. Several other domains of nature are linguistically encoded in a manner that allows claiming implicational universals [61, 62, 69-71]. An example is provided by plants. What linguists refer to as folk botanical life forms (tree and grass) are also implicationally related. For example, all languages containing a special word that refers to grass also contain one for tree but not vice versa. Similarly, there is evidence to the effect that worldwide languages show a distribution of names of zoological life forms (fish, bird, and snake) that also point to implicational universals. Thus all languages that contain a special word which refers to a large animal (mammal, crocodile, or iguana) also contain special words for fish, birds, and snakes but not vice versa.

In general, domains of nature which are lexically coded in a manner which allows one to derive implicational universals of the type illustrated above are classified or categorized conceptually in the form of a taxonomy. A folk taxonomy is a lay (naturally evolved) system of classifying, organizing, or categorizing a domain such that propositional relations of *class inclusion* hold among named categories of things. That is, things are named and classified in a hierarchic way by principles of class inclusion (oaks, evergreens, and maples are terms that fall under the category tree, and trees, vines, and grasses are part of the category plants).

Color terminologies seem to have a neurophysiologic basis whose properties have been analyzed with some fidelity. In fact, on the basis of recent studies, Bornstein claims that visual behavior of infants involving chromatic stimuli and spatially oriented gratings can be explained in terms of the way neurons are selectively activated (that is, feature extractors) [72]. Anthropologists are drawn to a different type of explanation in order to account for these apparent perceptual regularities. The existence of lexical universals in color and various other domains (words for plants, animal, and physical dimensions refer to the *same things* in nature) and the fact that certain domains of nature are (lexically) encoded sequentially are explained in terms of basic *principles of naming behavior*. As outlined by Witkowski and Brown, these principles reflect design properties of the brain which subserve perception-cognition, and hence their use is complementary to the explanations of physiologists and psychologists [62]. The first such principle is *conjunctivity* which can be illustrated by considering the physical dimension of depth. This dimension tends to be encoded linguistically by terms referring to its poles as deep/shallow; that is, by naming one or both ends. One could envision a word which codes the midregion and one which codes both extremes. However, to code both extremes with one word is disjunctive (it violates the principle of conjunctivity) and such a category rarely is found in human naming systems. By opposing the ends of the dimension in a binary fashion, the principle of conjunctivity is maintained.

A surface manifestation of the conjunctivity principle is that of binary opposition. The principle of *binary opposition* is evident in many adjectives. Thus dimensional concepts such as height and depth are usually encoded by two terms (tall/short, deep/shallow). The fact that languages acquire a word for tree first, and then a word which refers to a class of smaller items is explained by drawing on the principle of binary opposition: large plant/small plant. The principle of *criteria clustering* operates when key defining attributes of an object or item coalesce or bundle together. In other words, the presence of one attribute predicts that of others in a reliable way (feathers, wings, and a bill tend to go together in nature creating an expectancy leading to a conception of "birdness"). This principle in effect says that nature contains natural boundaries which languages pick up and which people use in order to classify things [73].

The principle of *dimensional salience* refers to the fact that certain dimensons are far more productive because they embrace a varied set of objects. For example, it is a fact that plants tend to demonstrate continuous variation along the dimensions of size and woodiness versus nonwoodiness; these two dimensions, then, are productive. Finally, the *principle of marking* also seems to operate behind the encoding uniformities of worldwide languages. Marking classically obtains in dimensions such as those listed above (height, depth). In languages that code these dimensions unequally, one finds that the term referring to the dimension is morphologically simpler and more general, tending to be neutralized in certain contexts. Contextual neutralization is illustrated in the fact that one usually says "She is five feet tall" as opposed to "She is five feet short," and one says "How deep is the river?" as opposed to "How shallow is the river?" Unmarked items (tall and deep) are those which usually refer to or possess the dimension in question (that is, height and depth), are more frequent in all languages, and tend to refer to similar aspects of the world. Unmarked items are also older and developmentally precede marked items in a particular language.

As stated above, the similarities in color terminologies can be explained in terms of neurophysiologic factors subserving perception. That is, the nervous system may be described as genetically preset to draw specific distinctions among colors. At the same time, the way in which the color spectrum is encoded can be explained in terms of principles of naming behavior as Witkowski and Brown have very lucidly indicated. They point out that two physical dimensions are held to be tapped by color terms: hue and brightness. From a linguistic viewpoint, red can be viewed as the unmarked pole of the hue dimension; yellow, green, and blue as marked. Of course, yellow is unmarked vis-à-vis brown, and pink and orange are marked in terms of it. On the other hand, light versus dark involves two binary oppositions, namely hue and brightness. This early color encoding sequence of light versus dark can thus be seen as an example of the principle of criteria clustering: the existence of the dark/light distinctions indicate that warm hues (yellows) predict brightness and cool hues (blues) darkness. There is thus a bundling together of one pole of the brightness dimension with one for the hue dimension. Because a domain such as color obviously has a neurophysiologic base yet its organization in language can also be explained by an appeal to general principles of naming behavior suggest that all these principles may themselves be based on neurophysiologic structures.

Work by developmental psychologists suggests that the principles of naming behavior may parallel and thus help explain the way children acquire words and make distinctions [54]. An example is that involving so-called classifier systems of language. As indicated by Greenberg [74], classifier systems are integral to languages and appear to reflect universal features of human categorization and perception. A classifier is a word or a participle attached to nouns or verbs which assigns entities to common categories on the basis of shared characteristics. Important distinctions in classifier systems involve animate versus inanimate things (usually based on perception of movement) and the domain of shape (round, long). The distinctions marked in classifier systems and the criteria children use in setting up early categories as they learn the semantics of their language bear a resemblance to each other as Clark and Clark have shown [54]. The following account is theirs. In early stages of language acquisition when children make mistakes in labeling categories they usually define a term (dog) on the basis of one (or more) central property (four-leggedness) and overextend the word to cover objects outside the adult category (cows, cats). The central properties used in overextensions include shape and movement. The criteria underlying children's overextensions of meaning repeatedly turn up in the classifier systems of all languages which, as stated, have universal properties. Along the same lines, in comprehension tasks children tend to prefer using unmarked (versus marked) adjectives which appear to be older and more basic in a language. Here again, then, language acquisition parallels structural properties inherent in languages. Particular dimensons which languages pick out are natural ones (vertical, horizontal) and these dimensions also have natural directions which are easier to handle conceptually. Thus upward and forward cover the optimal perceptible regions of space above the ground in front; these are positive directions and terms related to them are easier to process cognitively (seem more natural). In summary, one can think of languages and semantics as systems or devices which give (linguistic) form to basic psychologic processes. Language universals point to universals in the way psychologic processes operate. The organizing principles inherent in language and language use appear to derive from human perceptual-cognitive capacities which are presumably wired in the nervous system.

It should be mentioned that the word-distribution patterns of languages (which seem to reflect systematic ways in which domains are partitioned and encoded) bears an association to societal complexity. As an example, languages which contain but a few color terms are usually spoken by people living in small-scale societies, and as the number of lexical items for color increases so does the complexity of the society [75]. The association of language with societal complexity points to the complementariness between social and psycholinguistic phenomena. One can say that people from elementary societies have less need for certain lexical distinctions which their perceptual-cognitive apparatus is nonetheless able to make. As social development and technology proceeds, languages and people are able to encode distinctions in a way that reflects the complexity and importance of activities in a particular area of life. Color naming, for example, becomes more differentiated as painting and dye industries develop. However, linguistic distinctions appear to be based on perception-cognition uniformities having a neurologic basis.

The domain of the human body is another one which all languages seem to handle in such a way as to reflect universals [71, 76]. The domain viewed semantically is organized hierarchically into five (occasionally six) levels. The hierarchy is not termed a taxonomy (like that of plants) but rather is termed a partonomy since items referred to by terms located at different levels of the hierarchy are related by "part of" relations (hands are part of arms) rather than by kind of relations (in a taxonomy, an elm is a kind of tree) [61, 70, 77]. Visually perceptible properties such as shape (long and round) and location (upper versus lower) consistently turn up as being influential in the way the domain of the body is organized.

Universals in body-part terminology include, first of all, *what* is named. Thus there exist uniformities regarding what body parts are perceived and given separate recognition. Universals in body-part terminology also pertain to just *how* the perceived parts are named; that is, what part is labeled by a basic term as opposed to a derived term. All language recognize and label the head, trunk, and upper and lower extremities but divide these anatomical parts differently and terms referring to them do not have an exact correspondence across languages. Certain body parts are consistently given morphologically simple terms. The head invariably is labeled by a basic term which cannot be broken down into smaller lexical units (an unanalyzable term). Basic terms often have more than one meaning (polysemous), providing the source for so-called derived terms which refer to other parts of the body. When this occurs, the parts involved (those labeled by basic versus derived terms) are related in terms of structural similarity or spatial contiguity. The symmetry between parts of the upper and lower body is often reflected in body-part terminologies. In this case the basic term refers to a body part above the waist and the derived one to the part below the waist.

As indicated above, the way children acquire (developmentally) language terms of different domains have been studied and the principles which appear to inhere in language terminologies (apparent perceptual bases for labeling referents) bear a relationship to the cognitive processes children seem to go through as they learn to use language terms. The acquisition of body-part terms has not been studied directly but there exists diary studies and vocabulary lists of children which provide data on how they use body-part terms [71]. This information suggests that children acquire their vocabulary for body parts in parallel ways. Parts which tend to be labeled by basic terms are usually learned first. The face is the referent for most of the terms which are learned early. In general, the organizing principles behind body-part terminologies of all languages are held to be reflected in the way children acquire body-part terms.

In a very provocative way, White recently argued for a universal cognitive structure in terms of which all people make descriptions of personality [78]. Using multivariate statistical techniques applied to cross-cultural data, he shows that the same organization underlies the meanings of personality descriptors and their use in making judgments of persons. This evidence and the conclusions generated by White are counterintuitive since one supposes that the personality domain is a complex one involving events and acts, variably interpreted, which have few objective referents in nature. To explain these findings one must recall that the correlation between actual behavior and personality is known to be quite low. Moreover, as documented by D'Andrade and Shweder, high correlations exist between judgments about the meanings of key words (used to qualify personality) and the actual judgments which are offered about personality [79, 80]. The positing of universals in personality description is thus a claim about the abstract organization of meaning in terms of which persons categorize social life. The basic dimensions underlying personality descriptions parallel the evaluative and potency factors described by Osgood as universal modes of affective response in the use of adjective qualifiers [81]. Thus, universal psycholinguistic properties of language and thought appear to interact with general conditions of human social life to bring about universals in the cognitive structure underlying personality descriptions. The claim here is that at a fundamental level of experience all people are alike in the way in which they judge other persons in their social world. Obviously, dimensions such as evaluation and potency which in the social sphere can be equated with notions such as social dominance and social solidarity constitute very general schemata for the evaluation of personality and social behavior and say relatively little about cultural meanings. Cultural conventions about the manner in which solidarity and dominance are realized, the contexts in which these traits operate, and the actual interests and goals of the participants in question all serve to realize and give sense to these abstract dimensions of personality description. Thus, though there may exist general dimensions which people use to evaluate and describe comembers, the subtleties, refinements, and contexts for these evaluations rest on cultural conventions.

The linguistic relativity hypothesis of Sapir and Whorf was that language was not just a way of talking about or reporting thought and perception but rather a mold that actually shaped these cognitive activities. In acknowledging the complementarity between culture and language, Sapir and Whorf suggested that both the vocabulary (lexicon) and the rules for combining units of meaning (grammar) were influential in thought and perception.

The literature reviewed here points in the direction of commonalities and universals in all languages and in the mode of operation of perceptual cognitive processes of people. Implicit in this literature and in the orientation and thinking of researchers is that there exist elementary and universal modes of perceiving and also basic principles of cognition. At the most general level these universals involve a principle of cognitive economy in terms of which all people organize, categorize, and process information and a complementary principle which relates to the structure that is inherent in the (perceived) world which the "mind seizes." In short, it is held that in the perceived world information-rich bundles occur that form natural discontinuities and that human beings make basic cuts in categorization in terms of these discontinuities [73].

Cognitive psychologists have begun to extend their arguments to cover the domain of social events. Preliminary data reviewed by Rosch suggests that the principles of categorization posited for objects of nature may in fact apply to the domain of social events as well. For just as persons structure the physical world in terms of basic objects they may also structure the world of social happenings in terms of key basic events such as "going to the store" or "having a lunch break." When remembering, anticipating, or discussing social happenings it may be basic events of this type which furnish the content of information. Rosch suggests that the basic objects of nature which are products of the categorization process may be the ones which figure prominently in the social scripts of basic events [73].

The linguistic relativity hypothesis concerns the referential or denotative function of language. Its claim is about how language allows speakers to code and divide up the world. As this review suggested, analyses of the meaning of many languages point to basic commonalities or universals in this aspect of meaning. The semantic differential is a device for measuring connotative meanings: feelings or images conjured up by words or concepts. When a subject is administered this instrument, he is asked to rate words or concepts (for example, disease) in terms of pairs of adjective qualifiers (good-bad, light-heavy) on a seven-point scale. Analyses of many ratings of concepts by subjects of different cultural and linguistic communities disclosed a consistent factor structure underlying these ratings. The factors uncovered are termed evaluative (typical scale, good-bad), potency (strong-weak), and activity (fast-slow). Although the structure of connotative meaning appears similar across groups, individual concepts are rated differently. For example, the concept *mother* in group X might be rated as more active than in group Y. The seeming universal structure accounting for affective meaning suggested panhuman similarities in neurologic substrates subserving emotion. Similarities in connotative meaning are held to explain general capacities for metaphor, verbal-visual synesthesia (sad goes with arrow pointing down), and phonetic symbolism (link between sound of a word and its meaning). For reviews of this body of work see Osgood [81].

Studies in Cross-Cultural Psychology

Memory. The capacity of native or primitive people to remember has attracted the attention of explorers as well as anthropologists. A traditional view has been that primitive people have unusual memory capacities. There seems to be agreement in anthropology that in everyday affairs, advanced cultures place fewer demands for memory and recall on their members as compared to simpler societies, but data bearing on this impression have not been gathered systematically. Some nonliterate societies provide members with special mnemonic devices for transmission of esoteric knowledge [82].

As Cole and Scribner indicate, carefully controlled studies on memory capacities and functions of nonliterate people are relatively new in anthropology and psychology [82]. These studies do not support the notion of a general superiority of nonliterates or suggest that these subjects employ qualitatively different modes of remembering. Researchers usually compare unschooled with schooled native subjects and employ general tests drawn from developmental and cognitive psychology. When the amount and organization of recall of nonliterates are tested, they perform more poorly than literates. When memory tasks are rendered meaningful to the subjects or they are allowed to structure information in ways which are relevant and significant to them, unschooled native subjects generally perform better than when not provided such aids. Thus, it seems that the material to be remembered in formal tests of memory make little sense to the subjects and cannot be processed in a preexisting scheme developed to deal with dominant cultural themes. Ordinarily, it is the social sense of phenomena (its embeddedness in a meaningful social context) that facilitates recall.

Results of empirical studies led cognitive psychologists to emphasize the cognitive demands of tasks and the interaction of these demands with the cognitive skills of subjects. It seems clear that the superiority of educated versus uneducated subjects lies in tasks in which the structure of the material is not made explicit and the subject is forced to provide a mnemonic device for something which literally does not make much sense. These studies point to the uniqueness of the school as a social institution wherein remembering takes place as a distinct activity, an activity set apart from the application of what is to be remembered. Schools may thus be viewed as unusual inventions that give educated subjects an advantage in memorization through repeated practice. The possible differential ability of people for memory of natural events seems to be a critical factor to study.

Verbal Reasoning. A controversial question in anthropology and psychology (closely linked to the linguistic relativity hypothesis) involves reasoning. More specifically, do modern and traditional (primitive) people share the same logical processes of thinking? This problem was reviewed recently by Sylvia Scribner and the following account is based on her view [83].

One way to study verbal reasoning is to use syllogisms and other formal logical problems. Studies were conducted among different people, and schooled and unschooled natives were compared. In virtually all cultures studied, traditional or nonliterate people show just about a chance rate of solution to these problems. Within each culture, schooled subjects do better than unschooled subjects. A level of education of two or three years appears sufficient to ensure success in these syllogistic problems. Among subjects with the requisite schooling, there is little between-culture differences. While it appears that logical problems pose difficulties to nonliterates, the source of these difficulties does not stem from unique aspects of the culture but is linked somehow to factors associated with schooling.

The work of anthropologists attests to the fact that nonliterates are obviously logical in their practical daily activities. Similarly, analysis of protocols of subjects subjected to verbal-reasoning tasks indicated that the statements the subjects made in order to explain their error choices were in fact logical. They were thus able to reason inferentially using information presented in the verbal mode. Rather, it seemed that the evidence subjects used in reasoning was not that supplied by the experimenter. The subjects instead mentally "stepped outside" the context of the problem presented. For example, a nonschooled subject may support his wrong answer to a problem by appealing to fact, belief, or opinion and not to hypothetical information contained in the problem. Schooled subjects typically could rely on information contained in the problem. Scribner termed the appeal to real-world knowledge and experience in the solution to a formal theoretical problem an *empirical bias*; this bias seemed to act as a distractor, actually serving to organize the individual's entire mode of engagement with the material. At times, nonschooled subjects responded in a theoretical way to a logical problem and invariably provided the correct answer, again showing that they possessed the mental capacity to reason verbally in a logical way.

Scribner's evidence also indicated that unschooled subjects had difficulty remembering the content of the information provided in the story. This suggested that the basic aspects of understanding and assimilation of information were involved and not just verbal reasoning. This line of research led to an emphasis on the active and constructive process of comprehension. Comprehension involves relating information to *existing* lexical and nonlexical knowledge schemata. The failure of subjects to *recall* aspects of the test information suggests that the material was not integrated and assimilated to preexisting schemata.

This line of research led Scribner to emphasize the utility of the concepts of genre and performances initially used by Dell Hymes [84]. A genre is a stylistic structure or organized verbal form with a beginning and an end, and a prescription for a pattern in between. Examples are greetings, farewells, and proverbs. A performance refers to the use of a genre in a particular context. A verbal logical problem constitutes a special language genre that stands apart from others. Through experience with a particular genre (a socially evolved language structure) people acquire a distinctive cognitive schema through which they assimilate more complex examples of the genre. They will thus remember the form of the discourse and reasoning required in the setting or problem to which the genre applies. The schema for handling the discourse of a formal logical problem seems not to be salient among nonschooled subjects.

Cerebral Asymmetries and Cultural Differences. The existence of cerebral lateralization of function prompted researchers to specify what brain structures are involved (and how) in the performance of various intellectual tasks. It seems clear that there is some specialization of function in the two hemispheres and that during the performance of certain tasks there may exist active inhibition of one hemisphere by the other [85-87]. Left-sided structures appear especially suited for language and related analytical and linear sequential problems but less effective in handling visual-spatial problems. Conversely, visual-spatial tasks which appear to require a global, synthetic, and pattern-oriented form of analysis seem to be most effectively carried out by right-sided structures.

Neuropsychologists and neurologists stressed the interaction between culture and language during ontogenesis and suggested that different types of languages might be handled by the brain in different ways. For example, Critchley suggested that ideogrammatic languages might tap right-sided brain processes more so than European languages [88]. The overall dominance of the left hemisphere for language is clearly established, but there is evidence of right-hemisphere participation in many aspects of linguistic functioning [29-31]. The right hemisphere seems to participate more in the processing of nouns than English verbs. The question posed by certain researchers is whether different languages might force users to use their two brains differently.

The English and the Hopi (American Indian group) languages serve as useful vehicles for conceptualizing styles of cognitive processes in the two brains, propositional left versus appositional right. As classically described by Whorf, the Hopi language is said to create a participation with experience and perception, appearing to link speech with context. English, on the other hand, seems to orient its user so as to separate him from the environment; a context-free or abstracted universe of discourse is created. We draw sharp distinctions between objects and actions and represent them linguistically in a categorically different manner as nouns and verbs. To the Hopi these sorts of things are not categorically different but handled linguistically as eventuations of different durations. As an example, something which we view as a thing or object (say a mountain or an animal) and which syntactically we term a noun, to the Hopi is simply something which lasts a long time. Similarly, in English actions are categorically different from objects whereas in Hopi they appear to be similar, and to merely last a shorter amount of time. These differences involving the degree to which languages separate and isolate versus incorporate or join the speaker with reality has led researchers to posit different patterns of cerebral participation during language activities [89]. In particular, the extent of right-hemisphere participation in the processing of speech was hypothesized to be greater in Hopi than in English. Hopi bilingual right-handed schoolchildren were read Hopi and English stories and their electroencephalogram (EEG) activities recorded. Greater alpha desynchronization was observed in the right parietal area during the Hopi story indicating more right-sided participation. This suggested to the researchers that languages may in fact differ in the degree to which they serve as instruments of propositional versus appositional thought.

The correlation between interhemispheric asymmetries of ongoing brain electrical activity and differences between types of cognitive tasks (verbal versus spatial) was recently brought into serious question [90]. In a series of tasks which controlled for stimulus characteristics, limb and eye movements, and performance-related factors, recorded electrical asymmetry differences were all but absent. These findings thus did not support the claim that lateralized EEG differences seen in association with different tasks reflect cognitive processes. They suggest that large areas of both cerebral cortices are involved in the performance of higher-cortical functions. The pattern of increase in regional cerebral blood flow during automatic speech was also shown to involve both hemispheres, suggesting a general activation of the cerebral cortices during this basic cognitive task [91]. These results do not invalidate the claim that the hemispheres are specialized for types of cognitive tasks; the results are linked to the validity of the claim that the EEG or regional cerebral blood flow (RCBF) can differentially reflect highly discrete cognitive processes. In other words, it is possible that the hemispheres do in fact differ selectively in the way they carry out cognitive demands, but that the EEG or RCBF inadequately reflect these differences, recording instead general arousal and attentional correlates of cognition.

The possibility that cultures differentially engage right- versus left-cortical hemisphere obviously needs further study. Cerebral speech lateralization was also studied in the American Navajo [92]. Dichotically presented syllables were administered in this instance to Navajo and Anglo subjects. Navajo subjects demonstrated a left-ear advantage compared to the expected right-ear advantage found in Anglos. The authors conclude that the results only tentatively support the idea that Navajos process language in the minor hemisphere.

Psychophysiology and Sociophysiology. Some of the research in psychophysiology and sociophysiology falls within the scope of the problem of cultural programming of brain-behavior relations. Mandler made a useful distinction between psychologically functional physiologic variables and physiologically functional psychologic variables [93]. The former refer to physiologic responses which control psychologic events and processes; the latter (which on intuitive grounds should appear to anthropologists) refer to psychologic or behavioral events which control physiologic responses. To the extent that psychologic states are affected by cultural influences, they may control physiologic responses. Anthropologists have been attracted to the notion of personality and character as internalized correlates of culture. One would thus think that the idea of individuals and groups showing distinctive hierarchies of autonomic responses would have a similar appeal. It is theoretically plausible that just as cultural groups show differences in physiologic adaptation to physical environmental factors, they can show differences in psychophysiologic adaptation to their social environment; tasks and other demands of living which have a social and symbolic coloration may produce differing patterns of visceral and autonomic functioning and responsiveness. This general problem area is essentially uncharted by anthropologists.

The ability of persons to consciously modify the functioning of their autonomic nervous system through contingent reinforcement of responses which are fed back to the individual (biofeedback) is an established generalization in psychophysiology; biofeedback training techniques are used to treat many disease conditions. Just as it is reasonable to expect that groups may differ in psychophysiologic responsiveness, one may expect that they will differ in their ability to exert control over this responsiveness and that these differences can be traced to acquired or genetic influences. In this category of behavior, one may well find correlates of culture which individuals more-or-less consciously learn or which at the very least they acquire passively as a consequence of unique social experiences.

For example, Japanese subjects studied in a laboratory situation were compared to American subjects and showed a more general stress response to films than did Americans [94]. This study suggests that cultural or genetic factors accounted for differences in autonomic reactivity. In another study, Japanese subjects showed similar operant self-control of their skin potentials compared to Americans. This control appeared to be more immediate in the Japanese, however [95]. See [96] for a review of this literature.

Subjects belonging to different ethnic groups were compared in their reactions to pain [97-99]. In the study of pain, emphasis is usually placed on threshold discrimination of pain sensation and on tolerance for pain. A study by Sternbach and Tursky failed to show differences in the way ethnic groups estimate the magnitude of pain, reflecting a uniformity in the way pain is evaluated from a sensory point of view. Ethnic differences were noted in measures involving pain tolerance, which are judged to reflect the motivational-reactive component of pain. Attitudes and anxiety levels in subjects from different ethnic groups are ordinarily invoked in explanations of differences in pain tolerance. Ethnic differences in pain responses have also been explained in terms of psychophysical and autonomic functioning; for example, as reflected in habituation to pain stimuli.

The influence of language-cultural factors on the psychophysiology of pain raises the question of the influence of these factors on the bodily correlates of emotion. There is little work in this area as the literature review of Schwartz and Shapiro indicates [96]. The role of culture-language in emotion is a staple theme in cross-cultural psychology [100, 101]. At the same time, the influence of culture-language on facial expressions which accompany emotion have been carefully analyzed [46, 47, 102]. Eckman's work points to pancultural factors in the way certain basic emotions are registered in the face leading him in fact to posit a facial affect program, with neurologic substrate probably located subcortically. Indeed, this body of work constitutes yet another line of evidence which points in the direction of biologic uniformities. Nonetheless, the psychophysiologic correlates of emotions have not been systematically studied cross-culturally.

One can illustrate the relevance of psychophysiology for anthropology and its attendant problems by considering control of the cardiovascular system. In Western medicine, the search for predictors of hypertension and coronary heart disease (CHD) has implicated a number of physical, social, and psychologic factors [103, 104]. One line of research involves relating cardiovascular responses or their presumed precursors to the types of interactions which the individual has with comembers. Cardiovascular responses have traditionally been thought of as mediated at intermediate and lower levels of the nervous system, specifically at the level of brainstem and autonomic ganglia through reflexes affecting heart rate, stroke volume of the heart, and arteriolar constriction. The current perspective invoking sociopsychologic factors thus emphasizes the role of higher (cortical) levels of the nervous system in the control of (lower level) responses.

Intense competitiveness is a central feature of a specific behavior pattern, called type A, which has been linked to an increased likelihod of hypertension and CHD [105-111]. According to Rosenman et al. [111], the type-A person tends to be competitive, aggressive and hostile, hard-driving and ambitious, and restless and impatient. In style and manner the person exhibits brisk speech and body movements, fist clenching, taut facial muscles, and explosive speech. The type-A person acts as though he is in a chronic struggle with time, ever attempting to accomplish more in less time, and in a chronic struggle with people around him. His life-style is to live more rapidly and aggressively than his peers. Type-A behaviors are reportedly elicited more readily by such environmental conditions as deadlines, interruptions or delays, and competitive challenges. According to many, type-A behaviors are more typical of evolved and complex social systems [112]. Persons living in less disturbed, more organized, and simpler social conditions tend to show more normal blood pressures and less CHD despite similarities in diet and salt intake, which are also important influences in the genesis of these conditions.

A great deal of research on the type-A behavior pattern has led to a specific formulation of human-environment factors in hypertensions and CHD. Certain cultural conditions (competitive challenges and deadlines) must combine with certain susceptible individuals (type A whom one should view as more typically formed under certain cultural conditions) to produce specific motor behavior and associated changes (excess sympathetic response and reduced blood-clotting time) which if repeated sufficiently often cause permanent damage to the cardiovascular system. In essence one could say that adverse cultural conditions can lead to permanent maladaptive nervous system responses; the fixing of these is associated with increased levels of morbidity and mortality. All four parts of this model have been studied to some degree. According to the model, a limited part of the human environment, combining with susceptible people, is translated through the CNS into neurologic, neuroendocrine, and biochemical adaptations which contribute to hypertension and CHD.

Studies on Healthy Neonates and Infants

Emphasis on Child-Caretaker Interactions. Child-rearing influences are invoked in explanations of the differences in adult behaviors observed by anthropologists. In the past, these differences were generally analyzed from a culture and personality frame of reference and empirical studies of child socialization which implicitly or explicitly tended to rely on such a framework. The study initiated by William Caudill is an example of this type but was distinguished by its relatively rigorous methodology [113]. Caudill began with the observation that in Japan there is an emphasis on social interdependence and reliance on others, whereas in America the emphasis is on independence and self-assertion. To account for these differences in values, he hypothesized that Japanese mothers would spend more time with their infants, emphasize physical contact, treat them as objects to be acted upon rather than interacted with, and that the quality of the infant-mother interaction would point to mutual interdependence. On the other hand, he anticipated that American mothers would spend less time with infants, encourage physical activity, speak to infants more, treat them as separate objects to be interacted with, and that the quality of the infant-mother interaction would lead to self-assertion of child and a budding awareness of separateness from mother.

A time-sampling procedure was used with observations made in the actual homes of families. During a selected day researchers would arrive in the home to observe and record infant-caretaker (usually mother) interactions and behavior. The researcher made four observations each minute which were recorded for forty observation categories. Each observation period lasted ten minutes. A total of ten sheets or 400 observations were compiled per case, per day, over a two-day period. The independent variables were culture (American versus Japanese) and social class based on the father's occupation. Caudill's dependent variables were of two types: (1) infant behavior including such things as awake or asleep; feeding; finger or pacifier sucking; vocalization, happy or unhappy; active gross-body movements; and playing with an object; and (2) caretaker variables including feeds infant; diapers; dresses; positions; pats or touches; plays with; gives affection; looks at; talks to and rocks. Thirty American and thirty Japanese families whose four-month infants were in equally good health served as study subjects. No cultural differences were noted either in caretaker or infant behavior involving activities directed at or reflective of biological needs (food, sucking, and elimination). However, a large number of differences in behavior judged to have cultural significance were noted. The American baby appeared more physically active and happily vocal and more involved in exploration of his body and the environment than the more-subdued Japanese baby. The American mother seemed to have a more lively and stimulating approach to her baby: she positioned, looked at, and chatted with the baby more frequently than the Japanese mother, who was present more with the baby and seemed to have a more soothing and quieting approach.

These and additional results led Caudill to conclude that a great deal of cultural learning takes place by the age of 3 to 4 months. To Caudill, the presence of significant cultural differences in behavior in 3-to-4-month-old babies meant that the precursors of certain ways of behaving, thinking, and feeling that are characteristic of a given culture have become part of an infant's approach to his environment well before the development of language and hence not easily accessible to consciousness or change. Although Caudill never invoked the organization of the nervous system in this work, it is clear that his conclusions about behavior differences imply differences in brain organization and function involving lower-subcortical centers and the autonomic nervous system.

Brazelton's work among the Maya Indians of Zinacantan in the highlands of Chiapas, Mexico, constitutes another example of the ways in which child development has been studied cross-culturally [114]. In contrast to social scientists Brazelton, a pediatrician, brings a neurologic emphasis to his work. He performed neurologic examinations and unstructured observations of neonates at birth in the first week of life.

The Zinacantan Maya are an agricultural group that has retained its traditional indigenous way despite strong efforts by the national government to encourage Western values and principles. Brazelton notes that among these people indivdual self-expression is not encouraged, while conformity is highly valued and respected. The Zinacantecos show a high level of disease and illness; approximately 30 percent of children die before age 4 and 50 percent of these in infancy. Subclinical malnutrition is widespread though severe malnutrition which might permanently damage infant CNS is not present. Brazelton reports that among the Zinacantecos no pharmacologic agents are given during delivery and no obstetrical techniques are used. The infant is swaddled after birth and is soon thereafter carried by the mother in a rebozo or small blanket which she wraps around her shoulder. This mode of carrying ensures that infants have a higher level of kinesthetic and tactile stimulation during the first year. During this first year, infants are neither propped up so as to be able to look around nor are they talked to or stimulated by eye contact. Similarly, infants are not generally placed on the floor to allow them to explore and the mothers rarely try to elicit social responses from them. Finally, mothers engage in frequent breast feeding in response to any activity of the infant.

On the basis of observations made soon after delivery, Brazelton reports that with regard to physical size, Zinacanteco neonates appear much like American premature babies, but show no jerky movements or snapback of limbs as do American prematures. In appearance and behavior, the Zinacanteco neonates were mature and showed a high level of regulation and control of the autonomic nervous system. They were quiet with relatively low levels of motor activity, but displayed a striking sensory alertness. Compared to Caucasian controls Zinacanteco infants were distinguished by a higher freedom and fluidity of movement, low output of spontaneous movement, with no overshooting or overreaction to stimuli like American infants. The Zinacanteco's muted level of response noted at birth was maintained throughout the first week. American infants showed an increase in the intensity of their responses. Among Zinacantecos spontaneous startles were rare and the general disorganization and lack of coordination usually seen in days 1 and 2 in Americans were not observed. A quiet and alert mental state was maintained for long periods, with slow smooth transitions from state to state. Thus, the Zinacanteco child's apparent control of motor behavior and mental state appeared to be of higher order, permitting repeated and prolonged responses to auditory, visual, and kinesthetic stimuli during the first week.

Observations during the first year revealed a paucity of vocalizations among Zinacanteco infants; cries were brief and promptly terminated by mother's quieting activities. Infants rarely mouthed their hands, never sucked fingers, and did not use pacifiers. Zinacantecos appeared quieter and less demanding than middle-class American infants of comparable ages. During formal testing, Zinacantecos met novelty with impassive faces and showed little exploration or experimental play. Estimations of mental and motor ages of Zinacantecos lagged approximately one month behind those of American babies, but no increasing decrement with age was observed. Zinacanteco infants passed through the same developmental milestone sequences as did Americans and also at approximately the same rate as U.S. infants.

Brazelton concluded that American neonates are motoric and that reflex motor responses interfere with alertness. On the other hand, the mental states of Zinacanteco neonates appear to be less labile and peaks of sleep and awake states are leveled off. These differences in behavior could result from genetic or environmental factors. Thus the high level of regular physical activity of pregnant females in Zinacantan and the subclinical malnutrition might have produced slow liquid movements and what appeared to be a superb state of sensorimotor control. Zinacantecos showed a possible auditory or visual precocity, but this could have resulted from lack of competition from motor activity. At the same time, it appeared that the mother set up a mode of contingent responsiveness to the infant's needs before it expresses a need or makes demands. Thus, Zinacantecos appeared to have no experience during infancy which might lay the framework for a sequence of self-motivated demand, frustration, then gratification. Zinacanteco child-rearing emphasis on subdued motor activity and on averting demand-response patterns was noted during testing for when infant motor activity was elicited, the breasts of their lactating mothers leaked milk. Such a letdown response follows the baby's cry in American mothers. Results of this study suggest that the mothering responses of Zinacantecos reinforce the quiet passivity and lower-motor activity which was already present in early neonatal interactions. In Zinacantan culture a fussy baby is in fact judged to be ill and to be in need of a curing ceremony. Thus quiet nondemanding babies are a desideratum and child-rearing influences seem to contribute to their production.

Basic Neurobiologic Processes. A line of research directly suggesting genetic racial differences in sensorimotor behaviors is reported by Freedman [115]. He matched groups of Chinese American and European American newborns in terms of age, sex, mean Apgar scores, mean hours of labor, age of mothers, and use of medication during labor. Furthermore, behavior scales and neurologic examination were used to screen for neural damage. Observations were made on the behaviors of newborns using categories such as temperament, sensory development, autonomic and central nervous system maturity, motor development, and social interest and response. Neonates were tested hours after delivery. Multivariate analysis of variance indicated that on total performance the two groups were significantly different; the main difference stemmed from items measuring temperament and a variable termed excitability-unperturbability. Substantial overlap in range on all scales was found between Chinese and Caucasian infants. These results were attributed to differences in gene pool between the respective populations. In conformance with the results of this study are the observations of Wolff who studied the vasomotor responses to alcohol in Caucasoid and Mongoloid infants [116]. Group differences were observed, independent of geographic boundary or previous exposure to alcohol. He tentatively concluded that group differences among newborns may indicate differences in autonomic nervous system reactivity having a genetic basis.

Studies of young infants involving the discrimination of pitch indicate that discriminations are adultlike and probably continuous in character [117]. This parallels findings involving the perception of luminance [72]. At the same time, regarding the perception of speech sounds, preverbal infants are like adults in that they can discriminate meaningful units (phonemes) discontinuously. This is to say that they are able to tell the difference in acoustical properties which account for phonemic distinctions between b and p. This type of perception parallels the perception of wavelength regions as colors [67]. Discrimination of phonemes thus gives rise to perceptual features for the infant as it does in the adult. More specifically, infants show clear-cut between-phonemic-category discriminations but no within-phonemic-category discrimination. On the basis of these results one cannot conclude that infants are processing acoustic variations as though these had meaning, but it can be hypothesized that mechanisms underlying speech perception are innate. Categorical perception in infants in the auditory mode has also been demonstrated with nonspeech musical sounds [118]. Since similar categorical perception exists in adults these studies emphasize the ontogenetic stability of this perceptual capacity.

Studies involving color and speech perception point to the universal and neurobiologic nature of discriminability. Regions of the continua of voice onset time and wavelength wherein acute discriminations are possible represent points of transition among perceptual features. The latter thus reflect discontinuity in the operating characteristics of these particular sensory systems vis-à-vis particular physical continua. Sensory systems can thus be said to provide an infant with a kind of innate knowledge. The properties of sensory systems involving speech and hue were studied in infrahuman species and found to be similar in certain respects to those of humans, pointing to their evolutionary origins [119-122].

Recently Bornstein critically reviewed empirical data in infant sensory physiology and discussed its implications; the following account draws heavily from his analysis [123]. As he indicates, an important question in behavioral biology concerns the possible universality (pancultural distribution) of feature perception. Related to this is whether the neurologic substrates of feature perception are plastic and their development influenced by selective environmental experiences. With respect to universality of feature perception, it has been shown that babies can make discriminations of speech sounds that are intrinsic to some languages which are different from their native one, but not from others. In other words, the evidence indicates that infants are born with the capacity for categorical perception and can make many more discriminations than are actually made use of in their immediate language community. Conversely, adult perception is not necessarily congruent with infant perception indicating that new discriminations can be learned as a result of selective experiences. Since perceptual features can be added to the infant's endowed repertoire this indicates that initial discriminative capacities do not constrain the infant. At the same time, in some spheres adults retain the ability to make feature distinctions not capitalized in their language community; the neurologic machinery for these perceptions thus persists in the absence of relevant selective or reinforcing experiences, indicating that natural properties of the auditory and visual sensory systems are not easily eroded. General experience with a wide range of colors and sounds thus appears sufficient to maintain native feature sensitivities. In summary, "feature perception is ontogenetically canalized, and its pancultural validity biases the newborn system in the direction of mature perceptual analysis. Feature perception is adaptive, moreover, and during ontogeny it is subject to tempered modification, addition or attrition, but under somewhat rigid constraints" [123, p. 59].

Bornstein points out that discontinuous discriminality of energy in the environment gives rise to perceptual contrasts and opposition which serve to structure impressions into usable chunks of information which are stable and can be further organized by the organism. This reduction of variance which facilitates information encoding is the basis of categorization which itself underlies cognitive activity. Categorization speeds encoding time and facilitates recognition. Perceptual constancies made possible by innate capacities for categorical perception provide an initial guidance for the emergence of rules for communication and elementary cognitive behavior. In this way, perceptual constancies in vision and audition may be viewed as elementary visual and auditory concepts which facilitate learning, serve as templates for thinking, and form an "Anlagen for mature conceptual behavior and the treatment of transformations or variations of other stimulus sets" [123, p. 71].

Studies involving global aspects of the sensorimotor behaviors of newborns suggest an even more pervasive uniformity or universality rooted in the sociobiology of humans. Thus, observations of neonate interaction with caretaker show that infant whole-body movements are synchronized with the articulatory elements of adult speech as early as the first day of life [124]. From studies of adult behavior which rely on an ethological frame of reference, Condon derived the concept of *interactional synchrony* which refers to the configurational organization of units of a listener's body motions that synchronize with the speaker's speech. Interactional synchrony occurs out of awareness of the interactant. Condon applied his techniques of measurement of microbody movements to newborns. His study focused on interactional synchrony between sound segments of adult speech and points of change in the configuration of neonate movements. It was shown that the infant responds in a patterned and organized manner to adult speech. Segments of movements were synchronous with the adult speech, indicating a precise and sustained concurrence. No such concurrence was demonstrated when random neonate movements, filmed during silence, were analyzed in relation to adult sounds. This indicated that the correspondence was not due to a random fitting together of patterns of infant movement with patterns of adult speech. Furthermore, audiotapes containing English and Chinese were presented to American neonates and a clear correspondence between speech sounds and neonate movement emerged in both instances. Disconnected vowel and tapping sounds did not produce the correspondence associated with natural rhythmic speech, suggesting that meaningful speech was the organizing variable.

This study thus suggests that (at least American) infants are born with a general capacity to orient and relate organismically to human language and speech regardless of its morphology and syntax. Early in life the infant thus begins to move in a precise and rhythmic fashion with the organization of the speech structure of his culture. A developmental sociobiologic entrainment process appears to be set up between the body (and its motions-activities) and the linguistic system of a culture. Rhythm, syntax, and para-linguistic nuances are interlocked with body-motion styles and responses. This pattern of neonate responsiveness no doubt prepares and helps shape operational formats for later speech and may be held to provide a conditioning context for internal and external body activities in respect to non-verbal but still linguistic aspects of communication.

The material reviewed involving perception seemingly bears little relation to culture-language and points directly at neuropsychologic uniformities which are, as it were, built in to the nervous system. The similarities which these perceptual mechanisms have with analogous neuropsychologic processes in infrahuman groups raise the question of biologic determinism. Behaviors which one may wish to qualify as cultural are constrained by (or must conform to) the neurologic mechanisms outlined. However, as acknowledged by most of the researchers, such behaviors can also be said to be elaborated into a pattern which makes sense only when viewed socially and culturally. It is this complementariness between the neurobiologic and cultural-linguistic dimensions of behavior which leads some anthropologists to speak about the biocultural unity of human social behavior. The expression biocultural can also be given an evolutionary meaning. It is now held that at different points in the evolutionary time scale, prevailing social conditions served as factors that helped select for neurologic structures and changes; behavioral adaptations made possible by these changes had the effect of modifying the social conditions of people, thereby yielding a new context for natural selection [125-127]. All this implies a connectedness between social conditions and neurobiologic traits. This connection between social and neurobiologic factors in the evolutionary process is held to account for possible similarities in the social and cognitive behaviors of humans and other primates also explains why the precise origins and meanings of culture are problematic. A consequence of this is that higher-cerebral functions of humans must be continuous with those of humanoid groups and might be with those found in our closest relatives, the apes [128-131].

Research Involving Ideas of Piaget. The developmental cognitive psychology stemming from Piaget's work has implications for the problem of cultural programming of brain-behavior relations. This psychology posits universal cognitive structures which unfold during infancy in a predictable sequence of stages and are reflected in characteristic modes of functioning. It is obvious that this psychology reflects processes of brain maturation and development, though the exact centers and neurophysiologic mechanisms involved are not understood. An early strategy of research using ideas of Piaget was to test his propositions cross-culturally.

Research findings in cross-cultural Piagetian psychology indicate that the basic qualitative features and the sequencing of the sensorimotor stages of cognitive development for the most part appear to be similar among children of various cultures [132, 133]. The rates of development of these stages vary in relation to culture as well as to elements of the cognitive tasks. For example, though still controversial, evidence suggests precocity in African infants on some sensorimotor tasks [134]. Superior performance is explained in terms of the kinds or the amount of proprioceptive, tactile, and visual stimulation that African infants are given in the group. These experiences are assumed to enhance their psychomotor and postural development which by facilitating exploratory activities builds up sensorimotor schemata. In brief, differential rates of development are "linked to cultural characteristics, to the predominant mode or quantity of stimulation [and] to the cultural value placed on certain skills over others" [132, p. 165]. Information from cross-cultural experiments suggests that the structural properties of the schemata which are believed to develop and the way in which they are built into more complex action patterns are in some ways similar. The data thus suggest some similarities in the way the human infant interacts with his environment and begins to build up knowledge about it as a basis for further reasoning.

Cross-cultural research in the Piagetian stage of concrete operations (with conservation a key marker) suggests that many but not all children reach this particular state. In other words, groups differ in terms of the proportion of subjects who display concrete operations like conservation. Moreover, the evidence is clear that the stage of formal operations is not universal; several studies indicate that some people fail to show full development of this stage. Here then one sees a quantitative difference in cognitive development, and cultural factors seem to be influential. Western values, life-style, and demands linked to ecological conditions have in different instances been invoked as explanations. A working assumption in this area of research is the notion that indivduals possess the underlying potential to engage in cognitive behaviors appropriate to the more advanced stages of Piagetian psychology but may not be provided with experiences which tap the relevant abilities. Differences in the level of cognitive maturity are thus taken to reflect *performance* issues linked to cultural conditions rather than basic differences in competence. In general, conservation-of-quantity experiments yield information pointing to both similarities and differences among children of different cultures. The idea of invariance in the sequencing of stages and that of a basic cognitive structure corresponding to each stage has been challenged by empirical findings. Cognitive development as evaluated through these and other experiments appears to be arrested or significantly delayed among some non-Western subjects.

Summary and Conclusions

This review has covered information which points in a compelling way to universal aspects of perception, cognition, and language. Such information suggests that equally universal brain processes and functions underlie human higher forms of behavior. Statements about universals appear inconsistent with the data of cross-cultural psychiatry involving the specificity of culture-bound syndromes and the differences in manifestations of major psychiatric illnesses (as well as with speculations offered about culture-specific manifestations of neuropsychiatric entities). How is one to resolve or at least explain such an apparent inconsistency between universals and cultural differences?

A consideration of the basic aims and modes of inquiry of a neurobiologic as opposed to a culture-oriented psychiatrist can provide the beginnings of an explanation. A neuroscientist intent on demonstrating cultural influences on brain-behavior relations needs first to show that an association exists between a culturally relevant situation or stimulus and a brain event; or an association between a stimulus or situation and a behavior known to be an outcome of a specific brain event. Each of the three classes of phenomena (stimulus, brain event, and behavior) need to be clearly specified and measured. Given this, it would be necessary for the neuroscientist to show that there exist differences on the relevant measures across groups of individuals who belong to different language and cultural communities. The behavior involved would probably include a motor response of some sort with the researcher manipulating an expectancy based on the individual's culture. In this experimental context, the subject would be required to attend or to make a decision of some sort. It should be obvious that to show associations between culture and brain-behavior relations the neuroscientist is forced to reduce observations to discrete phenomena.

The above logic is essentially also that of the cognitive psychologist intent on demonstrating that cultural groups differ in ways of perceiving, making decisions, remembering, discriminating, or problem solving. The psychologist is required to make his test understandable and appropriate to the subject so as to motivate and engage equivalent cognitive processes. Moreover, he must assure that subjects' responses are discrete and unambiguous so that they can be reliably measured. When the neuroscientist evaluates behavior, he too will be guided by these restrictions. A key element in the strategy of the neuroscientist or cognitive psychologist is thus that of *abstraction* and *specificity*. In short, claims about cultural differences in neurologic or psychologic structures involve physical measures or behaviors which are highly discrete and isolated out of a social context.

A neurologically oriented psychiatrist pursuing the question of possible cultural differences in psychiatric illness can adopt the strategy of the neuroscientist or cognitive psychologist and concentrate on highly discrete phenomena. If he finds differences on measures of psychiatric illness which could be related to brain events or functions, he could claim that the brains of the persons with the disease-illness were different across cultural groups or that the disease-illness itself was different in the groups.

It is obvious that phenomena ordinarily studied by culturally oriented psychiatrists are at a quite different level of abstraction than that studied by neurologically oriented ones. Thus, such things as mental symptoms (delusions, hallucinations), social adjustment changes, or rate of onset or duration of psychotic disorganization are far removed from the discrete and abstract items engaging the neuroscientist or cognitive psychologist. It is in fact quite evident that culturally oriented psychiatrists tend to be interested in demonstrating differences in the configuration of psychiatric illness as a whole. That is, it is the logic or psychosocial rationale inherent in illness, viewed as an experiential and whole behavioral structure, which seems to claim his interest. Such a psychiatrist seeks to demonstrate that the illness, viewed in terms of the ill person or of group comembers, makes sense only when semantic aspects (that is, context or meaning) are taken into consideration. In other words, it is the symbolic dimension of social and psychologic behaviors which claims principal interest in this instance. A useful way to capture these differences in orientation is to say that culturally oriented psychiatrists are principally drawn to features of illness whereas neuroscientifically oriented ones are drawn to features of disease (physical changes in the brain).

In thinking about culture one has in mind the notion of symbols, rules, or conventions about such things as the world, others, the self, and work. We have seen that a host of uniformities underlie much of what is generally described as cultural differences in behavior. Indeed, one can say that culture influences and patterns social and psychologic behavior provided that this is examined in symbolic (cultural) terms. This obvious tautology can be made even more explicit by recalling that the idea of a cultural program arises as a result of an attempt to explain the basis or rationale for behaviors which are interpreted from a symbolic viewpoint. Although it is (tautologically) true that cultural programs somehow pattern social and psychologic behaviors, such behaviors nonetheless have a tangible form and organization and are the outcome of (produced by) brain programs or routines of some sort. One can thus inquire about the brain correlates of culture. Since social and psychologic (symbolic) behaviors differ across societies, one anticipates that such differences are correlated with differences in brain organization and function. How is one to understand cultural differences in terms of neural substrates?

The material discussed in this chapter offers few clear answers. Neuropsychologists speak of the engram as the physical brain substrate of memory. Although not often mentioned explicitly, it is very likely that part of what social scientists have in mind when speaking of culture and the symbolic can be equated with the engrams of the semantic memory system. As described by Tulving and illustrated by Warrington, it is this system which presumably embodies the repository of knowledge and beliefs that an individual requires as he learns his culture [135, 136]. Information of the semantic memory system may be judged to embrace such overlearned things as role prescriptions, attitudes, values, and beliefs all of which constitute the data of social scientists. In summary, one brain analog of culture can be thought of as involving protein changes which influence conduction properties of synapses and populations of neurons and serve as substrates for the posited semantic memory system. Molecular changes of this type may also be equated with the modules of Mountcastle and Edelman [8]; it is obvious that understanding how these molecular changes operate is at present beyond the reach of neuroscientists.

Another brain analog of culture (and also not explicitly mentioned as such in the literature) can be equated with what neuroscientists mean when they speak of "motor programs." That is, physical changes (again involving molecular arrangements, patterns of synaptic transmission, and neural nets) in the brain which mediate or serve to organize sequences of coordinated motor behaviors, including those underlying the use of language. Thus, motor progams presumably underlie the learning and performance of such things as basic neuromuscular skills, speech, and nonverbal ways of communicating and showing emotion. There is a suggestion that motor programs themselves may partly embody knowledge [137], though the information discussed above (as semantic memory) is best thought of as being represented in a physically separate manner. It is clear that the location, the neural organization, and the mode of operation of these motor programs vis-à-vis memory and cognitive systems are beyond understanding at present. In summary, motor programs in the brain can also be thought of as embodying neurologic correlates of culture though neuroscientists handle these programs as universals, disregarding the question of cultural specificities and differences.

The material reviewed indicates that when neurologically oriented researchers invoke cultural factors they refer to such things as patterns of cerebral asymmetry, relative amounts of brain tissue of a certain type which might be required (for cultural reasons) to carry out specific psychologic functions, or specialized ways in which basic neural structures are used in order to carry out culturally specific functions (ideographic reading in the Japanese). A basic assumption, in other words, is a quantum of plasticity in an otherwise highly specialized organ, whose organization and functioning is uniform across the species. Apparently, brain analogs of cultural differences are held to involve *quantitative* differences in the way specific brain regions are used, arranged, and coordinated.

Three aspects of the way culture may affect brain-behavior relations have been mentioned. First, cultural rules involving behavior and child rearing may, in a purely mechanical sense, regulate which physical environmental stimuli (and to what degree) impinge on the newborn and the developing infant. In this model, any cultural meaning which the stimulations may have is not considered important. Physical environmental agents typically are studied by neuroscientists, and to varying degrees each (given sufficient underload or overload conditions) can be expected to affect neural development and function and, by implication, behavior. The extent to which such stimuli have to be controlled in order to produce discernible effects on adult animal behavior is variable. Whether human infants are ordinarily subject to analogous levels of understimulation or overstimulation is questionable, and the possibility that culture (viewed by many as an adaptive system) could adversely (maladaptively) program physical stimuli which are required for normal brain maturation raises obvious philosophical questions. Nonetheless, on logical grounds alone, one should allow for the possibility.

Complementing this more-or-less mechanical view of cultural influences, we have also considered a dynamic one in which the rationale behind cultural conventions in child-rearing practices would play an influential role. Parental influences would be judged to reflect a code that is internalized by the infant and then helps regulate which level or pattern of stimuli are attended to, selected, processed, and integrated in the higher levels of the nervous system. This influence might take place not in primary sensory areas, but rather in secondary association areas wherein intermodal integrations and transformations are believed to take place [10]. At first verbally from the caretakers and also nonverbally (emotively, through cooing, touching, fondling, and directing), and later through the acquisition of actual language and speech, stimuli from the environment may be viewed as "packaged" or ordered in a meaningful way for the infant. Clearly, a great deal of brain maturation takes place under the influence of social stimulations, whose cultural meanings are not yet evident to the infant. Moreover, there are obvious limits to the extent to which neural representations of social symbols can filter physical stimuli and tune the nervous sytem. This effect of culture on brain functioning is clearly evident in the language which the infant eventually learns and as Condon suggests, prelinguistically as well. Moreover, culture and language together influence the way a person comes to recognize and like music, the way he shows emotion, and possibly the way he construes space and orients spatially. It may be that in an analogous way language and cultural conventions may regulate the way other brain capacities come to be realized, such as those for taste, emotion, pain, and other bodily states which are given cultural significance. Clearly so-called higher-cortical capacities (such as those underlying language) govern not only abstract (semantic) meanings but also hedonic ones (affective, emotional) which implicate subcortical structures. In contemporary interpretations of human brain organization, emphasis is given to the various brains (protomammalian, limbic, and so on) which are seen as somehow fused together. In these accounts, emphasis is given to the role which language and therefore culture play in modifying the functions of the "ancestral" brain [138, 139].

A final model of how cultural influences might affect the organization of the brain and behavior is suggested by considering an adult who migrates to a new social group and adopts its social practices. Such an individual will no doubt learn a great deal (nonverbally) simply by observation and imitation, though his native language system would obviously play an influential role in the process (through verbal introspection, rehearsal, and training). A better understanding of the conventions of the group would follow from learning its language. In both instances, neurolinguistic substrates play a critical mediating role. How and to what extent other structures and levels of the nervous system participate in this type of enculturation is not known. The literature dealing with recovery of aphasia among polyglots contains hints that emotion and language performance are linked together in complex ways [20, 21].

References

1. Keesing, Roger M. 1979. Linguistic knowledge and cultural knowledge: Some doubts and speculations. *Am Anthropol* 81:14-36.
2. Fabrega, Horacio, Jr. 1977. *The scope of ethnomedical science in culture, medicine and psychiatry.* Dordrecht, Holland: D. Reidel Publishing Co., pp. 201-228.
3. Fabrega, Horacio, Jr. 1979. Phylogenetic precursors of psychiatric illness: A theoretical inquiry. *Compr Psychiatry* 20:275-288.
4. Edgerton, Robert B. 1969. On the "recognition" of mental illness. In *changing perspectives in mental illness.* Eds. Stanley C. Plog and Robert B. Edgerton. New York: Holt, Rinehart and Winston, pp. 49-72.
5. Murphy, J.M. 1976. Psychiatric labeling in cross-cultural perspective. *Science* 191:1019-1028.
6. Westermeyer, Joseph, and Wintrob, Ronald. 1979. "Folk" criteria for the diagnosis of mental illness in rural Laos: On being insane in sane places. *Am J Psychiatry* 136:6.
7. Fabrega, Horacio, Jr. 1977. Culture, behavior and the nervous system. *Annu Rev Anthropol* 6:419-455.
8. Mountcastle, Vernon B., and Edelman, Gerald M. 1978. *The mindful brain.* Cambridge, Mass.: MIT Press.
9. Manschreck, Theo C., and Petri, Michelle. 1978. *Culture, medicine and psychiatry.* Dordrecht, Holland: D. Reidel Publishing Co., pp. 233-268.
10. Geschwind, N. 1965. Disconnexion syndromes in animals and man. *Brain* 88:237-294, 585-644.
11. Geschwind, N. 1970. The organization of language and the brain. *Science* 170:940-944.

12. Weinstein, Edwin A., and Friedland, Robert P., eds. 1977. *Advances in neurology: Vol. 18, Hemi-inattention and hemisphere specialization*. New York: Raven Press.
13. Gardner, Howard. 1974. *The shattered mind*. New York: Random House.
14. Stevens, J.R. 1973. An anatomy of schizophrenia? *Arch Gen Psychiatry* 29:177-189.
15. Koehler, Karl. 1979. First rank symptoms of schizophrenia: Questions concerning clinical boundaries. *Br J Psychiatry* 134:236-248.
16. Marsella, A.J. Forthcoming. Depressive experience and disorder across cultures. In *Handbook of cross-cultural psychology, vol. 5: Culture and psychopathology*. Eds. J. Draguns and H. Triandis. Boston: Allyn & Bacon.
17. Leff, J.P. 1973. Culture and the differentiation of emotional states. *Br J Psychiatry* 123:299-306.
18. Leff, J.P. 1977. The cross-cultural study of emotions. *Cult Med Psychiatry* 1(4):317-350.
19. Ekman, P. 1972. Universals and cultural differences in facial expressions of emotions. In *Nebraska symposium on motivation, 1971*. Ed. J.K. Cole. Lincoln: Univ. Nebraska Press.
20. Paradis, M. 1976. Bilingualism and aphasia. In *Studies in neurolinguistics*. Ed. H. Whitaker and H.A. Whitaker. New York: Academic Press.
21. Albert, Martin L., and Obler, Loraine K. 1978. *The bilingual brain*. New York: Academic Press.
22. Yamadori, Atsushi, and Ikumura, Goro. 1975. Central (or conduction) aphasia in a Japanese patient. *Cortex* 11:73-82.
23. Yamadori, Atsushi. 1975. Ideogram reading in alexia. *Brain* 98:231-238.
24. Sasanuma, S. 1975. Kana and Kanji processing in Japanese aphasics. *Brain Lang* 2:369-383.
25. Sasanuma, S., and Monoi, H. 1975. The syndrome of Gogi (word-meaning) aphasia: Selective impairment of Kanji processing. *Neurology* 25:627-632.
26. Sasanuma, Sumiko; Itoh, Motonobu; and Kobayashi, Yo. 1977. Tachistoscopic recognition of Kana and Kanji words. *Neuropsychologia* 15:547-553.
27. Hatta, Takeshi. 1977. Lateral recognition of abstract and concrete Kanji in Japanese. *Percept Mot Skills* 45:731-734.
28. Hatta, Takeshi. 1977. Recognition of Japanese Kanji in the left and right visual fields. *Neuropsychologia* 15:685-688.
29. Zaidel, Eran. 1978. Concepts of cerebral dominance in the split brain. *Cerebral correlates of conscious experience*. INSERM Symposium no.

6. Eds. Buser and Rougeul-Buser. New York: Elsevier/North Holland Biomedical Press.

30. Zaidel, Eran. 1978. Lexical organization in the right hemisphere. In *Cerebral correlates of conscious experience*. Proceedings. Ed. by P.A. Buser and A. Rougeul-Buser. New York: North-Holland.

31. Zaidel, Eran. 1978. The elusive right hemisphere of the brain. *Engineering and science*. California Institute of Technology, vol. 42, pp. 10-32.

32. Gardner, Howard; Silverman, Jen; Denes, Gianfranco; Semenza, Carlo; and Rosenstiel, Anne K. 1977. Sensitivity to musical denotation and connotation in organic patients. *Cortex* 13:242-256.

33. Franzen, E.A., and Myers, R.B. 1973. Neural control of social behavior: Prefrontal and anterior temporal cortex. *Neuropsychologia* 11:141-157.

34. Myers, R.E.; Swett, C.; and Miller, M. 1973. Loss of social group affinity following prefrontal lesions in free-ranging macaques. *Brain Res* 64:257-269.

35. Franzen, E., and Myers, R.D. 1973. Age effects on social behavior deficits following prefrontal lesions in monkeys. *Brain Res* 54:277-286.

36. Suomi, S.J.; Harlow, H.F.; and Lewis, F.K. 1973. Effects of bilateral frontal lobectomy on social preferences of rhesus monkeys. *J Comp Physiol Psychol* 71:448-453.

37. Deets, A.C.; Harlow, H.F.; and Lewis, J.K. 1973. Effects of bilateral lesions of the frontal granular cortex on the social behavior of rhesus monkeys. *J Comp Physiol Psychol* 72:452-261.

38. Luria, A.R. 1973. The frontal lobes and the regulation of behavior. In *Psychophysiology of the frontal lobes*. Eds. K.H. Pribrain and A.R. Luria. New York: Academic Press.

39. Teuber, H.L. 1972. Unity and diversity of frontal lobe functions. *Acta Neurobiol Exp* 32:615-656.

40. Nauta, W.J.H. 1971. The problem of the frontal lobe: A reinterpretation. *J Psychiatr Res* 8:167-187.

41. Rosvold, H.E. 1972. The frontal lobe system: Cortical-subcortical interrelationships. *Acta Neurobiol Exp* 32:439-460.

42. Hecaen, H., and Albert, M.D. 1975. Disorders of mental functioning related to frontal lobe pathology. In *Psychiatric aspects of neurological disease*. Eds. D.F. Benson and D. Blumer. New York: Grune & Stratton.

43. Teuber, H.L. 1975. Effects of focal brain injury on human behavior. In *The nervous system, 2: The clinical neurosciences*. Ed. D.B. Tower. New York: Raven Press.

44. Blumer, D., and Benson, D.F. 1975. Personality changes with frontal

and temporal lobe lesions. In *Psychiatric aspects of neurologic disease*. Eds. D.F. Benson and D. Blumer. New York: Grune & Stratton.

45. Teuber, H.L. 1964. The riddle of frontal lobe neurosciences. New York: Raven Press.

46. Ekman, P. 1973. Cross-cultural studies of facial expression. In *Darwin and facial expression: A century of research in review*. Ed. P. Ekman. New York: Academic Press, pp. 169-220.

47. Ekman, P. 1973. Cross-cultural studies of facial expression. In *Darwin and facial expression: A century of research in review*. Ed. P. Ekman. New York: Academic Press.

48. Blumer, D. 1975. Temporal lobe epilepsy and its psychiatric significance. In *Psychiatric aspects of neurologic disease*. Eds. D.F. Benson and D. Blumer. New York: Grune & Stratton.

49. Halgren, E.; Walter, R.D.; Cherlow, D.G.; and Crandall, H. 1978. Mental phenomena evoked by the human hippocampal formation and amygdala. *Brain* 101:83-118.

50. Penry, J.K., and Daly, D.D., eds. 1976. *Complex partial seizures and their treatment*. New York: American Elsevier Publishing Co.

51. Waxman, S.C., and Geschwind, N. 1975. The interictal behavior syndrome of temporal lobe epilepsy. *Arch Gen Psychiatry* 32:1580-1586.

52. Bear, D.M., and Fedio, P. 1977. Quantitative analysis of interictal behavior in lobe epilepsy. *Arch Neurol* 34:454-467.

53. Gloor, P. 1978. Inputs and outputs of the amygdala: What the amygdala is trying to tell the rest of the brain. In *Limbic mechanisms*. Eds. E.D. Livingston and O. Hornykiewicz. New York: Plenum Press, pp. 189-210.

54. Clark, H.H., and Clark, E.V. 1977. *Language and thought in psychology and language: An introduction to psycholinguistics*. New York: Harcourt Brace Jovanovich.

55. Sapir, E. 1949. *Selected writings in language, culture and personality*. Ed. D.G. Mandelbaum. Berkeley: Univ. of California Press.

56. Whorf, B.L. 1956. *Language, thought and reality*. Boston: MIT Press. New York: Wiley.

57. Fishman, J.A. 1960. A systematization of Whorfian hypothesis. *Behav Sci* 5:323-339.

58. Lucy, J.A., and Shweder, R.A. In press. Whorf and his critics: Linguistic and nonlinguistic influences on color memory. *Am Anthropologist*.

59. Lyons, J. 1977. *Semantics*. Vol. 1. Cambridge: Cambridge Univ. Press.

60. Witkowski, S.R., and Brown, C.H. 1977. An explanation of color nomenclature universals. *Am Anthropologist* 79:50-57.

61. Brown, C.H.; Kolar, J.; Torrey, B.J.; Truong-Quang, T.; and Volkman, P. 1976. Some general principles of biological and non-biological folk classification. *Am Ethnologist* 3:73-85.
62. Witkowski, S.R., and Brown, C.H. 1978. Lexical universals. *Annu Rev Anthropol* 7:427-451.
63. Bornstein, M.H. 1975. The influence of visual perception on culture. *Am Anthropol* 77:774-798.
64. Bornstein, M.H. 1973. Color vision and color naming: A psychophysiological hypothesis of culture difference. *Psychol Bull* 80:257-285.
65. Berlin, B., and Kay, P. 1969. *Basic color terms*. Berkeley: Univ. of California Press.
66. Kay, P., and McDaniel, C.K. 1978. Linguistic significance of meanings of basic color terms. *Language* 54:610-646.
67. Bornstein, M.H.; Kessen, W.; and Weiskoff, S. 1975. The categories of hue in infancy. *Science* 191:201-202.
68. De Valois, R.L.; Abramov, I.; and Mead, W.R. 1967. Single cell analysis of wavelength discrimination and the lateral geniculate nucleus in the macaque. *J Neurophysiol* 30:415-433.
69. Brown, C.H. 1977. Folk botanical life-forms: Their universality and growth. *Am Anthropologist* 79:317-342.
70. Brown, C.H. 1974. General principles of human anatomical partonomy and speculations on the growth of partonomic nomenclature. *Am Ethnologist* 3:400-424.
71. Andersen, E.S. 1978. Lexical universals of body-part terminology. In *Universals of human language, 4 vols.: Word structure*. Eds. J.H. Greenberg, Ferguson, C.A. and Moravcsik, E.A. Stanford, Calif.: Stanford Univ. Press.
72. Bornstein, M.H. 1978. Visual behavior of the young human infant: Relationships between chromatic and spatial perception and the activity of underlying brain mechanisms. *J Exp Child Psychol* 26:174-192.
73. Rosch, E. 1978. *Principles of categorization in cognition and categorization*. Eds. E. Rosch and B.B. Lloyd. Hillsdale, N.J.: Lawrence Erlbaum Associates, Publishers.
74. Greenberg, J.H. 1969. Language universals: A research frontier. *Science* 166:473-478.
75. Ember, Melvin. 1978. Size of color lexicon: Interaction of cultural and biological factors. *Am Anthropologist* 80:364-367.
76. McClure, E.F. 1975. Ethno-anatomy: The structure of the domain. *Anthropol Ling* 17:78-88.
77. Berlin, B.; Breedlove, D.E.; and Raven, P.H. 1973. General principles of classification and nomenclature in folk biology. *Am Anthropologist* 75:214-242.

78. White, G. 1977. Conceptual universals in personality description. Department of Anthropology, University of California, San Diego, La Jolla, California.
79. D'Andrade, R.G. 1965. Trait psychology and componential analysis. *Am Anthropologist* 67:215-228.
80. Shweder, R.A. 1977. Likeness and likelihood in everyday thought: Magical thinking in judgments about personality. *Curr Anthropol* 18:637-658.
81. Osgood, C.E.; May, W.H.; and Miron, M.S. 1975. *Cross-cultural universals of affective meaning*. Urbana: Univ. Illinois Press.
82. Cole, M., and Scribner, S. 1977. Cross-cultural studies of memory and cognition. In *Perspectives on the development of memory and cognition*. Eds. R.V. Kail, Jr., and J.W. Hagen. Hillsdale, N.J.: Lawrence Erlbaum Associates, Publishers.
83. Scribner, S. 1979. Modes of thinking and ways of speaking: Culture and logic reconsidered. In *Thinking: Readings in cognitive science*. Eds. D.B. Johnson, M. Laird, and L.C. Waron. Cambridge: Cambridge Univ. Press.
84. Hymes, Dell. 1974. *Foundations in sociolinguistics: An ethnographic approach*. Philadelphia: Univ. of Pennsylvania Press.
85. Levy, J., and Trevarthen, C. 1977. Perceptual, semantic, and phonetic aspects of elementary language processes in split-brain patients. *Brain* 100:105-118.
86. Levy, J., and Trevarthen, C. 1976. Meta-control of hemispheric function in human split-brain patients. *J Exp Psychol* 2:299-312.
87. Lazarus-Mainka, G., and Hörmann, H. 1978. Strategic selection (metacontrol) of hemispheric dominance in normal subjects. *Psychol Res* 40:15-25.
88. Critchley, M. 1974. Aphasia in polyglots and bilinguals. *Brain Lang* 1:15-27.
89. Rogers, L.; TenHouten, W.; Kaplan, C.; and Gardiner, M. 1977. Hemispheric specialization of language: An EEG study of bilingual Hopi Indian children. *Int J Neurosci* 8:1-6.
90. Gevins, A.S.; Zeitlin, G.M.; Doyle, J.C.; Yingling, C.D.; Schaffer, R.E.; Callaway, E.; and Yeager, C.L. 1979. Electroencephalogram correlates of higher cortical functions. *Science* 203:665-668.
91. Larsen, B.; Skinhøj, E.; and Lassen, N.A. 1978. Variations in regional cortical blood flow in the right and left hemispheres during automatic speech. *Brain* 101:193-209.
92. Scott, S.; Hynd, G.W.; Hunt, L.; and Weed, W. 1979. Cerebral speech lateralization in the native American Navajo. *Neuropsychologia* 17:89-92.
93. Mandler, G. 1967. The conditions for emotional behavior. In *Biology*

and behavior: Neurophysiology and emotion. Ed. D.C. Glass. New York: Rockefeller Univ., pp. 96-102.

94. Lazarus, R.S.; Tomita, M.; Opton, E.M., Jr.; and Kodama, M. 1966. A cross-cultural study of stress-reaction patterns in Japan. *J Pers Soc Psychol* 4:622-633.

95. Shapiro, D., and Watanabe, T. 1972. Reinforcement of spontaneous electrodermal activity: A cross-cultural study in Japan. *Psychophysiology* 9:340-344.

96. Schwartz, G.E., and Shapiro, D. 1973. Social psychophysiology. In *Electrodermal activity in psychological research.* Eds. W.F. Prokasy and D.C. Raskin. New York and London: Academic Press.

97. Sternbach, R.A., and Tursky, B. 1965. Ethnic differences among housewives in psychophysical and skin potential responses to electric shock. *Psychophysiology* 1:241-246.

98. Tursky, B., and Sternbach, R.A. 1967. Further physiological correlates of ethnic differences in responses to shock. *Psychophysiology* 4:67-73.

99. Weisenberg, M. 1977. Pain and pain control. *Psychol Bull* 84:1008-1044.

100. Tanaka-Matsumi, J., and Marsella, A.J. 1976. Cross-cultural variations in the phenomenological experience of depression. *J Cross-cult Psychol* 7:379-396.

101. Marsella, A.J.; Kinzie, D.; and Gordon, P. 1973. Ethnic variations in the expression of depression. *J Cross-Cult Psychol* 4:435-458.

102. Ekman, P. 1977. Biological and cultural contributions to body and facial movement. In *The anthropology of the body.* Ed. J. Blacking. London: Academic Press, pp. 39-84.

103. Jenkins, C.D. 1971. Psychological and social precursors of coronary disease. *N Engl J Med* 284:244-255, 307-317.

104. Proceedings of the National Heart and Lung Institute Working Conference on Health Behavior, Basye, Virginia, May 12-15, 1975. DHEW Publ. no. (NIH), pp. 76-868.

105. Friedman, M. 1969. *Pathogenesis of coronary artery disease.* New York: McGraw Hill.

106. Friedman, M., and Rosenman, R. 1974. *Type A behavior and your heart.* New York: Knopf.

107. Friedman, M.; Rosenman, R.; and Byers, K. 1964. Serum lipids and conjunctional circulation after fat ingestion in men exhibiting type A behavior pattern. *Circulation* 29:874-886.

108. Rosenman, R. 1974. The role of behavior patterns and neurogenic factors in the pathogenesis of coronary heart disease. In *Contemporary problems in cardiology (stress and the heart).* Ed. R.S. Eliot. Mount Kisco: Futura.

109. Rosenman, R., and Friedman, M. 1971. The central nervous system and coronary heart disease. *Hosp Pract* 6:87-97.
110. Rosenman, R., and Friedman, M. 1974. Neurogenic factors in pathogenesis of coronary heart disease. *Med Clin North Am* 58(2): 269-279.
111. Rosenman, R.; Friedman, M.; Straus, R.; Wurm, M.; Jenkins, C.; and Messinger, H. 1966. Coronary heart disease in the western collaborative group study. *JAMA* 195(2):130-136.
112. Eyer, J. 1975. Hypertension as a disease of modern society. *Int J Health Serv* 5(4):539-558.
113. Caudill, W., and Weinstein, H. 1969. Maternal care and infant behavior in Japan and America. *Psychiatry* 32:12-43.
114. Brazelton, T.B. 1977. Implications of infant development among the Mayan Indians of Mexico. In *Culture and infancy: Variation in the human experience.* Eds. P.H. Leiderman, S.R. Tulkin and A. Rosenfeld. New York: Academic Press, pp. 151-188.
115. Freedman, D.G. 1974. *Human infancy: An evolutionary perspective.* Hillsdale, N.J.: Lawrence Erlbaum Associates, Publishers.
116. Wolff, P.H. 1977. Biological variations and cultural diversity: An exploratory study. In *Culture and infancy: Variations in the human experience.* Eds. P.H. Leiderman, S.R. Tulkin, and A. Rosenfeld. New York: Academic Press, pp. 357-384.
117. Eimas, P.D.; Siqueland, E.R.; Jusczyk, P.; and Vigorito, J. 1970. Speech perception in infants. *Science* 171:303-306.
118. Cutting, J.E.; Rosner, B.S.; and Foard, C.F. 1976. Perceptual categories for musiclike sounds: Implications for theories of speech perception. *Q J Exp Psychol* 28:361-378.
119. Petersen, M.R.; Beecher, M.D.; Zoloth, S.R.; Moody, D.B.; and Stebbins, W.C. 1978. Neural lateralization of species-specific vocalizations by Japanese macaques (Macaca fuscata). *Science* 202:324-327.
120. Waters, R.S., and Wilson, W.A. 1976. Speech perception by rhesus monkeys: The voicing distinction in synthesized labial and velar stop consonants. *Percept Psychophys* 19:285-289.
121. De Valois, R.L., and De Valois, K.K. 1975. Neural coding of color. In *Handbook of perception*, vol. 5. Eds. E.C. Carterette and M.P. Friedman. New York: Academic Press.
122. Zoloth, S.R.; Petersen, M.R.; Beecher, M.D.; Green, S.; Marler, P.; Moody, D.B.; and Stebbins, W. 1979. Species-specific perceptual processing of vocal sounds by monkeys. *Science* 204:870-872.
123. Bornstein, M.H. In press. Perceptual development: Stability and change in feature perception. In *Psychological development from infancy*. Eds. M.H. Bornstein and W. Kessen. Hillsdale, N.J.: Erlbaum Publishers.

124. Condon, W.S., and Sander, L.W. 1974. Neonate movement is synchronized with adult speech: Interactional participation and language acquisition. *Science* 183:99-101.
125. Fox, R. 1975. Primate kin and human kinship. In *Biosocial anthropology*. Ed. R. Fos. London: Malaby Press.
126. Washburn, S.L. 1961. *Social life of early man*. Chicago: Aldine Publishing Co.
127. Wilson, E.O. 1975. *Sociobiology: The new synthesis*. Cambridge: Belknap Press of Harvard Univ.
128. Eisenberg, J.F., and Dillon W.S., eds. 1971. *Man and beast: Comparative social behavior*. Washington, D.C.: Smithsonian Institution Press.
129. Washburn, S.L., and Moore, R. 1974. Ape into man: A study of human evolution. Boston: Little, Brown & Company.
130. Napier, J. 1973. *The roots of mankind*. New York: Harper Torch Books.
131. Young, J.Z. 1974. *An introduction to the study of man*. Oxford: Oxford Univ. Press.
132. Dasen, P.R. 1977. Are cognitive processes universal? A contribution to cross-cultural piagetian psychology. In *Studies in cross-cultural psychology*, vol. 1. Ed. N. Warren. London: Academic Press.
133. Ashton, P.R. 1975. Cross-cultural Piagetian research: An experimental perspective. *Harv Educ Rev* 45:475-506.
134. Warren, N. 1972. African infant precocity. *Psychol Bull* 78:353-367.
135. Tulving, E. 1972. Episodic and semantic memory. In *Organization of memory*. Eds. E. Tulving and W. Donaldson. New York: Academic Press.
136. Warrington, E.K. 1975. The selective impairment of semantic memory. *Q J Exp Psychol* 27:635-657.
137. Geschwind, N.; Quadfasel, F.A.; and Segarra, J.M. 1968. Isolation of the speech area. *Neuropsychologia* 6:327-340.
138. MacLean, P.D. 1973. A triune concept of the brain and behavior. In *The Hincks memorial lectures*. Eds. T.J. Boag and D. Campbell. Toronto: Univ. of Toronto Press, pp. 6-66.
139. Isaacson, R.L. 1974. *The limbic system*. New York: Plenum Press.

2 Critical Periods of Brain Development Related to Behavior, Especially Epilepsies

Gilbert H. Glaser

There is a natural sequence in brain development, though the timing may be different in various animal species. This sequence produces a relatively correlated series of occurrences related to morphology: neuronal, particularly dendritic, and other tissue elements in the brain; biochemical: enzymes, proteins, lipids, ionic relations in membranes, neurotransmitters, hormonal regulations, particularly of various metabolic events in brain and especially modulated by the limbic-hypothalamic-pituitary control systems; electrophysiological, with regard to neurotransmission, development of the electroencephalogram (EEG), evoked potentials and receptor-effector activity, such as simple then complex reflexes; and behavioral activities, regarded as instinctual and learned [3, 7, 8, 14, 37, 62]. Many of these processes are "time-locked." They occur during certain periods of brain development. Only in certain instances do major specific correlations occur; there may be different critical time-locked periods for different processes.

Over the last twenty-five years at least, these concepts have been increasingly related to problems of teratogenesis, but in a more general sense the principles can be applied to other aspects of brain development and consequences in the development of various kinds of behavior. One important group of behaviors that will be emphasized in relation to the present discussion is that of epileptic seizure activity, which is abnormal behavior electrogenically induced and profoundly influenced by effects at or around certain critical periods of developmental timing. Clearly some of the controlling factors where "interference" with brain development may occur are related to actions of genetic influences, that is, when genes act to produce certain changes in the developing brain related to morphology and various chemical systems [23, 41, 66]. External environmental influences also are very significant, particularly effects of drugs and radiation as well as exposure to sensory input [5, 12].

In the present context there will be emphasis on the specific role of limbic control systems in brain, which are composed of a complex internal circuitry of neuronal aggregates much concerned with the development of behavior and very sensitive to effects which produce seizures (table 2-1). During both prenatal and postnatal development alterations in the activity of limbic system structures may produce significant changes in behavioral cycles of development of the individual animal particularly the history (or biography) of a developing seizure process, especially in humans. Structures such as the hippocampus and amygdala produce differential excitatory and inhibitory effects upon hypothalamus, and then directly upon pituitary functions which control the activities of the thyroid, adrenal, gonads, and growth hormone as major control systems. Implicit therefore in any considerations of behavioral changes, must be careful evaluation of gender differences which permeate even variabilities in the occurrence of different types of seizure activity [58].

The concept of critical periods in brain development received great impetus twenty-five years ago, when Flexner [20] presented his detailed observations on the development of the cerebral cortex of certain animals (such as the guinea pig, rat, and pig) which indicated that the differentiation of the neuroblast into the nerve cell entailed a series of physiological, chemical, and structural changes all closely related in time, and perhaps representing the complex end results of an interaction of an inductive stimulus with the neuroblast. Flexner was quite aware that the period during which these changes occur depended upon the maturity of the animal at birth. With regard to the guinea pig and pig, the critical period is about at the beginning of the last trimester of pregnancy. In the rat, it occurs at the tenth day postnatally. This was later emphasized by Dobbing [13] who preferred to use the concept of "vulnerable period." He regarded the period of vulnerability the time of fastest growth of brain, composed of an intricate sequence of many anatomical and neurochemical growth spurts, each one in a different region of brain probably having its own somewhat different period of heightened vulnerability. Dobbing further stated that, in its simplest form, the vulnerability concept indicated that if a develop-

Table 2-1
Limbic System Vulnerability

Susceptibility to anoxia, carbon monoxide, hypoglycemia, viruses (herpes, rabies)
Vascular supply: peculiar rakelike branching
Susceptibility to effects of herniation at tentorium
Low threshold for seizure activity, rapid spread of discharges
Distinctive chemical properties
   High rate of protein synthesis
   Zinc containing proteins, especially in dentate fibers
   Selective destruction by 3-acetylpyridine, methypyroxidine
   Isoniazid, thiosemicarbazide accumulation
   High methionine uptake
   High concentrations of serotonin and norepinephrine
   High level of choline acetylase
   Differential rates of synthesis of alpha-aminobutyric acid (GABA)
     and alpha-hydroxybutyric acid
   Hormonal binding to hippocampal cells
Genetic hippocampal abnormalities, both structural and chemical

mental process be restricted by any agent at the time of its fastest rate, not only will this delay the process but it will restrict its ultimate extent, even when the restricting influence is removed and the fullest possible rehabilitation obtained. Two important corollaries were then developed, first that the severity of the restriction required to produce the given ultimate effect may be less if earlier applied than at the time of fastest growth, and also that the same effect may be achieved later in the development but only by much greater application over a longer period of time. These periods therefore are most sensitive during the early life of the individual.

It is of interest that Flexner's conclusions from his research still have much relevance. These mainly were that electrophysiological activity in the cerebral cortex, both spontaneous and evoked, makes its first appearance only after a certain critical period of development has elapsed. In the guinea pig, this is between forty-one and forty-six days of gestation (the total period of gestation being about sixty-six days in this animal). Such a critical period was found to coincide with a development of nerve cell processes especially in the cortex, the appearance of Nissl bodies in the neurons, and the termination (or mature point of development) of the neuronal nucleus. Biochemically, this period also is at the time of maximum increase in the development of cytochrome oxidase, succinic dehydrogenase, and apyrase, and when the neurons become permeable to sodium. The latter finding has been regarded as too simplistic, but at least it had elements of neurophysiological significance. Exceptions were stated to the timing especially of other enzymatic changes. It was found that cholinesterase rose progressively and not suddenly, particularly though after the thirty-fifth day. Acid phosphatase levels in brain remained constant in cortex, then falling after birth. Various neurophysiological observations demonstrated that in the guinea pig reflex movements of the foreleg and neck could be elicited by the thirty-first day, of the fingers and toes on the thirty-fifth, and of the jaw on the thirty-eighth. These reflexes appeared before cortical stimulation was effective, before the electrical activity of the cortex was observed, and suggested that such reflexes probably were mediated subcortically by then more highly developed structures. By the forty-second and forty-fifth days, movements of the extremities and head structures could be obtained by electrical stimulation of the cortex. Flexner [20] found that rhythmic electrical potentials which resembled the EEG could be obtained from the cortex of the fetal guinea pig at about the end of the critical period for cellular differentiation and certain chemical changes as stated. These potentials in part arise from the cortex and not wholly from the underlying brain structures. The cortex also becomes responsive to stimulating drugs such as strychnine at this time, and the sensitivity of these electrical reactions was demonstrated by their elimination by experimentally induced anoxia produced by clamping the umbilical cord. At the time of appearance of cortical activity, there was some diminished reflex response to external stimulation in the animal, and in general it was felt that overall neuromuscular activity exhibited was greater in the younger fetus than in the older, with the implication that cortical inhibition was developing in the older animal. A similar sequence occurs in early human development (table 2-2) [24].

Particularly with regard to the electrophysiological activity in the brain, a great deal of work was done during the 1960s which indicated specific time-locked developments of various types of electrocerebral activity. These were carried out in fetal sheep and young cats (as well as certain studies in premature human fetuses) by a series of investigators, some of whom attempted correlations with the structural development of cortical neurons. For example, Bernhard, Kolmodin, and Meyerson in 1967 [4], reporting on the development of electrical activity in the sheep fetus, indicated that about sixty-five days after conception three significant indicators of maturing electrocortical activity appeared: the direct cortical response, the transcallosal response, and a negative shift of steady potential induced by repetitive cortical stimulation. Variations on this theme were reported by others in studies of brains of the newborn cat and rabbit. Investigation of the electrical activity of rat brain is important because of the many studies done on the biochemistry, morphology, and genetics of this animal [3, 8, 22, 31, 33]. With regard to the electrical activity of rat cerebeller Purkinje cells [68], action potentials were observed near the cells within hours after birth, with sustained electrical activity at one to two days. This increase occurred in conjunction with rapid rise in levels of brain lactate, succinate dehydrogenase, and other enzymes. Most significantly, between ten and fifteen days there was increase in spontaneous firing of these cells and decrease in spike duration. Synaptogenesis also increased in the molecular layer during this period. The studies of Purpura [46a, 46b] have added much during the last fifteen years to our knowledge regarding correlations between development of cortical neurons and their processes and neurophysiological activities. He recorded in young animals intracellularly, excitatory postsynaptic potentials as well as inhibitory postsynaptic potentials in neocortical and hippocampal neurons, and correlated these with the earliest synaptic contacts regarded as axodendritic. Purpura [46a] indicated that dendrites of immature cortical neurons were capable of generating and propagating spikes, a property which was stated as lost with maturation, except in selected areas such as the hippocampus. He emphasized the necessity of correlating such results with stimulus type, particularly influences of strength and duration of stimulus, and how these related to the occurrence of repetitive firing. A strong correlated activity of hippocampal cortex ontogenesis [46c] was seen in the repetitive firing of neurons in excess of 20 Herz (Hz), rarely in the newborn where spike potentials were relatively of long duration, but noted distinctly in more mature animals.

Table 2-2
Maturation of the EEG and Cerebral Activity Related to Behavior in the Human

	Birth	3 months	5 months
Electroencephalogram			
Topography	Undifferentiated	1. Topographical organization of the EEG	
Occipital activity	S1. Response to eye opening Responses to photic stimulation	2. Occipital 3-4 cps 3. Responses to photic stimulation	Occipital activity: rhythmic 5-6 cps +
Reactivity during sleep	General flattening responses Diffuse, irregular discharges Diphasic responses, increased amplitude, then flattening	4. Diffuse sharp waves	Progressive differentiation
Neurological-Psychomotor Maturation			
Archaic reflexes	Moro Automatic walking Creeping Static straightening Grasping		
Motor tonus		Control of tonus of head	Voluntary prehension Sitting position
Vision	Light perception	Oculomotor coordination Sweeping of space	Macular vision
Hearing	Generalized reactions Moro	Arrest of movements	Mimicry responses Rotation of head
Speech	Cooing sounds		Murmuring Repetition of syllables

There have been many studies of evoked cortical potentials using auditory, visual, and somatosensory stimulations in developing animals and humans, and these techniques have been increasingly used clinically in recent years in determining the functional integrity of the specific sensory pathways [17, 18]. The details of the configuration and development of these evoked responses vary in different species. Also there is distinct variability in human infants at different times of day especially in relation to the waking-sleep cycle. Auditory evoked potentials during development have been more constant and stable compared with the visual. This complex field of brain ontogeny is only beginning to be understood.

The development of the human EEG ontogenetically has been studied by many [14, 17, 24] and will be commented upon briefly. It is of great interest that the appearance of alpha activities mainly occipitally, though present in the newborn, become definitively dominant in late adolescence. In the premature infant, there are frequent periods of relative electrocerebral silence alternating with rhythms occasionally in the alpha range of 8-12 Hz and even in the beta range. These are less common in the normal-term newborn. The electrical activity of the awake newborn contains mixtures of delta (1½-3 Hz) and theta (4-7 Hz) activities of varying amplitudes, often up to over 100 microvolts. During the first year, there is increasing theta activity, particularly from the temporal regions, and the gradual occurrence of more alpha occipitally along with asymmetries, fluctuating from side to side, particularly during sleep. The development of sleep activity in the EEG has achieved much attention with differentiation of various spindle frequencies and sharp waves, especially biparietally, during the first year (table 2-2).

A number of studies attempted to correlate brain structure with electrophysiological events, especially in the brain of the newborn cat, by Purpura [46a, b]. At birth the apical dendrites are well-developed and extend into the molecular layer with axodendritic synapses; however, the basilar dendrites and axon collaterals are poorly developed. During the period between the first and third weeks of postnatal life, there is rapid proliferation of basilar dendrites, great increase in the number of collateral branches of apical and basilar dendrites, and marked proliferation of dendritic spines, suggesting more axodendritic synaptic connections. These investigators correlated the development of both evoked responses and the early electroencephalographic activities with development of axon collaterals, increased spines, and synaptic connections. There also has been a certain amount of correlation between changes in lipids forming various neuronal membranes and these electrical activities, but the associations are not yet clear [52].

Recently, there has been a considered analysis of the concept of critical periods in brain development by Dodge, Prensky, and Feigin [14], making the following generalizations and critique. They indicate that there are critical periods for most functions occurring mainly in intrauterine or early postnatal life, but without a single critical period. For example, myelin lipids may be in the state of rapid synthesis when synaptic structure of the cortex may be in a lesser state of development. It is emphasized that specific events in their maturation may be different in different areas of the nervous system. This would particularly apply to subcortical timing being earlier than cortical. Although there is a rough similarity in processes in different mammalian species there is species variation, especially in relation to time of birth. The maturation of psychological functions does have considerable variation, but they do state that modifications of such functions can be made by manipulations of the developmental sequence. These authors further feel that it has not been proved unequivocally that the development of a function is most susceptible to injury during the period of most rapid maturation, especially with regard to nonspecific insults. The question of irreversibility, particularly with regard to behavior and modifications of behavior, still remains to be solved. It is regarded that after insults of limited duration early in infancy, some "catch up in the anatomic and biochemical development of brain can be observed." The relationship of data from lower mammalian species to human infants requires a great deal of further study, and this particularly applies to evidence that maturation of the nervous system can be accelerated by various manipulations of hormones or by electrical stimuli, for example, early in neonatal life.

However, there appears to be little doubt that, at certain times of brain development, influences do exist either biologically or environmentally which can modify brain development and the behavior derived from such development. Two important such periods are the postnatal, which is expanded into a time phase varying from the immediate neonatal to several months during the first year (especially in the human), and puberty, during which significant changes in hormonal balance occur which modify behavior, and particularly seizure activity and its course during adolescence.

Recently, much attention is being paid to febrile convulsions in infancy [19, 34, 42, 48, 59]. These seizures when severe are now regarded to be of major importance in the pathogenesis of further spontaneous epileptic seizures, particularly partial complex seizures or temporal lobe-limbic epilepsy [1, 19, 26, 34, 42]. Important factors relate to the individual susceptibility of the infant (which in many instances is genetically determined), the actual age, the fever, and the existence of already present evidence of some neurological disorder [39, 63]. Febrile convulsions have been noted since the time of the Hippocratic writings. They occur frequently enough to have been described in the midnineteenth century as appearing in a third of all children, with a 20 percent mortality. A detailed analysis and reappraisal of febrile convulsions was published by Lennox-Buchthal [34]. These have also been the subject of an extensive International Brain Research Organization symposium (1976). The syndrome (convulsions with fever) appears when susceptible children have a febrile illness, with the most susceptible age being between 9 and 20 months; febrile convulsions are rare below 6 months and above 5 years. Susceptibility is inherited probably by a single dominant gene with incomplete penetrance. The syndrome is present more often in boys than in girls, which prevalence might be due entirely to an excess of all-boy over all-girl sibships in many series. The incidence varies in different populations from 2 to 9 percent and must be distinguished from such processes that occur in this age group as breath-holding spells and similar phenomena. The importance of this syndrome in relation to the present context of critical period is that there may be a significant variation in the sensitivity of the infant to temperature, represented by a predetermined threshold, which when exceeded results in convulsions. Experimental work relating to this in animals is discussed later. The threshold also relates to the rate of the rise of temperature, with a rapid rise being more effective as a seizure-trigger mechanism. Lennox-Buchthal [34] emphasized that febrile convulsions are highly age-determined. The significance of their unusual occurrence in humans below the age of 6 months is not clear. However, experimental studies in the newborn period of normal animals (such as mice, rats, kittens, and monkeys) confirm an infrequent ability to elicit seizures during that time by electrical stimuli, drugs, sound, or fever. As indicated in some of the above studies of the development of brain, correlated with its electrophysiology and morphology, in higher mammalian forms (particularly human) it has been difficult to elicit repetitive discharges from neocortical neurons along with sustained seizure discharges in the newborn or very young. However, prolonged after-discharges could be elicited in the hippocampus. These features were correlated with poor development of basilar dendrites.

Douglas [15] presented interesting theoretical implications concerning the development of hippocampal function. His major thesis is that the hippocampus may have two different but related modes of functioning. The simpler is present in infancy and at times in adulthood and consists of a gross or nonspecific inhibition of an emotional reactivity in general. This nonspecific inhibition requires only that the hippocampal pyramidal cells be functionally developed and that they be driven by some synchronized input, such as a theta-pacing system. The second functional mode is regarded as a stimulus-specific inhibition, since it corresponds to a specific inhibition of an emotional reaction to a particular stimulus or set of stimuli. This can be carried out only when the hippocampal pyramidal cells are "informed" of the stimulus by the temporoammonic tract to its major target, the dentate gyrus. These are at best only rudimentally developed at birth and develop in synchrony with the maturation of the dentate gyrus, apparently in all species. Douglas states that this type of inhibition is sensitive to early stressful experience, and that the harmful effects of such early stress on adult behavior appear to be counteracted by drugs which enhance cholinergic transmission. His approach is essentially Pavlovian, based upon deductions that internal inhibition must be an actively generated process which suppresses or inhibits other actively generated processes of excitation, the latter determining direction and magnitude of behavior and comparable more to motivation than arousal. Stimulus strength is important in this concept and involves processes of attention, reinforcement, and orientation. Fluctuations in the general state of arousal and fatigue, and changes related to handling are variable factors which can be contained or ruled out in controlled experiments. Douglas pointed out that animals with hippocampal lesions appear to lack habituation; in addition, they are highly deficient in passive avoidance. The relationship to amygdalar functions is not clear. Douglas' studies utilized a spontaneous alternation paradigm of measurement of the mammalian tendency to avoid stimulus reexposure during investigatory or exploratory behavior. The ability of a mammal (such as a rat) to respond in various tests with spontaneously alternating behavior can be abolished by large hippocampal lesions, and just reduced by smaller lesions. This function is present mainly in adult animals but totally lacking in animals age 2 to 3 weeks, though they are capable of exploratory behavior. The correlation can be made with developmental studies of morphology which indicate that the dentate gyrus of the rat and mouse (in hippocampus) is not fully developed at birth and is populated by granule cells which, though undergoing postnatal mitosis and then migration, have not finished their structural differentiation which tends to occur at about 2 weeks of age, leveling off by 1 month. The development of spontaneous alternation behavior, then, requires a well-developed dentate gyrus and predictably matures at the age of about 1 month, in this animal. The phenomenon further can be correlated with development of so-called cholinergic inhibition, maturing in synchrony with the maturation of hippocampal morphology and with the alternation behavior. Testing with various drugs indicated that the hipppocampal-cholinergic inhibitory system matures at about 25 to 30 days of age. For example, the adult-dose response curve for scopolamine effects does not emerge until about 25 days, as does stimulant effects of amphetamine. Since guinea pigs are born with an already developed dentate gyrus, these animals at birth had essentially well-developed alternation behavioral traits in various tests. Destruction of granule cells (by radiation) in the hippocampus of rats in later life produced effects resembling hippocampectomy when the animals were tested for spontaneous alternation, passive avoidance, open-field behavior, and shuttle-box learning.

Douglas also described investigations concerned with the DBA/2J inbred strain of mice which is sensitive to audiogenic stimuli, producing seizures in a time-locked period early in development. He studied older animals in the range of 100 days of age, and concluded that they may have hippocampal defects. They have been reported to be excellent shuttle-box learners, deficient in passive avoidance and habituation, and overactive in the open field. Additional studies suggest weak or aberrant memory processes. Other data indicate that the cholinergic system may operate at reduced efficiency in the DBA strain. In studies correlating the age of the animals with sensitivity to other stimuli and behavior characterized as jumpiness, it is felt that this indicates a high arousal or reactivity tendency, especially in the younger animals. In this mouse strain, the hippocampus and its internal inhibitory functions appear to develop late, and this development could be very susceptible to disruption because of the high reactivity and an unusually prolonged period of vulnerability. If these animals are not subjected to repeated emotion-provoking experiences during development, they appear to mature into adults with normal or even supernormal inhibition. Douglas concludes that it may be possible to exploit the young DBA mouse as a naturally hippocampectomized subject, and studies of its postnatal neurogenesis should be carried out.

Douglas studied further the effect of electroconvulsive seizure (ECS) administration as well as administering an adrenal steroid (such as cortisol) which is known to reduce seizure thresholds in the production of behavioral changes in these animals, most prominent in the very young, and correlated with what may be regarded as a critical developmental period. ECS was found to abolish an inhibitory-conditioned reflex for over a week, while having no effect on excitatory behavior. It was interesting that pretreatment with barbiturates prevented the ECS from producing its prolonged disinhibitory effect. He concludes that in infancy such a disruption of function is more serious because it occurs during a critical developmental state. However, behavioral factors that must be considered are early handling of the animal and placing it in an enriched stimulating environment, compared to isolation. Solitary confinement results in a stress reaction of chronically elevated adrenal steroid hormones and at times behavior resembling that of hippocampal lesions. Even a morphological correlate was found [64]: the thickness of the dentate gyrus became "thin" in animals subjected to solitary confinement. This remains a complex area to unravel but indicates the significance of interplay between intrinsic developmental factors and environmental ones, especially postnatally, in the evolution of certain kinds of behavior which may have application to abnormal behavior in the human, consequent upon seizures and abnormal environmental influences occurring early in life. Over the last twenty-five years there has been increasing interest in the animal model of seizures triggered by a specific stimulus, the audiogenic seizure (AS) state, in young mice, rats, and rabbits, which is genetically determined and present in inbred strains [2, 23, 29, 51, 53, 54]. In mice the susceptibility to sound is time-locked, being most intense at the third postnatal week then gradually subsiding with age to about 7 weeks. This is particularly true of the DBA/2J strain, and the susceptible period varies slightly in different inbred strains studied in different countries; the susceptibility to ECS, febrile seizure, and drug-induced seizure (pentylenetetrezol) also is increased in these animals. A number of mechanisms have been related to this susceptibility and low threshold, particularly cellular hydration (abnormal concentrations of extracellular and intracellular sodium and potassium) but the evidence concerning an electrolyte fault has never been conclusive. Some time ago [2] it was found that mice with ASs had a reduction in cerebral oxidative phosphorylation produced by presumed genetic retardation of an enzymatic system. Studies using histochemical techniques localized an ATPase difference in the brains of mouse strains to the granular cell layer of the dentate fascia in the hippocampus. Other differences were noted in relation to nucleoside triphosphates, but the genetic details are not clear. At the age of peak susceptibility to ASs, but not before or after, the brains of DBA mice were found to have a marked diminution of sodium-potassium-activated ATPase, diminished concentration of potassium, diminished potassium-stimulated release of gamma-aminobutyric acid (GABA), diminished oxygen uptake [29], and diminished GABA, norepinephrine, and 5-hydroxytryptamine [51]. These neurochemical alterations pointed to genetically determined age-dependent enzyme deficits in the brain, with resultant ionic and metabolic changes contributing to seizure susceptibility. The DBA mice are much more apt to die when subjected to anoxia. As a result of severe seizures, this might account for the fact that human infants might suffer severe anoxic damage in the course of prolonged convulsions, whereas such damage is relatively rare after the age of peak susceptibility. The DBA mice, with specific susceptibility to audiogenic stimuli, also were susceptible during the same time period to elevation of body temperature, a parallel to febrile seizures in human infants [29]. It is possible that the audiogenic mouse paradigm could be a valid model of febrile seizures in human infants. Furthermore, the concentration of potassium in brain slices from the mice was diminished in the DBA strain compared with the C57 nonseizure susceptible strain, indicating a deficient mechanism for cellular accumulation of potassium and probably related to the deficit in sodium-potassium ATPase. This low potassium content was present only during a specific time period in the strain studies at about 30 days, but not at 20 or 40 days. The significance of this finding was emphasized, since the level of potassium that affects GABA release was lower in the DBA than in the C57 mice. Low levels of GABA might dispose these mice to seizures.

During the past two years in our Yale Neurology Research Laboratories, an attempt has been made to study other underlying mechanisms responsible for the AS state genetically determined in the mouse model [53, 54, 55]. Our initial studies indicated that the levels of cerebroside and GM1 ganglioside, which are generally enriched in myelin, were significantly higher in the brains of AS-susceptible DBA/2J mice than in the brains of the resistant C57BL/6J strain [53]. These results suggested that the DBA mice possessed a more heavily myelinated central nervous system (CNS). An elevated level of myelin could increase the excitability of the CNS by lowering the threshold for electrical conductivity in transmitting structures such as axons and dendritic bundles. In addition, the cerebellum of the DBA mice was less developed than that of the nonsusceptible mice at 21 days of age [54]. The cerebellum (because of its intense inhibitory efferent function) is thought to play an important role in the control or modulation of seizure activity. A hypothesis was proposed that the AS susceptibility of the DBA mice could result from a combination of accelerated myelinogenesis and underdeveloped cerebellum, as at least one genetically determined constellation. Because of evidence available in the literature concerning relationships between level of thyroid hormone and various aspects of brain development [3, 10, 16a, 22, 28, 31, 44, 45, 56, 60, 61, 67], thyroxin content of the blood of these animals was studied. Thyroid hormone is well-known to have profound effects on several aspects of early postnatal brain development, and certainly a deficiency of thyroid hormone in the young human is correlated with marked retardation of brain development and a multitude of learning processes. Further, it had been determined that thyroid hormone was known to stimulate myelinogenesis in mammalian brain and that the growth of cerebellum also could be affected by alterations in the level of thyroid hormone. It has been reported that the presence of an excess level of thyroid hormone during early stages of brain development could significantly advance and exaggerate responsiveness to various types of environmental stimuli in young mammals. Hence, the inherent susceptibility of the DBA mice to sound-induced seizures could be related to an elevated level of thyroid hormone during the early critical period of brain development. Our investigations demonstrated [55] that the levels of serum thyroxine (T4) peak earlier and are significantly higher in DBA mice than in the nonsusceptible mice during their critical stage of brain development with seizure susceptibility (figure 2-1). Second, we found that the susceptibility of these mouse strains to AS could be reversed by artificial manipulation of their thyroid hormone levels (figure 2-2). It was noted that the serum T4 levels were significantly higher in the DBA mice during earlier ages, with maximum levels reached at 14 days of age, then being almost twofold higher than the values in the nonsusceptible mice. After 16 days of age the T4 levels of both mouse strains fell sharply, and by 21 days, at which time seizure susceptibility clearly was different, there were no changes in the hormonal levels. Therefore the actual significant effect had been produced during the earlier time period. Also not only were the levels of T4 higher during the early period of brain development, but the maximum level was reached two days before the control mice. Since the free, or unbound, T4 is the fraction available for physiological action, differences observed between the strains for these levels assumed special importance, and it was felt that both the increased level of CNS myelin and the early underdevelopment of the cerebellum observed in the DBA mice could be consequences of the elevated T4 levels. This early increase in T4 levels could also disburb normal balance between excitatory and inhibitory actions, and exaggerate responsiveness to auditory stimulation.

The hypothesis was tested further by inducing hypothyroidism in DBA mice with two agents: propylthiouracil (PTU) and I 131. These exposures significantly reduced susceptibility to seizure at 18 days of age. PTU given in the mother's diet from two days before birth and then to the newborn produced a marked reduction in seizure susceptibility. If the PTU was administered just six hours before the sound stimulus or for three days before the sound stimulus, there was no significant change in the seizure susceptibility, so that the substance was apparently not specifically acting as an antiseizure agent but was having an influence on certain developmental factors in the animal's metabolism and brain structure by inhibiting thyroid function.

In another series of experiments, thyroid hormone was administered to normally resistant mice to determine if seizure susceptibility could be enhanced. The daily injection of small doses (0.6 μg) T4 into the C57 nonsusceptible mice from birth until 18 days did not influence their seizure susceptibility, nor did a single large dose of T4 at 21 days. However, a series of high T4 doses (20 μg per mouse per day) administered from 5 to 8 days significantly enhanced seizure susceptibility at a later age. Thus, timing and dosage appeared to be critical factors affecting the influence of thyroid hormone on seizure susceptibility. Interestingly the phenotype appeared identical in both the seizure-susceptible DBA mice and the thyroxine-treated, previously nonsusceptible mice, with similar earlier eye opening, longer and more pointed snouts, more pointed ears, and a peculiar smallness in overall body size. These results are preliminary and in an early state of evaluation, but they demonstrate a genetically controlled relationship between thyroid function and susceptibility of an animal to a seizure disorder which occurs during a critical period postnatally. It must be determined if thyroid hormone acts alone or in conjunction with other hormones which influence seizure susceptibility such as adrenal steroids.

In relation to these findings, it is of great interest that Raskin and Fishman [47] in their studies on the effect of thyroid on permeability, composition, and electrolyte metabolism of brain and other tissues produced ex-

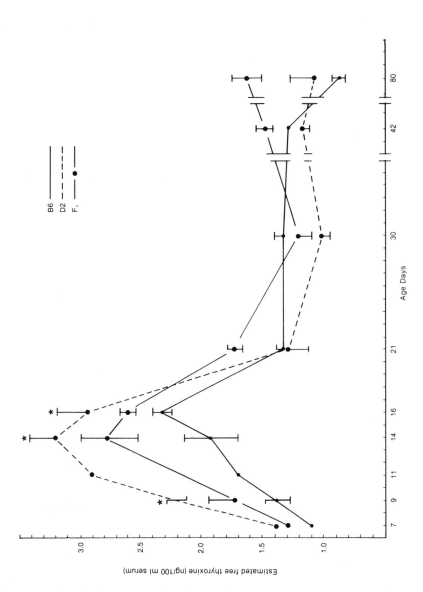

Note: Values are expressed as means (±SEM) and from three to five samples were analyzed for each point (the number of animals analyzed per sample ranged from three to nine). The t-test was used to compare the mean of the B6 and D2 strains only. Asterisks indicate $p < 0.01$.

Figure 2-1. Development Profile of Estimated Free Thyroxine Levels in Serum from B6 (nonsusceptible), D2 (seizure susceptible), and Their F_1 Hybrid Mice

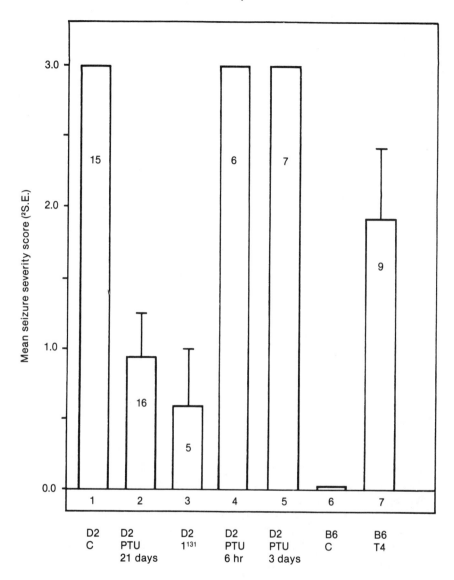

Note: The number of animals tested is shown above each bar. 1, untreated D2 controls; 2, D2 mice exposed to PTU (in diet) from two days before birth until sound treatment; 3, D2 mice treated with I^{131}; 4, D2 mice treated with PTU (10 ug/g body wt) 6 hours before sound treatment; 5, D2 mice treated with PTU (10 ug/g body wt/day) for three days before sound treatment; 6, B6 controls; 7, B6 mice treated with %4 (20 ug/mouse/day) on 5 to 8 days of age.

Figure 2-2. Influence of Thyroid Hormone Manipulation on the AS Susceptibility of Eighteen ±1-day-old B6 and D2 Mice

perimental hyperthyroid states in adult male rats by administration of thyroxine. They found that in the hyperthyroid brain there was greater permeability, permitting more rapid entry of sucrose and free sulfate ion. The rate of entry of radioactive sodium was increased in hyperthyroid brain and decreased in hypothyroid brain. They did not find any change from normal in ATPase activity in hyperthyroid brain, but felt that this might be related to the limitations of the methods available at that time. Also they found a retarded entry rate of potassium into hyperthyroid brains, paralleling the finding of reduced rate of uptake of radioactive potassium into erythrocytes of thyrotoxic patients. They noted that a laboratory study had shown that ouabain (which inhibits sodium-potassium ATPase) reduced both potassium uptake and exchangeable potassium in this system. These characterizations strengthened the consideration that there is a deranged sodium and potassium exchange in hyperthyroid brain, resulting from an inhibition of the sodium-potassium pump. Woodbury [67] showed that thyroxine rapidly decreased the electroshock seizure threshold in rats, while thyroidectomy increased it. An inhibited pump-related enzyme system in brain that provokes seizures and a stimulated enzyme associated with a raised seizure threshold are intriguing possibilities. Raskin and Fishman [47] hypothesized that the hyperthyroid brain was a seizure-susceptible brain.

The issue of early-life seizure susceptibility achieves additional importance in considerations of pathogenesis of the complex partial seizures of temporal lobe-limbic epilepsy. Many studies demonstrate that over 50 percent of the resected temporal lobes, from patients with medically uncontrollable seizures, contain the lesion of mesial temporal sclerosis [11, 19]. This lesion is characterized by a basic process of neuronal atrophy and glial scarring with indications, especially from the studies of the Scheibels [50], that discrete episodes of seizures early in the life of the individual and consequently (revealed by Golgi methods) produce an ongoing structural pathology characterized by neuronal damage in early as well as in advanced states of pathological change, involving dendritic formations. The question of adjacent vascular pathology also is raised, with possible compromise of the integrity of the blood-brain barrier. Whatever the original insult, the significance of severe seizure postnatally is high in relation to future complications, and this is emphasized further by the studies of Wasterlain and Plum [65] on the vulnerability of developing rat brain to repetitive ECS. These investigations found marked reduction in brain weight, brain protein, and brain RNA but not DNA, suggesting a reduction of cell size throughout. Species differences are important, and there is no doubt that the age of 30 days at which these animals were studied represents a postmitotic period in the rat, but it was felt that a comparable decrement in young human brain could represent a highly significant reduction in viable cells. A number of studies not only indicate the later development of temporal lobe-limbic epilepsy, but reduction in overall intelligence related to frequent seizures, and marked intellectual deterioration after severe febrile seizures in infancy [1, 42, 48] and even later status epilepticus [1, 42, 43]. In humans, onset of seizure before the age of 1 year can be correlated with learning difficulties, even though seizure after that age period might be controlled. Again further studies in other mammalian species including primates, relating vulnerability to seizures of the immature brain to later brain dysfunction and lesions are necessary. The aspect of the possibility of an abnormality in a hormonal-control system clearly opens another area even with genetic implications for investigation.

In recent years, emphasis on these hormonal factors relating to brain development was presented by Timiras and her group [60, 61]. The regulatory role of several hormones in the development of the CNS has been established. It appears quite clear that studies in humans and animals demonstrate that appropriate thyroid-hormone levels are necessary at an early age for normal maturation of the brain. However, Timiras further states [61] that with specific respect to the role of thyroid hormones, the critical age at which these hormones exert their organizing action on the brain (particularly the cerebral cortex) generally encompasses the late fetal and neonatal periods in humans, and can be circumscribed precisely from the tenth to the fifteenth postnatal days in rats. In her studies with rats, she found that when thyroid hormones are lacking or insufficient during this critical period, the brain failed to develop normally in terms of structure and, conversely, thyroid hormones administered to the hypothyroid animal within this critical age period restored normal brain maturation and assured functional competence at later ages. Again once the critical age was past, administration of thyroid hormones, even in large doses, failed to prevent the severe impairment in physical and functional development that inevitably resulted when hypothyroidism remained untreated. Critical periods during prenatal and postnatal development also have been identified for other hormones besides those of the thyroid gland as well as for a variety of environmental influences. Thus the future potential of any given organ, tissue, or function, in addition to genetic factors, will depend on environmental inputs, and the interplay between the two becomes maximally effective at a specific critical time during ontogeny.

The mechanisms that underlie the increased sensitivity of the brain to hormones at critical periods remain for the most part unknown. Recently, it was found that the mechanism by which developing brain alters its response to thyroxine during the critical period may involve changes in thyroxine-binding sites at the level of subcellular membranes [16b, 40]. Thyroxine-phospholipid interactions also have been theoretically implicated in the mechanism of action of thyroxine. Abnormal membranous bodies in neuronal and glial cytoplasms and in synapses of hypothyroid rats have been found, suggesting that there may be a peculiar change in lipid synthesis as well as abnormal protein synthesis [22]. Since mitochondria seemed to undergo a marked increase in their affinity for thyroxine during the period when thyroxine most profoundly affects the developing brain, it seems probable that the mitochondria also may be intimately involved in the mechanism of action of this hormone. The developing brain certainly increases its sensitivity to thyroxine during the critical period, both by removal of more of the hormone from the circulation and by an alteration of thyroxine-binding sites on subcellular membranes.

Further hormonal brain-function correlations are being made increasingly with regard to the circadian cycles related to the onset of puberty and menses in females, and even the onset of puberty in males [32]. In the female, there is a strong correlation between hormonal changes and flurries of epileptic seizure activity. These phenomena are increasingly being related to the associated fluctuations in hormonal balance. There is a known feedback relationship between the hormonal environment and the functions of the CNS. As previousy indicated, certain cerebral activities (especially those involving limbic-hypothalamic circuits) regulate many endocrine and their associated physiological functions, particularly adrenal, thyroid, and gonadal. In turn, the endogenous levels of these hormones modulate the activity of the involved cerebral structures. The cerebral limbic system components prominent in these functions are the hippocampus and the amygdala, the structures dominating the known pathology of temporal lobe-limbic epilepsy. Timiras and her group [36, 60, 61] demonstrated that in experimental rates the hippocampus and the amygdala show cyclical changes in their electrical excitability which correlate with stages of the oestrous cycle. Seizure thresholds in the dorsal hippocampus were decreased from the morning of prooestrous through the morning of oestrous, then increased afterward. The medial amygdala pattern was similar, but that of the latter amygdala reversed. Progesterone administration increased seizure threshold in dorsal hippocampus and has antiepileptic effects in human patients. Massive destructive lesions of the temporal lobe and deeper limbic structures produce a syndrome of hypersexuality along with a peculiar visual agnosia (the Kluver-Bucy syndrome). However, studies of human individuals (postpubertal) with temporal lobe-limbic epilepsy emphasized diminished sexuality [6, 21, 35, 57]. More controlled longitudinal studies of altered psychosexual development in temporal lobe-limbic epilepsy, particularly beginning in childhood, are needed for a more adequate understanding of these processes.

There have been many reports that seizures tend to be more frequent and severe just prior to and during the follicular phase of the menstrual period and less frequent during the luteal phase, when progesterone activity is maximal. Anticonvulsant action of progesterone and lower-seizure thresholds related to estrogens have been demonstrated in animal studies, suggesting a link between the levels of these hormones, and sensitivity to seizure activity during critical periods postpuberty in females, related to the longer circadian cycles of the menses. In our recent studies [J. Kamer, R.H. Mattson, and G.H. Glaser, unpublished] of precipitating factors in epileptic patients, we found that over 50 percent of women with epilepsy experience an association between seizure occurrence and the menstrual cycle, with 85 percent of these noting an increase in seizures during premenstrual and midmenstrual phases. Determinations of possible premenstrual fluid retention and changes in sodium metabolism refute the suggestion that these factors are altering seizure thresholds under these circumstances. But there is some physiologic evidence of changes in cerebral excitability during different phases of the menstrual cycle. Studies of the EEG have been of interest with findings, using frequency spectral analyses, that theta waves dominate before ovulation and increase midcycle, with alpha rhythms increasing after ovulation. Creutzfeldt et al. [9] studied EEG changes during the menstrual cycle, and in women taking (progesterone-containing) oral contraceptive drugs. Power spectrum frequency analyses of EEGs showed slight increase in alpha frequency during the luteal phase until menstruation in women not taking oral contraceptive drugs. Performance of simple psychometric tests was increased during the luteal phase, with shortest reaction times observed at onset of menstruation. Observations correlating levels of the sex steroid hormones, the electroencephalographic spectra, psychological state of the individual, and psychometric test performance are being accumulated to clarify some of these relationships. The development of temporal lobe-limbic seizure activity on or about the time of puberty or earlier in childhood and continuing through puberty into adolescence is extremely important in the development of the individual's sexual behavior through adolescence into adult life.

Several studies concerned with sexual behavior and temporal lobe-limbic epilepsy have been published over the last twenty-five years [6, 21, 35, 57]. These emphasized the frequent incidence of sexual indifference, especially notable clinically in the male patient. In a number of patients this was relieved by posttemporal lobectomy. Recently, this problem has been looked at in detail by Lindsay, Ounsted, and Richards in their intensive follow-up analysis of the long-term outcome of children with temporal-lobe seizures [35]. They addressed one aspect of the study to marriage, parenthood, and sexual indifference. The importance of this study is that a large number of patients were followed from early childhood onset of such epilepsy, into adult life. This type of investigation is fundamental to understanding the long-term effects of childhood seizures, even when the seizures themselves might have ceased at a particular time. In their original group of 100 children, all being followed, the seizures started in childhood, with 86 percent entering the study before the eleventh birthday. It is of interest in the present context that in the original series thirty-seven girls and sixty-three boys entered at random. Although it seemed clear that boys were twice as likely as girls to develop temporal lobe-limbic epilepsy, an analysis of marriageability indicated that males and females with prolonged occurrence of seizure activity were equally likely to be so handicapped that parenthood was barred to them. Females who were not grossly handicapped had a good prognosis for marriage. Males, even those not seriously handicapped, more often than not refrained from matrimony. Of great importance was the factor of early remission of seizures. Early remission was defined as that occurring by the age of 12 or younger and such early remission, the corollary of nonseizure during adolescence, and marriage were strongly linked. Among twenty-nine patients who remitted early, twenty-six were married by the end of the follow-up period in 1977, and only three were single. Among thirty-seven who did not remit early, fourteen were married and twenty-three were single. More females than males had an early remission. Virtually all marriageable females did marry: all fourteen who remitted early were married, but nine of the eleven who did not remit early also were married. However, in the male group, the problem was more complex. Only three males who did not marry remitted early, but the group of seventeen who did marry contained twelve who remitted early and five who did not; this was considered to be highly significant. The problems of sexuality were not related to the side of the epileptic focus.

Taylor's [57] account concerned with the absence of sexual appetite in adults with temporal lobe-limbic epilepsy was paralleled completely in the study by Lindsay, Ounsted, and Richards [35]. The important behavioral aspect was that at least fourteen of the twenty-four single men (in the latter series) clearly had no attraction to sexual activity. The attitude or absence of sexual drive emerged repeatedly in consultations, and was evident in the life-style which was evaluated over a long period of time. The only significant discriminating factor was that of early remission, when the subgroup of "sexless men" was compared with the apparently more sexually adjusted married group. The important consideration from the standpoint of applied neuropathophysiology is that early remission meant cessation of temporal lobe-limbic seizure activity at or about the time of puberty. In cases with asexuality, seizure activity continued throughout adolescence and adult life. The concept of temporal lobe-limbic epilepsy therefore must be qualified in terms of the critical time periods of its occurrence, when one is considering culturally oriented and instinctually oriented behaviors of sexuality, marriage, and parenthood. The fact that nonearly remission carried a poor prognosis for marriage applied with greater force to male patients, but not to female. This syndrome of sexlessness or sexual apathy, especially in male patients, has been noted by all who studied the patricular problem in temporal lobe-limbic epilepsy. Taylor [57] regarded this as a loss of a "vital synergism" rather than some positive psychiatric syndrome. None of the patients in the Lindsay, Ounsted, and Richards series was known to be homosexual and this has been remarked upon in other studies as well. None was eunuchoid in appearance.

There clearly is a significant difference in the behavior controlled by neuoroendocrine processes in the male and female with temporal lobe-limbic epilepsy past the age of puberty. As is known in animals with sexual cycles, rhythmic and reciprocal changes in the electrophysiological activity in the hippocampus and amygdala [36] parallel the rise and fall in sexual drive. Of importance, therefore, in the present context is that most of the single males and virtually all those known to have sexual indifference probably suffered frequent "epileptic" disturbance of hippocampal and amygdala limbic functions, and hence limbic-hypothalamic functions, during the developmental period when sexual appetite and behavior develops and become manifest, at puberty and afterward. Children who had frequent limbic seizures but showed early remission before puberty grew as normally sexually appetitive. It is of further interest that in the Lindsay, Ounsted, and Richards series four of the five married men who had not remitted early were psychiatrically disturbed, and three of the five marriages broke down within a few years. The part played by sexual indifference could not be disentagled from their psychiatric disorders, but it was suspected to be a contributory factor.

This study [35] emphasizes that etiological group (that is, presence of mesial temporal sclerosis, tumor, or hamartoma), frequency of limbic seizures, frequency and intensity of grand mal seizures, and various factors related to alterations in cognitive functions did not discriminate between the two groups of males. Seizures continuing during postpuberty and the adolescent period emerged as the only significant discriminant discerned. This problem could be subjected to an experimental approach utilizing certain animal replicas of limbic seizures. For example, Mellanby et al. [38] and Glaser and Yu [27] devised a model using tetanus toxin injected into hippocampus that produced a self-limited period of clinical and electrographic seizure activity followed by a more prolonged period of both behavioral and cognitive functioning disturbance. The model is well-suited to test the hypothesis that such seizures differently disrupt adult sexual activity, dependent upon the ontogenetic epoch in which they are induced. Experimental protocols are being devised to examine these hypotheses and functions in young animals of both sexes, with carefully planned timing of the epileptogenic induction.

There is another interesting point that relates to the effect of the critical period of temporal lobe-limbic seizure activity proceeding through adolescence. This phenomenon leads to the conclusion that females with

temporal lobe-limbic epilepsy contribute more than males to the next generation of children. Many epidemiological studies of epilepsy found more afflicted relatives on the female side in the pedigree of epileptic probands. The
data of Lindsay, Ounsted, and Richards [35] indicate that there is at least a
threefold greater chance of transmission of a genetic seizure-trait activity
through females, because of the lack of sexual behavior on the part of the
males having seizure activity persisting to adult life. The likelihood of marriage and parenthood among those patients who have children appears to
rest on the few recognizable biological factors which can usually be discerned before the end of childhood.

Many other aspects of critical or vulnerable periods in brain development related to various aspects of behavior could have been discussed. The
concept of critical periods has been taken in a wide sense, and in a variable
sense related to certain specific factors which could have an effect on the
development of a kind of behavior as indicated in the epilepsies, and the
various secondary behavioral traits derived from the interference of brain
function produced by epileptic activity. An attempt was made to show that
prenatal and perinatal factors are important, especially those genetically
determined, and particularly those which might relate to the sensitivity of
brain to the development of specific kinds of seizure activity which are time-
locked into periods shortly after birth. Considerations in species differences
apart, there are factors which indicate certain highly suggestive parallels
between specific kinds of seizure susceptibilities in certain mammals related
to sensory stimuli such as the AS paradigm of the mouse, and the possibility
that there are parallels with the occurrence of the febrile-seizure state in the
young human. This state is particularly important, at least in the concep-
tualizations concerned with the pathogenesis of temporal lobe-limbic
epilepsy, with its production of the limbic lesion of mesial temporal
sclerosis.

In addition, the other vulnerable or critical period under discussion
related to that concerned with sexual functions, especially the exacerbation
of seizure activity in the female at the time of puberty and then cyclically
related to the menses. Male individuals with temporal lobe-limbic epilepsy,
especially those who experience seizures beyond puberty through
adolescence, are afflicted with significant behavioral dysfunction (sexual
apathy and indifference) which again secondarily leads to a multitude of
varying behavioral patterns. The interplay between the limbic-system structures and functions and the various hypothalamic-endocrine circuits and
relationships are emphasized throughout. The possibility also is raised, at
least from some experimental data relating to the AS model, that a form of
genetically determined hormonal imbalance during a specific period of
development is of particular importance in the production of some types of
seizure disorders.

References

1. Aicardi, J., and Chevrie, J.J. 1971. Convulsive status epilepticus in infants and children: A study of 239 cases. *Epilepsia* 11:187-197.
2. Abood, L.G., and Gerard, R.W. 1955. A phosphorylation defect in the brains of mice susceptible to audiogenic seizure. In Waelsch, H., ed. *Biochemistry of the developing nervous system*. New York: Academic Press, pp. 467-472.
3. Balazs, R.; Lewis, P.D.; and Patel, A.J. 1975. Effects of metabolic factors on brain development. In Brazier, M.A.B., ed. *Growth and development of the brain*. New York: Raven Press, pp. 83-115.
4. Bernhard, C.G.; Kolmodin, G.M.; and Meyerson, B.A. 1967. On the prenatal development of function and structure in the somesthetic cortex of the sheep. *Prog Brain Res* 26:60-72.
5. Blakemore, C. 1975. Development of functional connections in the mammalian visual system. In Brazier, M.A.B., ed. *Growth and development of the brain*. New York: Raven Press, pp. 157-169.
6. Blumer, D., and Walker, A.E. 1967. Sexual behavior in temporal lobe epilepsy. *Arch Neurol* 16:37-43.
7. Brazier, M.A.B., ed. 1975. *Growth and development of the brain: Nutritional, genetic and environmental factors*. New York: Raven Press.
8. Cheney, D.L.; Costa, E.; Racagni, G.; and Zsilla, G. 1976. Cholinergic and adenylate cyclase systems in rat brain nuclei during development. In Brazier, M.A.B., and Coceani, F., eds. *Brain dysfunction in infantile febrile convulsions*. New York: Raven Press, pp. 41-53.
9. Creutzfeldt, O.D.; Arnold, P.-M.; Becker, D.; Langenstein, S.; Tirsch, W.; Wilhelm, H.; and Wuttke, W. 1976. EEG changes during spontaneous and controlled menstrual cycles and their correlation with psychological performance. *Electroencephalogr Clin Neurophysiol* 40:113-131.
10. Davenport, J.W.; Hagquist, N.W.; and Hennies, R.S. 1975. Neonatal hyperthyroidism: Maturational acceleration and learning deficit in triidothyronine-stimulated rats. *Physiol Psychol* 3:231-236.
11. Davidson, S., and Falconer, M.A. 1975. Outcome of surgery in 40 children with temporal lobe epilepsy. *Lancet* 1:1260-1263.
12. Denenberg, V.H. 1968. A consideration of the usefulness of the critical period hypothesis as applied to the stimulation of rodents in infancy. In Newton, G., and Levine, S., eds. *Early experience and behavior: Psychobiology of development*. Springfield, Ill.: Charles C. Thomas, pp. 142-167.
13. Dobbing, J. 1968. Vulnerable periods in developing brain. In

Davison, A.N., and Dobbing, J., eds. *Applied neurochemistry*. Philadelphia: F.A. Davis Co., chapter 7, pp. 287-316.

14.   Dodge, P.R.; Prensky, A.L.; and Feigin, R.D. 1975. *Nutrition and the developing nervous system*. St. Louis: C.V. Mosby Co., pp. 1-157.

15.   Douglas, R.J. 1975. The development of hippocampal function: Implications for theory and for therapy. In Isaacson, R.L., and Pribram, K.H., eds. *The hippocampus*. New York and London: Plenum Press, vol. 2, chapter 11, pp. 327-361.

16a. Eayrs, J.T. 1971. Thyroid and developing brain: Anatomical and behavioral effects: in Hamburgh, M., and Harrington, E.J.W., eds. *Hormones in development*. New York: Appleton-Century-Crofts, pp. 345-355.

16b. Eberhardt, N.L.; Valcana, T.; and Timiras, P.S. 1976. Hormone-receptor interactions in brain: Uptake and binding of thyroid hormone. *Psychoneuroendocrinology* 1:399-409.

17.   Ellingson, R.J. 1964. Studies of the electrical activity of the developing human brain. *Prog Brain Res* 9:26-53.

18.   Ellingson, R.J.; Lathrop, G.H.; Dansky, T.; and Nelson, B. 1973. Variability of visual evoked potentials in human infants and adults. *Electroencephalogr Clin Neurophysiol* 34:113-124.

19.   Falconer, M.A. 1976. Surgical treatment of sequelae of severe febrile convulsions. In Brazier, M.A.B., and Coceani, F., eds. *Brain dysfunction in infantile febrile convulsions*. New York: Raven Press, pp. 307-326.

20.   Flexner, L.B. 1955. Enzymatic and functional patterns of the developing mammalian brain. In Waelsch, H., ed. *Biochemistry of the developing nervous system*. New York: Academic Press, pp. 281-295.

21.   Gastaut, H., and Collomb, H. 1954. Etude du comportement sexuel chez épileptiques psychomoteurs. *Ann Medicopsychol* 112:565-696.

22.   Geel, S.E., and Timiras, P.S. 1970. The role of hormones in cerebral protein metabolism. In Lajtha, A., ed. *Protein metabolism of the nervous system*. New York: Plenum Press, pp. 335-354.

23.   Ginsburg, B.E. 1969. Genetic assimilation of environmental variability in the organization of behavioral capacities of the developing nervous system. In Wolstonholm, G.E.W., and O'Connor, M., eds. *Ciba Foundation Symposium*. London: J & A. Churchill, Ltd., pp. 286-299.

24.   Glaser, G.H. 1959. The neurological status of the newborn: Neuromuscular and electroencephalographic activity. *Yale J Biol Med* 32:173-191.

25.   Glaser, G.H. 1967. Limbic epilepsy in childhood. *J Nerv Ment Dis* 144:391-397.

26. Glaser, G.H. 1975. On the development and manifestations of temporal lobe epilepsy. *Bull Acad Med Toronto* 48:59-62.
27. Glaser, G.H., and Yu, R.K. 1977. A model of hippocampal epilepsy produced by tetanus toxin. *Neurology* 27:337.
28. Grave, G.D., ed. 1977. *Thyroid hormones and brain development.* New York: Raven Press.
29. Hertz, L.; Schousboe, A.; Formby, B.; and Lennox-Buchthal, M. 1974. Some age dependent biochemical changes in mice susceptible to seizures. *Epilepsia* 15:619-631.
30. Hirano, A., and Zimmermann, H.M. 1973. Aberrant synaptic development. *Arch Neurol* 28:359-368.
31. Hodge, G.K.; Butcher, L.L.; and Geller, E. 1976. Hormonal effects on the morphologic differentiation of layer VI cortical cells in the rat. *Brain Res* 104:137-141.
32. Krieger, D.T., ed. 1979. *Endocrine rhythms.* New York: Raven Press.
33. Legrand, J. 1977. Morphologic and biochemical effects of hormones on the developing nervous system in mammals. In Berenberg, S.R., ed. *Brain: Fetal and infant.* The Hague: Martinis Nijhoff Medical Division, pp. 137-164.
34. Lennox-Buchthal, M.A. 1973. Febrile convulsions: A reappraisal. *Electroencephalogr Clin Neurophysiol* 32:1-138.
35. Lindsay, J.; Ounsted, C.; and Richards, P. 1979. The long term outcome in children with temporal lobe seizures. (1) Social outcome and childhood factors. (2) Marriage, parenthood and sexual indifferences. (3) Psychiatric aspects in childhood and adult life. *Dev Med Child Neurol* 21:285-298, 433-440, 630-636.
36. McGowan-Sass, B.K., and Timiras, P.S. 1975. The hippocampus and hormonal cyclicity. In Isaacson, R.L., and Pribram, K.H., eds. *The hippocampus.* New York and London: Plenum Press, vol. 1, chapter 13, pp. 355-374.
37. McIlwain, H., and Bachelard, H.S. 1971. *Biochemistry and the central nervous system.* Edinburgh and London: Churchill Livingstone, pp. 406-444.
38. Mellanby, J.; George, G.; Robinson, A.; and Thompson, P. 1977. Epileptiform syndrome in rats produced by injecting tetanus toxin into the hippocampus. *J Neurol Neurosurg Psychiatry* 40:404-414.
39. Nelson, K.B., and Ellenberg, J.H. 1976. Predictors of epilepsy in children who have experienced febrile seizures. *N Engl J Med* 295:1029-1033.
40. Oppenheimer, J.H.; Schwartz, H.L.; and Surls, M.I. 1974. Tissue differences in the concentration of triiodothyronine nuclear binding sites. *Endocrinology* 95:897-907.

41. Ounsted, C. 1976. Genetic messages and convulsive behavior in pyrexia. In Brazier, M.A.B., and Coceani, F., eds. *Brain dysfunctions in infantile febrile convulsions*. New York: Raven Press, pp. 279-290.

42. Ounsted, C.; Lindsay, J.; and Norman, R. 1966. *Biological factors in temporal lobe epilepsy*. London: William Heinemann Ltd.

43. Oxbury, J.M., and Whitty, C.W.M. 1971. Causes and consequences of status epilepticus in adults. *Brain* 94:733-744.

44. Pelton, E.W., and Bass, N.H. 1973. Adverse effects of excess thyroid hormones on the maturation of rat cerebrum. *Arch Neurol* 29: 145-150.

45. Phelps, C.P., and Leathem, J.H. 1976. Effects of postnatal thyroxine administration on brain: Development, response to postnatal androgen and thyroid regulation in female rats. *J Endocrinol* 69:175-182.

46a. Purpura, D.P. 1972. Intracellular studies of synaptic organization in the mammalian brain. In Pappas, G.D., and Purpura, D.P., eds. *Structure and function of synapses*. New York: Raven Press, chapter 12, pp. 257-302.

46b. Purpura, D.P. 1976. Structure-dysfunction relations in the visual cortex of preterm infants. In Brazier, M.A.B., and Coceani, F., eds. *Brain dysfunction in infantile febrile convulsions*. New York: Raven Press, pp. 223-240.

46c. Purpura, D.P.; Prelevic, S.; and Santini, M. 1968. Structural characteristics of neurons in the feline hippocampus during postnatal ontogenesis. *Exp Neurol* 22:379-390.

47. Raskin, N.H., and Fishman, R.A. 1966. Effects of thyroid on permeability, composition and electrolyte metabolism of brain and other tissues. *Arch Neurol* 14:21-30.

48. Rodin, E.A. 1968. *The prognosis of patients with epilepsy*. Springfield, Ill.: Charles C. Thomas.

49. Schapiro, S.; Vukovich, K.; and Globus, A. 1973. Effects of neonatal thyroxine and hydrocortisone administration on the development of dendritic spines in the visual cortex of rats. *Exp Neurol* 40:286-296.

50. Scheibel, M.E.; Crandall, P.H.; and Scheibel, A.B. 1974. The hippocampal dentate complex in temporal lobe epilepsy: A golgi study. *Epilepsia* 15:55-80.

51. Schlesinger, K., and Griek, B.J. 1970. The genetics and biochemistry of audiogenic seizures. In Lindzey, G., and Thiessen, D.D., eds. *Contributions to behavior-genetic analysis: The mouse as a prototype*. New York: Appleton-Century-Crofts, chapter 9, pp. 219-257.

52. Schmitt, F.O., and Samson, R.E., Jr., eds. 1969. Brain cell microenvironment. *Neurosci Res Program Bull* 7:277-417.

53. Seyfried, T.N.; Glaser, G.H.; and Yu, R.K. 1978a. Cerebral, cerebellar and brain stem gangliosides in mice susceptible to audiogenic seizures. *J Neurochem* 31:21-27.

54. Seyfried, T.N.; Glaser, G.H.; and Yu, R.K. 1978b. Developmental analysis of regional brain growth and audiogenic seizures in mice. *Genetics* 88:590.
55. Seyfried, T.N.; Glaser, G.H.; and Yu, R.K. 1979. Thyroid hormone influence on the susceptibility of mice to audiogenic seizures. *Science* 205:598-600.
56. Stone, J.M., and Greenaugh, W.T. 1975. Excess neonatal thyroxine: effects on learning in infant and adolescent rats. *Dev Psychobiol* 8:479-488.
57. Taylor, D.C. 1969a. Sexual behavior and temporal lobe epilepsy. *Arch Neurol* 21:510-516.
58. Taylor, D.C. 1969b. Differential rates of cerebral maturation between sexes and between hemispheres. *Lancet* 2:140-142.
59. Taylor, D.C., and Ounsted, C. 1971. Biological mechanisms influencing the outcome of seizures in response to fever. *Epilepsia* 12:33-45.
60. Timiras, P.S. 1969. Role of hormones in the development of seizures. In Jasper, H.H.; Ward, A.; and Pope, A., eds. *Basic Mechanisms of the Epilepsies*. Boston: Little, Brown and Co., pp. 727-736.
61. Timiras, P.S., and Luckock, A.S. 1974. Hormonal factors regulating brain development. In International Society for Psychoendocrinology. Psychoendocrinology; proceedings of the workshop conference. Ed. N. Hatotani. Basel, N.Y.: Karger, pp. 206-213.
62. Vernadakis, A., and Woodbury, D.M. 1969. The developing animal as a model. *Epilepsia* 10:163-178.
63. Wallace, S.J. 1976. Neurological and intellectual deficits: Convulsions with fever viewed as acute indications of life-long developmental defects. In Brazier, M.A.B., and Coceani, F., eds. *Brain dysfunction in infantile febrile convulsions*. New York: Raven Press, pp. 259-277.
64. Walsh, R.N.; Budtz-olsen, O.E.; Penny, J.E.; and Cummins, R.A. 1971. The effects of environmental complexity on the histology of the rat hippocampus. *J Comp Neurol* 137:361-366.
65. Wasterlain, C.G., and Plum, F. 1973. Vulnerability of developing rat brain to electroconvulsive seizures. *Arch Neurol* 29:38-45.
66. Wimer, R.E.; Wimer, C.C.; Vaughn, J.E.; Barber, R.P.; Balvanz, B.A.; and Chernow, C.R. 1976. The genetic organization of neuron number in Ammon's horns of house mice. *Brain Res* 118:219-243.
67. Woodbury, D.M. 1954. Effect of hormones on brain excitability and electrolytes. *Recent Prog Horm Res* 10:65-104.
68. Woodward, D.L.; Hoffer, B.J.; and Lapham, L.W. 1969. Postnatal development of electrical and enzyme histochemical activity in Purkinje cells. *Exp Neurol* 23:120-129.

3

Behavioral Test for Detection of Subclinical Brain Damage: An Experimental Model

Michael J. Zigmond and
Edward M. Stricker

Introduction

Damage to the central nervous system (CNS) is often accompanied by obvious behavioral symptoms. However, for the past several years we have been studying lesions which do not result in clear loss of function. Furthermore, even conventional histological examination fails to reveal damage. These lesions involve the destruction of catecholamine (CA)-containing neurons in brain using the neurotoxin, 6-hydroxydopamine (6-HDA). Present neurological and histological methods are often inadequate for the detection of such lesions. Thus, animals with selective destruction of central catecholaminergic neurons usually will appear neurologically intact. (Abbreviations: CA, catecholamine; 2-DG, 2-deoxy-D-glucose; DOPAC, dihydroxyphenylacetic acid; DA, dopamine; ED50, dose needed for 50 percent of the effect; 6-HDA, 6-hydroxydopamine; NE, norepinephrine; TH, tyrosine hydroxylase.)

The reasons for many of the difficulties in detecting damage to CA-containing systems may lie in the biochemical characteristics of these neurons. Much of our thinking about the nervous system is based on an understanding of the mammalian neuromuscular junction at which acetylcholine produces a rapid alteration of membrane conductance, thereby generating a postsynaptic potential of millisecond duration. This is not the only form of synaptic transmission, however; it may not even be the most common one. Many transmitters, including the CAs, norepinephrine (NE), and dopamine (DA), do not act directly to affect ion channels. Instead they act through several intervening steps resulting in a slower and often more

Based on a paper presented at the Fifth Symposium on the Effects of Foods and Drugs on the Development and Function of the Nervous System sponsored by the U.S.P.H.S. Food and Drug Administration in Arlington, Virginia, 10-12 October 1979, and reprinted in HHS Publication No. (FDA)80-1076.

Much of the research presented here was carried out in collaboration with Ann L. Acheson, Thomas G. Heffner, and other members of our laboratory. The work was supported in part by grants from the U.S.P.H.S. (MH-20620, NSMH-16359, MH-29670 and MH-00058).

subtle response. An important characteristic of synapses utilizing such transmitters is that they operate at a low and relatively constant frequency which tends to resist change. The homeostatic mechanisms responsible for this constancy might be expected to respond to subtotal destruction of CA-containing neuronal systems by initiating presynaptic and postsynaptic events which return the basal output toward normal. Our observations support this hypothesis.

In this chapter we briefly review some of the basic characteristics of catecholaminergic neurons in the brain. (For more detailed reviews and specific literature citations see [1-3].) Then we present evidence for compensatory neurochemical changes which appear to minimize the functional impairments produced by 6-HDA. Finally, we discuss the implications of these adaptive responses for the development of clinical instruments to detect such neuronal damage.

Characteristics of Catecholaminergic Neurons in the CNS

The catecholaminergic cell bodies of the CNS are located primarily in the brainstem reticular formation. DA-containing cells are concentrated in and around the substantia nigra and send their axons rostralward to the striatum and several other telencephalic structures. The largest groups of NE-containing cells is found in locus coeruleus and projects throughout the CNS (figure 3-1). The gross anatomy of these systems suggests a diffuse action. This possibility is reinforced by more detailed structural analyses. For example, the terminal regions of these axons are characterized by extensive branching and each branch contains multiple presynaptic boutons "en passage." Moreover, electron microscopic examination of these varicosities often indicates an absence of discrete presynaptic and postsynaptic specialization.

The CAs are synthesized from phenylalanine and tyrosine by a sequence of reactions which begins with the action of the rate-limiting enzyme, tyrosine hydroxylase (TH). The amines are stored in vesicles from which they are released during depolarization to act on a postsynaptic receptor. The transmitters are then inactivated, largely by reuptake due to high-affinity transport systems located at the nerve terminals, and are either stored in vesicles for reuse or metabolized (figure 3-2).

Pharmacological studies suggest that catecholaminergic synapses can provide a relatively constant output even in the face of changing input. This homeostasis is the net result of several types of regulating processes. First, transmitter release is monitored at both the terminal region (through presynaptic and postsynaptic receptors) and the cell body (for example, through the influence of recurrent collaterals). When the availability of transmitter at these sites is altered a compensatory change in release is rapidly initiated. Second, sensitivity of the postsynaptic cell is tuned to

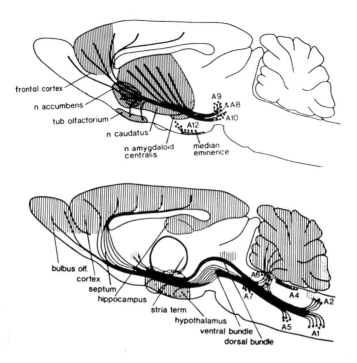

Note: Stripes indicate the major nerve terminal areas. (Upper) The cell bodies of the DA-containing neurons include a large group in the mesencephalon within and adjacent to the substantia nigra (A8-10, according to the designations of Dahlstrom and Fuxe [4]) and a smaller group in the hypothalamus (A12). Axons from A8-10 ascend in the ipsilateral crus cerebri and internal capsule through the globus pallidus to terminate in several areas including the caudate-putamen, nucleus accumbens, and frontal cortex. Axons from A12 innervate the median eminence. (Lower) NE-containing cell groups are present in the medulla and pons (A1, A2, A4, A5, and A7), and innervate the lower brain stem, hypothalamus, preoptic area, and septum. The largest NE cell group is in the locus coeruleus (A6), which projects diffusely throughout the CNS. (Modified from the work of Ungerstedt [5]) and others; (see [1] and [2]).

Figure 3-1. Sagittal Projections of the Ascending NE and DA Pathways in the Rat Brain

transmitter availability. Its membrane appears to adapt to changing levels of stimulation both by the modification of existing receptors and, more gradually, by the alteration of the rate at which new receptors are formed. Finally, several processes operate to maintain a steady-state level of transmitter stores within the catecholaminergic nerve terminal. Thus, changes in transmitter release and degradation are accompanied by parallel changes in transmitter synthesis. Long-term changes in CA synthesis appear to result from changes in the synthesis of TH in the cell body, while more rapid changes may be accomplished in the terminal region by altering the activity of existing enzyme.

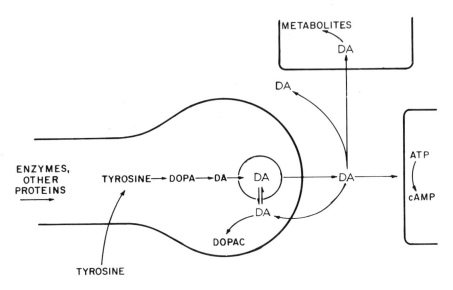

Note: Tyrosine is transported into the nerve terminal where it is converted first to dopa (catalyzed by tyrosine hydroxylase) then to DA which is transported into vesicles. (In some cells DA is subsequently converted to NE.) CA is released into the synaptic cleft by exocytosis. There it acts on the postsynaptic membrane, perhaps by influencing adenylate cyclase, an enzyme which catalyzes the conversion of adenosine triphosphate (ATP) to adenosine $3',5'$-cyclic monophosphate (cAMP). The CA is removed from the synapse either by diffusion or by uptake into surrounding cells, the most important of which are the NE and DA-containing terminals themselves. Once within the cytoplasm, the CA can either be metabolized (by one of several routes involving the enzymes monoamine oxidase and catechol-O-methyltransferase) or taken up and stored in vesicles for reuse. The enzymes involved in the synthesis or catabolism of CA are formed in cell bodies and transported to their sites of action, as are various other proteins which may be important in the construction of vesicles, cell membranes, transport systems, and receptors.

Figure 3-2. The Life Cycle of Catecholamines

6-Hydroxydopamine: Gross Histological and Behavioral Effects

6-HDA is a structural analog of the CAs (figure 3-3). It does not cross the blood-brain barrier in adult animals but may be administered into the CNS either by direct injection into central neural tissue or by injection into the cerebrospinal fluid. Such injections have relatively little effect on the gross histological appearance of cerebral tissue. However, if the tissue is stained in such a way as to convert the amines to fluorescent derivatives, the relative absence of CA-containing structures is apparent (figure 3-4). Similar results can be obtained by direct biochemical analysis of the tissue [6]. As expected, the decrease in CAs is accompanied by an equivalent loss of high-affinity CA-uptake sites (figure 3-5). In short, while conventional histological examination would detect few toxic effects of 6-HDA, a more detailed analysis suggests that the agent causes selective degeneration of

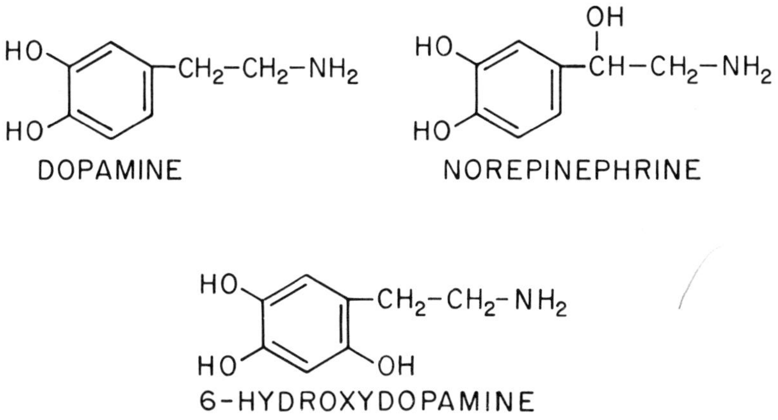

HO—⟨benzene ring⟩—CH$_2$—CH$_2$—NH$_2$
HO—

DOPAMINE

OH
|
HO—⟨benzene ring⟩—CH—CH$_2$—NH$_2$
HO—

NOREPINEPHRINE

HO—⟨benzene ring⟩—CH$_2$—CH$_2$—NH$_2$
HO—   OH

6-HYDROXYDOPAMINE

Figure 3-3. Structural Formulas of Dopamine, 6-Hydroxydopamine, and Norepineprine

catecholaminergic terminals. This hypothesis has been confirmed in the peripheral nervous system following systemic injections of 6-HDA [6].

The general mechanism by which 6-HDA produces these effects is well understood. Because of its structural similarity to CAs, the toxin is concentrated in CA-containing terminals by their specific high-affinity uptake system. However, 6-HDA is highly unstable and rapidly oxidizes to form several toxic compounds, which destroy the terminals [6]. Conventional histological analyses are generally inadequate for detecting this sort of damage because the axons and terminals of aminergic neurons are both too thin (1μ) and too diffuse [1, 2].

Conventional behavioral analyses are not much better at detecting the damage. Despite the permanent depletion of up to 95 percent of the NE and DA in brain, animals given intracerebral injections of 6-HDA show little impairment in food and water intake, locomotor activity, sexual behavior, or performance on a wide variety of tasks. Overall appearance is quite normal, and neurological tests for responsiveness to sensory stimuli and for motor coordination also show no signs of impairment. Obvious dysfunctions are seen only after the near-total destruction of dopaminergic terminals, or the acute pharmacological blockade of dopaminergic synaptic activity [8, 9].

Compensatory Neurochemical Changes

One possible explanation for the absence of obvious functional impairments following 6-HDA-induced brain damage is that the processes which normally serve to keep synaptic activity constant also help to restore

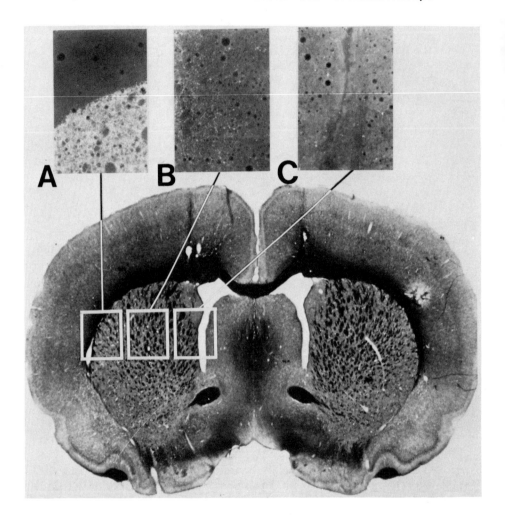

Note: Twenty microliters containing 200-250 μg of 6-HDA were administered to the lateral ventricle several days prior to histological examination. Coronal section prepared by perfusing with 10 percent formalin and saline, and staining with luxol fast blue (fiber tracts) and safranin-O (nuclei). (A-C) Insets (from a separate animal) were prepared by exposing unperfused tissue to buffered glyoxylic acid and then photographing the flurophore derived from endogenous catecholamines through a fluorescent microscope: (A) Far lateral edge of the striatum showing normal varicosities; (B) middle of striatum showing a transition zone in which fluorescent varicosities begin to disappear; (C) periventricular portions of striatum (left) and septum (right) showing absence of fluorescent varicosities. (Fluorescent microscopy by Gregory Kapatos.)

Figure 3-4. Effect of 6-Hydroxydopamine on the Histological Appearance
                of Brain

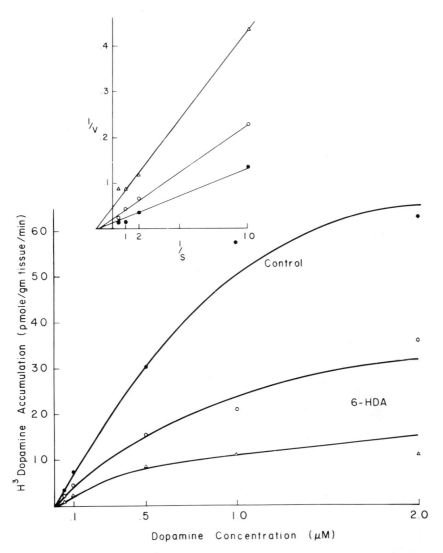

Note: Synaptosome-rich P2 fractions were prepared from the striatum of control rats and from animals treated two months previously with 6-HDA. Aliquots for the resuspended P2 fraction were taken for determination of endogenous DA and protein content. A third fraction was incubated in Krebs-Ringer phosphate buffer (pH 7.4) containing 0.05-2.0 μM 3H-dopamine. After five minutes tissues were separated by filtration and net tritium uptake determined. The apparent Vmax for DA uptake decreased in proportion to the loss of endogenous DA (r = 0.92); Kt was unchanged. Shown are results from representative control animal (●) and two 6-HDA-treated animals (o) 53 percent DA depletion; (Δ) 77 percent DA depletion (from [7]).

Figure 3-5. 3H-Dopamine Uptake into Striatal Synaptosomes

activity after extensive brain damage. Recent evidence from our laboratory and others supports this hypothesis.

Increased CA Turnover. Following the administration of 6-HDA, changes in the levels of DA metabolites are less marked than the reduction in DA levels. For example, we find that the loss of 74 percent of striatal DA is accompanied by only a 45 percent decline in dihydroxyphenylacetic acid (DOPAC), one of the principal metabolites of DA (table 3-1). In fact, for DA depletions above 50 percent the ratio of DOPAC to DA rises steadily with increasing lesion size (figure 3-6). If one takes CA content (or in vitro CA uptake) to reflect the number of residual dopaminergic terminals, this observation suggests an increase in the accumulation of DOPAC per terminal. Furthermore, the relative increase in DOPAC does not appear to result from a decline in DOPAC efflux but instead suggests an increase in DA turnover in these residual neurons [1]. This hypothesis is consistent with the relative increases in the production of homovanillic acid (another metabolite of DA) and in the synthesis of DA following subtotal destruction of dopainergic neurons [11, 12]. It may also be analogous to the increase in DA turnover that results when DA receptor antagonists are administered to normal animals [13, 14]. In each case a decrease in DA receptor activation appears to elicit a compensatory increase in activity of DA neurons.

Increased TH Activity. As with DOPAC content, the effect of 6-HDA on striatal TH activity is less severe than is the decline in DA (table 3-1). There appear to be two components to this apparent increase in TH activity in residual nerve terminals: an activation of existing TH molecules and an increase in the number of functional TH molecules. This hypothesis is based on parallel studies of the noradrenergic projection from locus coeruleus to

Table 3-1
Effect of 6-HDA on Dopamine, Dihydroxyphenylacetic Acid, and Tyrosine Hydroxylase Activity in Striatum

	Control	6-HDA	Control, %
DA (μg/g)	7.00 ± .33	1.55 ± .50	22.14
DOPAC (μg/g)	2.78 ± .39	1.52 ± .12	54.68
TH (nmoles/mg/min)	.950 ± .023	.474 ± .046	49.89

Note: Rats were given 250 μg 6-HDA twenty-one days prior to sacrifice. Tyrosine hydroxylase was measured at pH 5.6 (pH optimum for this area) and in the presence of a saturating concentration of cofactor. Values represent the means ± S.E.M. for groups of four. (A.L. Acheson, unpublished observations.)

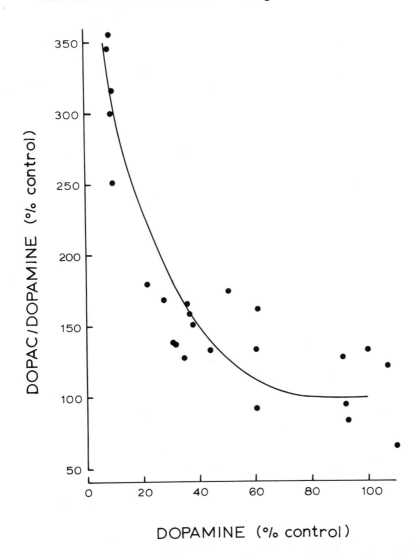

Note: Animals given 6-HDA were sacrificed three to twenty-one days later and the DOPAC and DA content of striatum was determined. Since DA content appears to be an index of the number of residual terminals (for example, it correlated with the number of high-affinity DA uptake sites, see figure 3-5), we expressed our results as a ratio of DOPAC to DA. An increase in this ratio may indicate an increase in the amount of DOPAC formed per residual terminal. (Ann L. Acheson, unpublished observations.)

Figure 3-6. DOPAC Concentration in Striatum as a Function of DA Depletion

hippocampus, a pathway whose considerable length facilitated analysis of the temporal pattern of changes in TH activity. In the days immediately following 6-HDA administration, the NE content (and in vitro high-affinity NE uptake) in hippocampus is markedly decreased whereas TH activity is little changed (table 3-2). This discrepancy between TH activity and NE content only exists when the enzyme is assayed well above the pH optimum for the enzyme and in the presence of a subsaturating concentration of cofactor [15]. Since these conditions are the same as those required to permit detection of the effects of in vitro TH activation [16, 17], the findings suggest that the elevation in TH activity results from activation of existing enzyme molecules. By three weeks following 6-HDA treatment, however, an increase in TH activity can be detected under optimal, saturating assay conditions (figure 3-7) [18]. Apparently, an initial activation of TH is gradually replaced by an increase in the availability of enzyme.

These short- and long-term increases in TH activity may serve to maintain a high rate of CA synthesis in residual terminals and thereby permit the increase in CA turnover that occurs there. Such changes in TH activity have also been produced by DA receptor antagonists and by reserpine [19-22].

Decreased CA Inactivation. The decrease in CA uptake represents another adaptive change. This does not appear to be an active response to the lesion but simply results from the loss of CA terminals and their high-affinity transport sites (figure 3-5). Nevertheless, it may serve an important function. Since many CA nerve terminals do not appear to make conventional synapses [23], it seems reasonable to assume that transmitter released from one terminal normally gains access to receptors which are in the proximity of other terminals. A decrease in the number of uptake sites following 6-HDA treatment should decrease the rate at which transmitter diffusing from residual terminals is inactivated. This in turn should increase the effectiveness of transmitter acting on these more distant target cells in a

Table 3-2
Effect of 6-HDA on Norepinephrine and Tyrosine Hydroxylase Activity in Hippocampus

	Control	6-HDA	Control, %
NE (μg/g)	2.21 ± .2	.62 ± .03	28
TH (pmoles/mg/min)			
pH 6.2	9.39 ± .07	2.90 ± .08	31
pH 6.6	3.11 ± .1	2.88 ± .07	93

Note: Rats were given 250 μg 6-HDA five days prior to assay. Tyrosine Hydroxylase was measured at pH 6.2 (pH optimum for this area) or pH 6.6 in the presence of a subsaturating concentration of cofactor. Values are the mean ± S.E.M. for groups of four animals. (A.L. Acheson, unpublished observations.)

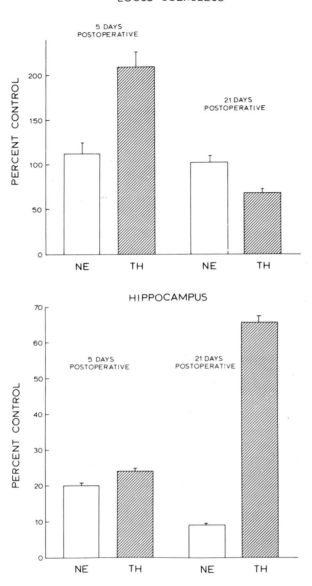

Note: Animals received 250 ug 6-HDA. All values are expressed as mean percentage of control ± S.E.M. for at least seven samples. Mean control values: NE, 47 μg/pair (locus coeruleus) and 400 ng/g (hippocampus); TH activity, 5.5 pmoles/pr/min (locus coeruleus) and 4.7 pmoles/mg protein/min (hippocampus). (From [18].)

Figure 3-7. Effect of 6-HDA on NE Content and TH Activity in Locus Coeruleus and Hippocampus

manner analogous to the "presynaptic supersensitivity" to adrenomedullary CAs that is seen after destruction of peripheral noradrenergic neurons [24].

Increased CA Receptors. Finally, destruction of CA terminals by 6-HDA, like chronic receptor blockade in intact systems, is followed by an increase in the number of apparent postsynaptic receptors. This is evident both in an increase in the response of NE- and DA-sensitive adenylate cyclase to catecholaminergic agonists [25-27] and an increase in the number of apparent CA receptors [28, 29]. The increase begins within a week after the lesion and develops gradually over the subsequent weeks. As with the loss of high-affinity CA-uptake sites, this increase in receptors may permit residual terminals to influence more distant targets.

To summarize, the functional impact of lesions induced by 6-HDA may be offset by two types of compensatory changes. First, CA release may be enhanced, with this increase supported by a parallel increase in the rate of CA synthesis. Second, the efficacy of the released transmitter may be enhanced due to a decrease in CA inactivation and an increase in target-cell sensitivity (figure 3-8).

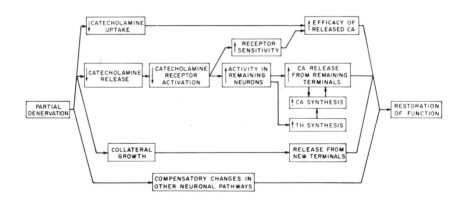

Note: According to this scheme the destruction of catecholaminergic terminals by 6-HDA or other neurotoxin results in an initial decrease in CA release and thus in CA receptor activation. This in turn triggers an increase in firing rate in residual neurons and an increase in CA release, from their terminals. The increased release is supported by increased CA synthesis which is facilitated by an increase in the availability of TH. The CA released in this way is made more effective by loss of uptake sites for the amines and, in the case of large lesions, by an increase in the availability of CA receptors. Growth of additional catecholaminergic terminals was observed in rats treated with 6-HDA as neonates [30, 31] and could also serve a compensatory function. (We find no evidence for such growth in rats lesioned as adults.)

Figure 3-8. A Model of Recovery of Function Following Subtotal Damage to Central Catecholamine-containing Neurons

Implications for Diagnostic Tests

The neurochemical responses described in the previous section may account for the absence of prominent symptoms in animals given 6-HDA. They also provide the basis for tests which indicate the presence of neurological damage despite or even because of these compensatory changes. We will describe two groups of such tests.

Pharmacological Challenges. A number of psychoactive drugs appear to affect behavior through their actions on dopaminergic synapses. 6-HDA, by destroying a large proportion of CA terminals and producing changes in remaining terminals and their target cells, might be expected to alter the drug-induced behavioral responses. Three examples are cited: The response to a direct receptor agonist, such as apomorphine, should be increased owing to the increased number of DA receptors. In contrast, the behavioral response to an indirect agonist, such as amphetamine, should be reduced since there will be fewer terminals which release DA, and those present will already be releasing transmitter at a high rate. The response to drugs which block DA receptors, such a spiroperidol, should be enhanced because the antagonists encounter less competition from endogenous DA.

To test these hypotheses we made use of our previous observations that food intake is related to dopaminergic activity by an inverted U-shaped curve; that is, either large decreases or large increases in dopaminergic activity disrupt feeding in association with hypokinesia and hyperkinesia, respectively [32]. The effects of various DA agonists and antagonists were examined in intact rats and in animals previously lesioned with 6-HDA. In most cases the effects were as predicted [27, 32]. For example, the anorexic effect of d-amphetamine was markedly reduced (figure 3-9) while the effects of apomorphine (figure 3-10) and of spiroperidol (figure 3-11) were enhanced. Thus though basal behavior was unaffected by 6-HDA, the behavioral responses to certain psychoactive drugs were altered in predictable ways.

Stress Test. Although the compensatory neurochemical changes that we have described may permit the lesioned animal to operate under basal conditions, the destruction of 80 to 95 percent of the CA-containing neurons and the neurochemical changes that follow must have a cost. In attempting to detect that cost, it is appropriate to consider the possible functions of these systems in the intact animal. Several lines of evidence point to a role for CAs in modulating arousal and the attendant responsiveness to environmental stimuli. As noted above, nearly all of the CA-containing neurons have their cell bodies located within the classical reticular formation and project diffusely to various areas of the CNS. DA agonists increase

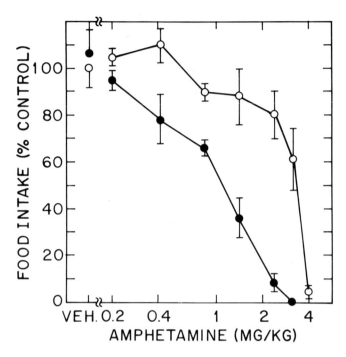

Note: In figures 3-9 through 3-11 rats were housed one per cage and feeding was restricted to four hours per day (1,300 to 1,700 hours) with water available continuously. Food intake was measured at the end of the first hour and is expressed as a percentage of mean control food intake (7 gm). Rats were given 200 μg 6-HDA (o) or vehicle (●) at least two weeks prior to testing. d-Amphetamine sulfate was administered intraperitoneally thirty minutes before onset of feeding test. All doses are given as milligram free base per kilogram body weight. Each point represents the mean ±S.E.M. of six animals. 6-HDA increased the dose of amphetamine needed to inhibit 50 percent of food intake (ED50) by 138 percent ($p < .01$) [32].

Figure 3-9. The Effect of 6-HDA on the Anorexic Action of d-Amphetamine

behavioral arousal, while antagonists decrease it. Moreover, electrophysiological and biochemical indexes of CA activity are often increased during periods of heightened arousal [33-35]. Thus, we believe that during arousal CA release is increased from many of the CA terminals in brain and that this release is a prerequisite for appropriate behavioral responses. However, we have proposed that after 6-HDA treatment CA release is already elevated in residual terminals. If so, the ability of these neurons to further increase CA release might be severely constrained and the behavioral responses to a stressor might therefore be reduced.

This hypothesis is analogous to that offered for reduced sensitivity to amphetamine. To test it, we examined the behavioral effects of several acute homeostatic challenges. One such stressor is 2-deoxy-D-glucose (2-DG), an analog of glucose that blocks glucose transport and utilization

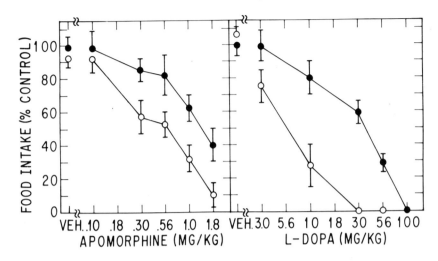

Note: Apomorphine HCl was administered intraperitoneally ten minutes prior to testing. L-Dihydroxyphenylaline methylester hydrochloride (L-dopa) was administered ten minutes prior to testing and thirty minutes after the peripheral decarboxylase inhibitor seryl-trihydroxybenzyl-hydrozine (Ro4-4602, 50 mg/kg). All drugs administered intraperitoneally and doses expressed as milligram free base per kilogram body weight. Each point represents the mean ±S.E.M. for six to eight 6-HDA-treated (200 μg,o) or sham-operated (●) animals. 6-HDA decreased the ED50 for apomorphine by 68 percent ($p < .01$), for L-dopa by 75 percent ($p < .01$) [32].

Figure 3-10. Effect of 6-HDA on the Anorexic Actions of Apomorphine and L-dopa

and thus produces a functional glucoprivation. Intact rats increase their food intake after 2-DG administration, an apparent attempt to offset the metabolic impact of the drug. We administered 2-DG to control animals and to rats sustaining damage to central CA neurons, produced either by 6-HDA treatment or by electrolytic lesions along the medial forebrain bundle. As expected, control animals increased their food intake by 4-6 grams over the next six hours. However, the lesioned animals did not increase feeding (figure 3-12) but showed the severe sensorimotor impairments that are characteristic of hypofunction at central dopaminergic synapses.

To quantify the apparent debilitation we used a battery of neurological tests adapted for this purpose. For example, akinesia was assessed by placing the rats on a flat surface and measuring the latency for limb movement. Catalepsy was measured by placing the animal with its forelimbs or hindlimbs raised on a block and measuring the amount of time needed to climb down. Orientation to touch and pain stimuli were measured after delivering probes to specific points along the body. Scores on each test were combined to provide an overall sensorimotor index. Under basal conditions,

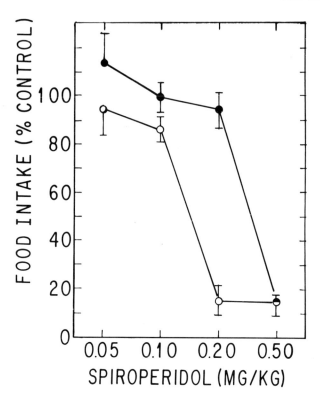

Note: Spiroperidol was administered intraperitoneally one hour prior to testing. Doses expressed as milligram free base per kilogram body weight. Each point represents the mean ± S.E.M. for six to eight 6-HDA (200 μg, o) or sham-operated (●) animals. 6-HDA decreased the ED50 for spiroperidol by 48 percent (p < .01) [32].

Figure 3-11. Effect of 6-HDA on the Anorexic Action of Spiroperidol

lesioned rats did not differ from control animals on any of these tests. Thus, by themselves, such tests were not effective in distinguishing lesioned animals from intact ones. In contrast, thirty minutes after the administration of 2-DG, neurological performance in lesioned animals differed markedly from controls (figure 3-13) [38, 39].

These and other experiments suggest that the differences between lesioned and control animals depends on three variables: the size of the lesion, the intensity of the stressor, and the demand of the test. For example, the difference between the two groups was greatest when the DA depletion was relatively large, the dose of 2-DG was relatively large, or the test was relatively stringent (requiring animals to move all four limbs rather than a single limb in evaluating akinesia). Thus, the toxic effects of 6-HDA

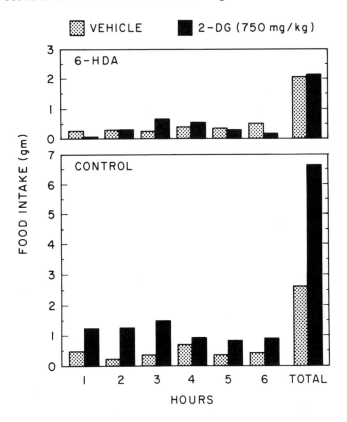

Note: Animals previously treated with 200 μg 6-HDA received 2-DG (750 mg/kg, intraperitoneally) or saline. Food intake was then measured hourly for six hours. Bars represent food intake for six animals.

Figure 3-12. The Behavioral Response of 6-HDA-treated Rats to 2-Deoxy-D-glucose

became clearly evident when behavior was examined under extreme conditions rather than in the basal state.

Conclusions

Extensive destruction of central catecholaminergic neurons has little observable impact on behavior. The explanation for this phenomenon is beginning to emerge. Following such lesions several neurochemical changes occur in residual terminals and target cells. These changes are predictable from pharmacological studies of synaptic homeostasis in intact brain and may serve to

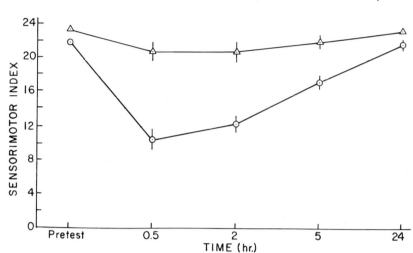

Note: Rats with electrolytic lesions along the nigrostriatal bundle (o) or sham-operated rats (Δ) received 2-DG (500 mg/kg, intraperitoneally) and sensorimotor tests were performed at various times thereafter. Values are the means ± S.E.M. for thirteen animals in each group. (For additional details of the testing procedure see [38].)

Figure 3-13. The Effect of 2-Deoxy-D-glucose on Sensorimotor Performance in Control and Brain-Damaged Rats

obscure the extensive neural damage. From these neurochemical effects we have been able to derive pharmacological challenges as diagnostic tools for detecting the presence of damage to these neuronal systems. A second approach for detecting damage has been to expose the animal to conditions which are outside the limits of the compensation, thereby eliciting measurable neurological dysfunctions. Studies of intact neuronal systems suggest that the tendency of synapses to maintain a constant output is probably not unique to the CAs; for example, similar regulatory processes have been reported for serotonergic systems and for muscarinic, cholinergic systems [40-43]. Thus, the principles discussed here may help to explain the phenomenon of subclinical brain damage and form the basis for a rationale whereby various types of neuronal degeneration may be assessed.

References

1. Moore, R.Y., and Bloom, F.E. 1978. *Ann Rev Neurosci* 1:129-169.
2. Moore, R.Y., and Bloom, F.E. 1979. *Ann Rev Neurosci* 2:113-168.
3. Iversen, L.L.; Iversen, S.D.; and Snyder, S.H., eds. 1975. *Handbook of psychopharmacology*, vol. 3. New York: Plenum Press.

4. Dahlstrom, A., and Fuxe, K. 1964. *Acta Physiol Scand Suppl* 237:1-55.
5. Ungerstedt, U. 1971. *Acta Physiol Scand Suppl* 367:1-48.
6. Breese, G. 1975. In *Handbook of psychopharmacology* (Iversen, L.L.; Iversen, S.D.; and Snyder, S.H., eds.) vol. 1, pp. 137-189. New York: Plenum Press.
7. Zigmond, M.J., and Stricker, E.M. 1977. In *Animal models in psychiatry and neurology* (Hanin, I., and Usdin, E., eds.), pp. 412-429. New York: Pergamon Press.
8. Zigmond, M.J., and Stricker, E.M. 1973. *Science* 182:717-720.
9. Stricker, E.M., and Zigmond, M.J. 1976. In *Progress in psychobiology and physiological psychology* (Sprague, J., and Epstein, A.N., eds.), vol. 6, pp. 121-188. New York: Pergamon Press.
10. Acheson, A.L.; Zigmond, M.J.; and Stricker, E.M. 1979. *Trans Am Soc Neurochem* 10:142.
11. Agid, Y.; Javoy, F.; and Glowinski, J. 1973. *Nature, (New Biology)* 245:150-151.
12. Bernheimer, H.; Birkmayer, W.; Hornykiewicz, O.; Jellinger, K.; and Seitelberger, F. 1973. *J Neurol Sci* 20:415-455.
13. Carlsson, A., and Lindquist, M. 1963. *Acta Pharmacol Toxicol* 20:140-144.
14. Nyback, H., and Sedvall, G. 1968. *J Pharmacol Exp Ther* 162:294-301.
15. Acheson, A.L., and Zigmond, M.J. 1980 *Neurosci Abstr* 6:666.
16. Acheson, A; Kennedy, L.; Kapatos, G.; and Zigmond, M. 1979. *Neurosci Abstr* 5:395.
17. Hegstrand, L.R.; Simon, J.R.; and Roth, R.H. 1979 *Biochem Pharmacol* 28:519-523.
18. Acheson, A.L.; Zigmond, M.J.; and Stricker, E.M. 1980. *Science* 207:537-540.
19. Zivkovic, B.; Guidotti, A.; and Costa, E. 1975. *J Pharmacol Exp Ther* 194:37-46.
20. Roth, R.H.; Walters, J.R.; Murrin, L.C.; and Morgenroth, V.H. 1975. In *Pre- and postsynaptic receptors* (Usdin, E., and Bunney, W.E., eds.), pp. 5-48. New York: Marcel Dekker.
21. Black, I.B. 1975. *Brain Res* 95:170-176.
22. Zigmond, R.E. 1979. *J Neurochem* 32:23-29.
23. Beaudel, A., and Descarries, L. 1978. *Neuroscience* 3:851-860.
24. Cannon, W.B., and Rosenblueth, A. 1949. *The supersensitivity of denervated structures*. New York: Macmillan.
25. Kalisker, A.; Rutledge, C.O.; and Perkins, J.P. 1973. *Mol Pharmacol* 9:619-629.
26. Mishra, R.K.; Gardner, E.L.; Katzman, R.; and Makman, M.H. 1974. *Proc Natl Acad Sci* 71:3883-3887.
27. Zigmond, M.J., and Stricker, E.M. 1980. *Experientia* 36:436-437.
28. Creese, I.; Burt, D.R.; and Snyder, S.H. 1977. *Science* 197:596-598.

29. Staunton, D.A.; Wolfe, B.B.; Groves, P.M.; and Molinoff, P.B. 1979 *Neurosci Abstr* 5:572.

30. Jonsson, G., and Sachs, C. 1976. *Med Biol* 54:286-297.

31. Oke, A.; Keller, R.; and Adams, R.N. 1978. *Brain Res* 148:245-250.

32. Heffner, T.G.; Zigmond, M.J.; and Stricker, E.M. 1977 *J Pharmacol Exp Ther* 201:386-399.

33. Thierry, A.M.; Tassin, J.P.; Blanc, G.; and Glowinski, J. 1976. *Nature* 263:242-244.

34. Kennedy, L.; Saller, C.; and Zigmond, M. 1979 *Neurosci Abstr* 5:339.

35. Chiodo, L.A.; Caggiula, A.R.; Antelman, S.M.; and Lineberry, C.G. 1979. *Brain Res* 176:385-390.

36. Zigmond, M.J., and Stricker, E.M. 1972. *Science* 177:1211-1214.

37. Stricker, E.M., and Zigmond, M.J. 1974. *J Comp Physiol Psychol* 86:973-994.

38. Stricker, E.M.; Cooper, P.H.; Marshall, J.F.; and Zigmond, M.J. 1979. *J. Comp Physiol Psychol* 93:512-521.

39. Marshall, J. 1979. *Brain Res* 177:311-324.

40. Mandell, A.J., and Knapp, S. 1979. *Fed Proc* 36:2142-2148.

41. Wang, R.Y., and Aghajanian, G.K. 1977. *Brain Res* 132:186-193.

42. Hadhazy, P., and Szerb, J.C. 1977. *Brain Res* 123:311-322.

43. Simon, J.R., and Kuhar, M.J. 1975. *Nature* 255:162-163.

4 Gabaergic Aspects of Neurologic and Psychiatric Disorders

O. Carter Snead III

Gamma-aminobutyric acid (GABA) was first synthesized in 1883 [1], sixty-seven years before its presence as a normal constituent of mammalian central nervous system (CNS) was established [2-4]. The first evidence that this compound might be biologically significant came in 1956 when physiologic studies involving topical application of GABA to cerebral cortex showed that it exerted inhibitory effects upon electrical activity in brain [5, 6]. Since that time, a prodigious research effort has confirmed the inhibitory properties of GABA [9-12], demonstrated that it is probably a neurotransmitter in brain [13, 14], and elucidated many of its basic neuropharmacologic and neurophysiologic properties [15-20].

This chapter first considers those biochemical and pharmacologic properties of GABA necessary toward an understanding of any role that this ubiquitous substance might play in deranged CNS states and then reviews the evidence (human and animal) for involvement of GABA in a number of psychiatric and neurologic disease states.

Metabolism

Most if not all of the GABA formed in mammalian CNS derives from L-glutamic acid (figure 4-1). The formation of GABA from glutamic acid is catalyzed by L-glutamic acid decarboxylase (GAD), an enzyme which has a coenzyme requirement for pyridoxal phosphate in vitamin B_6. Once formed, GABA is transaminated with γ-ketoglutarate via a reaction catalyzed by an amino transferase, GABA transaminase (GABA-T), which is a mitochondrial enzyme. The product of this reaction, succinic semialdehyde, is then converted to succinic acid by succinic semialdehyde dehydrogenase (SSDH). The succinate is then metabolized via the Krebs cycle [16, 19, 20]. Alternatively, succinic semialdehyde may be metabolized to γ-hydroxybutyrate (GHB) by a Nicotinamide adenine dinucleotide phosphate (NADPH) dependent succinic semialdehyde reductase [21, 22]. This latter pathway is of uncertain significance but presumably exists in the human because GHB has been identified in human brain [23].

113

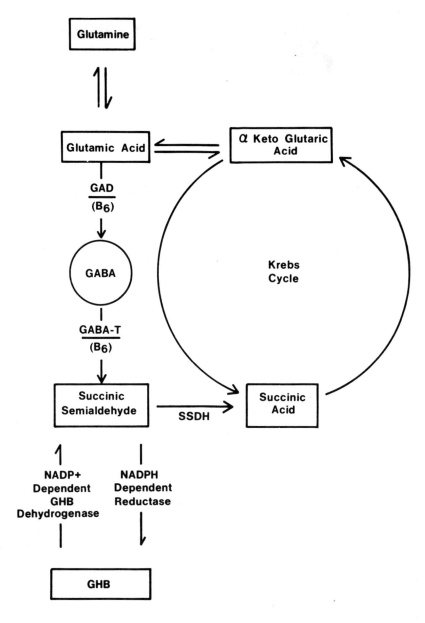

Note: GAD = glutamic acid decarboxy-lase; GABA-T = GABA transaminase; SSDH = succinic semialdehyde dehydrogenase.

Figure 4-1. Metabolism of GHB

Regional Distribution

Extensive regional-distribution studies of GABA and the enzymes involved in its metabolism have been done in human, rhesus monkey, and other species [24-29]. GABA is present in brain, spinal cord, and retina but not peripheral nerve. In brain, it occurs predominantly in gray matter with the highest concentration in humans occuring in globus pallidus and substantia nigra (table 4-1). The next highest amounts are found in hypothalamus and nucleus accumbens. GAD activity parallels GABA concentrations in human (table 4-1) and other species, with the highest activity occuring in hypothalamus, limbic system, and globus pallidus as demonstrated by elegant neuroanatomical and immunocytochemical techniques [29, 30]. Because of the close correlation between GAD activity and GABA levels in brain, GAD is used as a marker enzyme to identify gabaergic neuronal pathways. Although the data in human studies are not complete, animal data suggest that little or no correlation exists between other enzymes in the GABA metabolic pathway and the concentration of GABA in discrete areas of brain [24]. GABA-T and SSDH both have their highest activity in the striatum, but in the caudate and putamen (table 4-1) rather than the globus pallidus where GAD has its highest activity.

Although GABA levels in cerebellar cortex are less than half those in

Table 4-1
Regional Distribution of GABA and Enzymes of Gabaergic Pathways in Human Brain

	Regions of Brain	GABA[a]	GAD[b]	GABA-T[c]	SSDH[c]
High GABA	Substantia nigra	5.31	214 ± 20	—	—
	Globus pallidus	5.69	163 ± 11	149	132
	Nucleus accumbens	3.72	141 ± 11	166	255
	Hypothalamus	4.26	214 ± 20	—	—
	Dentate nucleus	—	213 ± 21	—	276
Medium GABA	Putamen	2.20	105 ± 10	203	293
	Caudate	3.03	100	176	279
	Thalamus	2.52	101 ± 16	133	207
	Amygdala	2.47	59 ± 4	107	183
	Temporal cortex	2.14	113 ± 29	—	—
Low GABA	White matter	0.26	28 ± 11	51	49-77
	Red nucleus	1.86	59 ± 7	164	—

Note: Data from [24-27, 62, 65, 68, 173].
[a]Mmoles/g frozen tissue.
[b]Percentage of enzyme activity in caudate nucleus.
[c]Mmoles product formed/g wet weight/hour.

globus pallidus and substantia nigra, much interest has centered about the metabolism, distribution, and function of GABA in cerebellum. The reasons for this interest are twofold. First, other neurotransmitters such as dopamine and serotonin are conspicuous by their low levels or absence in cerebellum [31] while GABA is present in clearly definable amounts and secondly, the output of the cerebellum is solely inhibitory [32] via the Purkinje cells that utilize GABA as their inhibitory neurotransmitter [14, 33-37]. Immunocytochemical techniques with visualization of GAD at the light and electron microscopic levels have thus demonstrated well-defined gabaergic pathways in the cerebellar Purkinje system which terminate in subcellular nuclei and Deiter's lateral vestibular nucleus. To date such techniques have also demonstrated gabaergic pathways from caudate, putamen, or globus pallidus to substantia nigra and possibly from the stria medullaris to the lateral habenular nucleus [28, 30, 38-40]. The ubiquitous distribution of GABA and its synthetic and catabolic enzymes throughout the CNS [24] suggest that there may be many other yet-to-be defined gabaergic pathways, perhaps involving local inhibitory circuits throughout the brain.

Interaction with Other Neurotransmitters

A brief consideration of the interaction of the gabaergic with other transmitter systems is crucial to an understanding of any postulated role for GABA in disease states since gabaergic neurons do not function as a unitary system but rather are intricately involved in the functioning of other neuronal systems in brain and vice versa. We have seen that GABA is more extensively and evenly distributed throughout various brain regions than other known neurotransmitters such as acetylcholine, dopamine, norepinephrine, or serotonin. Such a distribution is indirect evidence that GABA, given its inhibitory properties, may play a major role in neuronal inhibition throughout the brain. Based on this premise, Eugene Roberts postulated a system of neurochemical organization of the CNS called "disinhibition" [16, 41]. Simply put, this theory states that the CNS is maintained under a tonic state of inhibition and that excitatory events result from release of this inhibition. This release of inhibition or disinhibition, itself results from inhibition of an inhibitory neuron. This principle is shown schematically in figure 4-2, where a neuronal circuit in which two neurons are inhibitory and one excitatory is demonstrated. Neuron C is under tonic inhibition from neuron B and thus is inactive; however, when neuron A fires, neuron B is inhibited and neuron C is disinhibited and thus fires resulting in excitation. Although a gross oversimplification, this serves to illustrate the concept of disinhibition, for which there is mounting supportive experimental evidence.

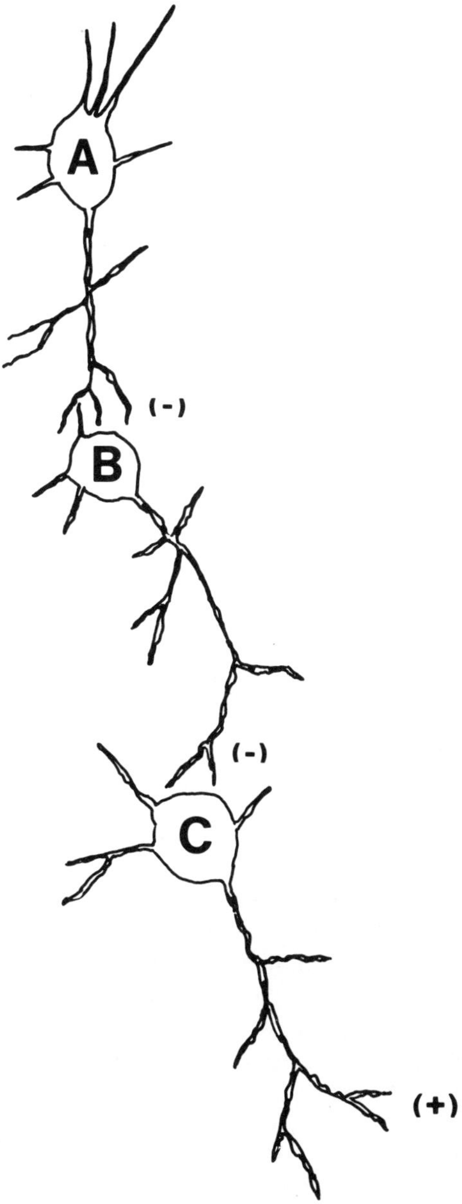

Note: Excitatory event caused by firing neuron C is produced by firing neuron A which inhibits neuron B, hence releasing the tonic inhibition normally imposed on C by B.

Figure 4-2. Illustration of the Principle of Disinhibition

A schematic of GABA interaction with other systems in the striatum is shown in figure 4-3 which is a postulated neuronal circuit diagram [42, 43] of striatonigral pathways. Most of the pharmacologic and physiologic studies done to date have been directed at striatonigral [44-48], mesolimbic [49-52], and hypothalamic [53, 54] pathways in brain particularly in regard to dopamine metabolism and the regulation of dopamine release and synthesis by other neurotransmitters. These studies indicate that dopamine synthesis in these areas is regulated by multineuronal feedback loops involving gabaergic neurons as well as presynaptic enkephalinergic receptors located on dopamine neurons. Although studies involving the regulation of other neuronal systems (such as gabaergic and cholinergic) are less extensive than those of dopamine, there is no reason to think that the mechanisms of interaction controlling these systems are any less complicated than those outlined above for dopaminergic systems.

Disease States

The diagram of neuronal circuits in figure 4-3 serves to illustrate the complicated nature of neuronal interaction. Such complexity needs to be borne in mind when one is evaluating studies that make a claim for involvement of a single neurotransmitter or its metabolites in any disease state of the CNS. Such simplistic explanations of neurochemical pathogenesis of psychiatric and neurologic disease states merit more skepticism than they usually receive. The evidence for involvement of various neurotransmitter substances including GABA in a number of diseases comes from four sources: (1) pharmacologic studies in animals and animal models; (2) data from studies on postmortem human brain; (3) human cerebrospinal fluid (CSF) studies usually consisting of measurement of the neurotransmitter or its metabolites; and (4) studies of drugs known to affect a particular neurotransmitter system in vivo, in a specific disease process. Of these four lines of evidence the first obviously has the greatest experimental precision while the last is most often fraught with error, particularly with gabaergic drugs. For example, a drug such as sodium valproate is said to exert its antiepileptic action by inhibition of GABA-T with a resultant increase in brain GABA [55-57] when in fact the situation is much more complicated [22]. The problem with both postmortem and CSF GABA studies is that GABA levels rapidly increase after death [58, 59] and also in CSF upon standing [60]; further, CSF and postmortem studies do not reflect turnover of GABA or does a CSF value tell us which gabaergic systems in human brain might be involved in a specific disease process. Thus we are somewhat

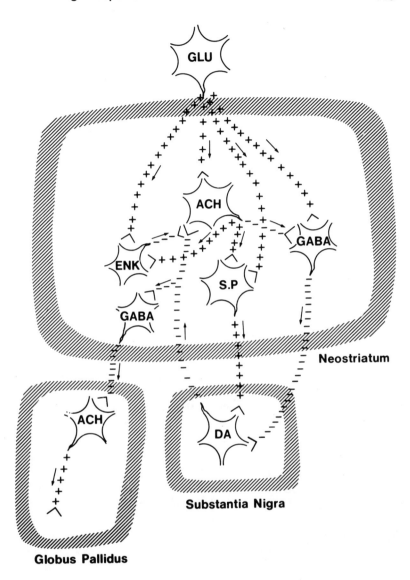

Note: GLU indicates glutaminergic neurons; ACH, cholinergic neurons; DA, dopaminergic neurons; ENK, enkephalinergic neurons; S.P. Substance P neurons; GABA, gabaergic neurons. Neuronal circuit diagram is modified after Costa et al. [42, 43]. +++ equals excitatory pathways; – – – indicates inhibitory pathways.

Figure 4-3. Schematic of Neuronal Interaction in the Striatum

limited concerning information regarding GABA metabolism that we can relate to human diseases. There are, however, some diseases in which gabaergic systems are severely enough involved that a combination of the above techniques allows one to at least speculate about the presence or absence of gabaergic involvement in some diseases if not hypothesize in what way GABA may play a role in the pathogenesis of such diseases. The CNS diseases in which a GABA deficiency has been implicated are listed in table 4-2.

Huntington's Chorea

This is the disorder for which there is the most solid evidence of gabaergic involvement. Huntington's disease is an autosomal dominant, progressive, degenerative brain disease in which the basal ganglia is most severely involved [61]. In 1973 Perry et al. [62] first described a deficiency of GABA in the substantia nigra, caudate, and putamen-globus pallidus complex. Subsequently GAD has been shown to be markedly decreased in caudate-putamen and to a lesser extent in nucleus accumbens. Except for the nucleus accumbens, the decrease in GAD (the marker enzyme for gabaergic neurons) seems to be confined to the extrapyramidal system [63-68]. There is a 70 to 80 percent decrease in the density of GABA binding sites in the striatum [69, 70], though there is some debate concerning these data [71, 72]. Another recently described abnormality in choreic brain is an elevated GHB content [73]. Although no correlation was found between high GHB and low GABA levels, there was a trend toward an inverse relationship. This has been explained by Stahl and Swanson's work [66] showing a decreased activity of succinate dehydrogenase in choreic brain which would theoretically slow the metabolism of GHB via succinate [74, 75] (figure 4-1). CSF levels of GABA are significantly depressed in patients with Huntington's chorea [76-78] but are probably not reliable in predicting at-risk individuals [76].

The animal-model evidence for involvement of gabaergic neurons in Huntington's chorea is the use of a substance called kainic acid. This is a rigid analog of L-glutamic acid which, when injected into rat striatum, causes degeneration of neuronal cell bodies located at the site of injection while axons passing through or terminating in the area of injection are not affected. Histological, neurochemical, and behavioral abnormalities resulting from intrastriatal injection of kainic acid are similar to those occuring in Huntington's disease [79-88] with decreased GABA and GAD as well as increased GHB levels in striatum [89]. Further ^{3}H-kainic acid binding density has been shown to be decreased both in striata of human choreic brains as well as rat striata after kainic acid lesioning [90].

Table 4-2
Evidence for GABA Involvement in Human CNS Diseases

Disease	Animal Model	Human Brain			Gabaergic Drugs Useful	
		GABA Conc.	GAD Activity	CSF GABA Conc.	Experimentally	Clinically
Huntington's chorea	Kainic acid	↓ Striatum	↓ Striatum	↓ Striatum	γ-acetylinic-GABA muscimol	? Isoniazid glutamine
Parkinson's disease	Reserpine; nigral lesions	↓ Striatum	↓ Striatum	Normal	None	None
Schizophrenia	Mesolimbic kindling	? ↓ Nucleus accumbens	? ↓ Nucleus accumbens	Normal	Muscimol	None
Epilepsy	GAD inhibition GABA receptor blockade	? Normal	No data	↓	Muscimol γ-acetylinic-GABA γ-vinyl GABA valproic acid	? Valproic[a] acid
Analgesia	GABA-T inhibition and GABA receptor agonism potentiates opiate analgesia	No data	No data	No data	Muscimol γ-acetylinic-GABA γ-vinyl GABA	No data
Alzheimer's disease	None	No data	↓ Temporal cortex	↓	No data	No data
Anxiety	None[b]	No data	No data	No data	No data	No data

↓ = Decreased.
? = Hypothesized.
[a] Although valproic acid is a useful anticonvulsant, there is some question as to whether Gabaergic mechanisms are involved in its mode of action.
[b] Anxiety was included because of the close biochemical relationship of anxiolytic agents, that is, benzodiazepines and GABA.

In addition to the gabaergic deficiencies described above, activity of choline acetyltransferase (a marker enzyme for cholinergic systems) has also been demonstrated to be decreased in caudate and putamen [63, 65, 66-68]. Dopamine and tyrosine hydroxylase levels are normal in choreic brains [65], but dopamine receptor density is reduced in the striata of patients with Huntington's [91].

Because of the apparent involvement of gabaergic neuronal systems in Huntington's chorea a number of therapeutic modalities aimed at increasing gabaergic tone have been attempted. Since GABA does not cross the blood-brain barrier [92], any attempt to increase GABA concentration or activity in brain must be aimed at decreased catabolism, decreased uptake, increased endogenous release of GABA, or direct stimulation of gabaergic receptors [93]. The results of such attempts in Huntington's chorea have for the most part not been encouraging, using a GABA receptor agonist [94] or sodium valproate [95-98] as an inhibitor of GABA catabolism. Some preliminary data suggest that isoniazid may be useful [99, 100]. Again this is based on the theory that one is inhibiting GABA catabolism though isoniazid at higher dosages inhibits GABA synthesis as well [101]. Also glutamine therapy has reportedly produced beneficial effects in a single patient associated with elevation of CSF GABA levels [102]. There are several reasons why a therapeutic approach addressed toward correcting a GABA deficiency in brain has not been successful in alleviating the symptomatology of Huntington's disease. First, although gabaergic systems may be the most severely involved, Huntington's chorea is a multineuronal system disease. It is not at all clear whether or not correcting the GABA deficiency alone will improve whatever symptoms might be due to the cholinergic derangement. Second, the pharmacologic methods used clinically in this disease have not been selectively aimed at a single aspect of gabaergic function as outlined above. The reason for this is that such selective drugs are not clinically available. For example, GABA-T blockers which have been demonstrated to correct the deficiency in the kainic acid animal model [103] may be too toxic for clinical use. Third, even if one were able to manipulate a selective facet of GABA metabolism, the problem of affecting only those gabaergic systems involved versus all systems in brain would remain. Fourth, Huntington's disease is a degenerative process in which the physical number of neurons and receptor sites are markedly diminished. Hence one may be limited in what one could achieve even if a selective increase in gabaergic tone by pharmacologic techniques was possible. We tried a different therapeutic tack [104], equally unsuccessful, of attempting to lower brain GHB levels in two Huntington patients. We used ethosuximide, based on the ability of this drug to lower subcortical endogenous GHB levels experimentally [105]; however, to date the drug has had no beneficial effect on the clinical course of these two patients.

Parkinson's Disease

Parkinson's disease is a degenerative disease of brain characterized by progressive impairment of basal ganglia function which is clinically manifest as rigidity, tremor, facial immobility, abnormal speech, and impaired postural stability [106, 107]. Animal data that provided clues to the biochemical defect in this disease came from the use of reserpine [108-111], a drug which induces catecholamine deficiency in brain by inhibition of reuptake mechanisms [31]. This drug induces rigidity and immobility in animals. The suggestion that catecholamines were involved in parkinsonism was initially substantiated by the observation that afflicted patients excreted less dopamine in urine than normally [112, 113]. Direct evidence for involvement of dopamine came in the early 1960s when it was demonstrated that dopamine was virtually absent from the striatum of humans with parkinsonism [114, 116]. In addition there was a marked decrease in the level of homovanillic acid (HVA), tyrosine, hydroxylase, and dopa decarboxylase in the basal ganglia, globus pallidus, and substantia nigra [116]. Since the initial description of the dopaminergic aberrations, other neuronal systems have also been implicated in Parkinson's disease. GAD has been found to be depressed in the globus pallidus, substantia nigra, nucleus accumbens, and a number of cortical areas in Parkinson's disease [68, 115, 117-120]. Brain GABA levels are normal in Parkinson's disease [62, 119] but GABA receptor binding in substantia nigra is significantly decreased in parkinsonian brain [121]. CSF concentrations of GABA in parkinsonian patients have been found to be normal [78].

The profound deficiency of dopamine and dopaminergic enzyme systems in parkinsonism and the successful therapeutic use of L-dopa [122-124] and dopaminergic agonists [125, 126] belie the fact that this disease involves more than just dopamine systems in brains. In addition to evidence for cholinergic involvement [127] and that cited above for gabaergic involvement, there are also data suggesting that there is a response of gabaergic systems to L-dopa therapy since such treatment is associated with an increase in GAD activity in brain [117, 119, 128]. Theoretically this increase in GAD activity may be due to a "trophic" influence of dopaminergic neurons on gabaergic neurons; that is, stimulation of the postsynaptic dopaminergic receptor which resides on the gabaergic neuron results in increased activity of GAD. Although the clinical significance of these neurochemical data is not known, it may be that the abnormalities of GABA in parkinsonism contribute to the constellation of clinical findings in this disease. Partial correction of these abnormalities by L-dopa may play a role in the therapeutic potential of that compound additive to its direct effect on dopaminergic systems.

Schizophrenia

The idea that schizophrenia might have a biochemical substrate was first conceived in 1884 by Thudichum [129]. Since that time a number of hypotheses concerning the biochemical basis of schizophrenia have been put forth [130-134]. The proposal that gabaergic systems may be involved in this thought disorder is a spin-off from the dopamine hypothesis of schizophrenia [135-142] which states that schizophrenic symptoms result from hyperactive dopaminergic systems in brain and further that anti-psychotic agents exert their beneficial effects by reversal or attenuation of this increased dopaminergic tone. This theory arose from a number of observations: (1) amphetamine which increases dopamine in brain by a number of different ways produces a schizophreniform psychosis character-ized by paranoid ideation [143-147]; (2) amphetamine and L-dopa both ex-acerbate clinical symptoms of thought disorders [147-149]; (3) all known antipsychotic drugs have dopamine receptor blocking properties [141, 150-152]; (4) the antipsychotic potency of antischizophrenic drugs can be predicted by their affinity for the dopamine receptor [153]; (5) kindling of the mesolimbic dopamine system in animals produces behavioral patterns believed to be a model for schizophrenia [154]; and (6) dopamine has been reported to be elevated in nucleus accumbens in postmortem brains of schizophrenic patients but normal in the putamen [155].

   The dopamine hypothesis presumes that mesolimbic dopaminergic pathways [140, 156-158] are involved in the pathogenesis rather than stria-tonigral pathways [139]. Antipsychotic drugs, according to this theory, produce their antipsychotic effect by acting on mesolimbic dopaminergic systems and produce their extrapyramidal side effects by acting on striatonigral dopaminergic systems [135]. Crow et al. [137] recently pointed out that the dopamine hypothesis is in fact two separate hypotheses: one saying that hyperactivity of dopaminergic systems is responsible for schizophrenia and the other that dopamine receptor blockade is the mode of therapeutic action of antischizophrenic drugs. Cur-rent pharmacologic evidence supports the latter but there are a number of reasons to doubt the former. The evidence against a hyperactive dopamine system involves CSF HVA studies in normal humans [159, 160]. Further treatment with antipsychotic drugs causes an increase in CSF HVA in-dicating that baseline dopaminergic activity is below maximum [135]. In addition, blockade of dopamine synthesis is not an effective therapeutic modality in schizophrenia [161]. Finally, schizophrenia can occur in Parkinson's disease [162], a disorder characterized by profound dopamine deficiency. As an alternative to a simple excess of dopamine in brain, one could propose, in view of the neuronal circuitry illustrated in figure 4-3, that there is a *relative* increase in dopaminergic tone in schizophrenia which could be secondary to either increased excitatory input from peptidergic or cholinergic neurons, or decreased inhibitory input from gabaergic neurons. In other words, the dopaminergic system per se may be normal but seems to be in excess due to a deficiency in some neuronal system which normally serves to counterbalance dopaminergic influence.

In 1972 Roberts [163] first proposed that an imbalance in gabaergic systems might be involved in the biochemical pathogenesis of schizophrenia. Since that time evidence both supporting and refuting this supposition has accumulated. Pharmacologic evidence to support involvement of gabaergic mechanisms consists of GABA turnover studies which show that antipsychotic drugs known to be dopamine receptor blockers produce an increase in GABA turnover, possibly by blocking postsynaptic inhibitory dopamine receptors on gabaergic neurons which in turn would lead to increased firing of the gabaergic neuron with the resultant increase in turnover of GABA. The increased GABA turnover in mesolimbic areas of brain in response to these drugs may be a pharmacologic marker for their antischizophrenic properties [164-169].

Additional support for the involvement of gabaergic neurons in schizophrenia comes from the work of Stevens et al. [170, 171] who demonstrated that instillation of the GABA antagonist, bicuculline, into the ventral tegmental area produces psychotic behavior in cats while instillation of this substance in substantia nigra produces stereotypic behavior. All these changes could be blocked by haloperidol. In the course of these studies, Stevens [170] also pointed out the analogies between the neostriatum and limbic striatum with respect to histoarchitecture, and suggested that similar mechanisms for regulation of dopamine release may exist for both striatal structures. Thus the neuronal circuitry diagram shown in figure 4-3 may apply to the limbic striatum; however, pharmacologic studies suggest that there may be a crucial difference in limbic striatum due to insertion of cholinergic interneurons in the mesolimbic area [164].

The evidence in humans for gabaergic involvement in schizophrenia is less compelling than that from animal experiments. Roberts [172] demonstrated decreased GAD activity in thalamus of postmortem schizophrenic brain. Other workers also show a decrease in GABA content as well as GAD activity in thalamus and nucleus accumbens in postmortem schizophrenic brains [155, 173]. These data were challenged by others [137, 174] who found no difference in either GABA content or GAD activity between control and schizophrenic brains. CSF GABA levels in schizophrenic patients are no different from controls; nor is the CSF concentration of GABA affected by haloperidol therapy [175, 176]. Therapeutic trials of such gabaergic agents as baclofen and muscimol have for the most part been un-successful and may actually worsen symptoms [136, 174, 177-180].

Failure of the human data to support the GABA hypothesis of schizophrenia is probably more a reflection of the crudity of available techniques to measure finite biochemical events in human CNS than an invalidation of the theory that GABA may play a role in the biochemical pathogenesis of schizophrenia. For example, if patients with schizophrenia indeed had some deficiency of gabaergic systems in mesolimbic areas of brain, one would not expect this to readily show up as decreased CSF GABA since CSF concentration probably reflects whole brain gabaergic activity of which the mesolimbic proportion represents a very small part. Similarly, a shotgun approach stimulating all GABA receptors in brain, given the fact that such pharmacologic manipulation were possible, could produce a massive increase in brain gabaergic tone the results of which could mask any beneficial effect caused by stimulation of the relatively small receptor population in mesolimbic area of brain. These concepts should be considered when setting out to assign or deny a role of GABA to any CNS disease process as well as when designing drug therapies to correct a presumed GABA deficiency in brain.

Epilepsy

This term refers to a group of disorders of brain characterized neurophysiologically by paroxysmal, excessive neuronal discharge and clinically by seizure activity which may manifest itself in a variety of ways. There has long been considerable interest in the involvement of gabaergic systems in the pathogenesis of epilepsy [183-191], the reason being that epilepsy is often thought of by both clinicians and basic scientists as representing an imbalance of inhibitory and excitatory events in brain [192, 193], with aberrant neuronal paroxysms representing the result of a predominance of excitation or a deficiency of inhibition. Since GABA is considered to be a primary inhibitory neurotransmitter in brain, any derangement of inhibitory systems leading to a chronic seizure state would presumably involve gabaergic neurons in some way. Various animal models of seizures have been used in three ways to support this thesis of GABA involvement. First, GABA has been shown to be anticonvulsant in a number of experimentally induced seizures [194-202]. Second, the impairment of GABA synthesis by GAD inhibition [7, 8, 203-212] or blockade of its postsynaptic action [213-221] reduces seizure threshold and results in seizure activity. Third, experimentally induced seizures associated with decreased brain GABA content can often be successfully treated with GABA-T inhibitors. The increased brain GABA resulting from GABA-T inhibition can be correlated with anticonvulsant efficacy of the enzyme inhibitor [222-233]. In addition the GABA receptor agonist, muscimol, has been reported effective against metrazol seizures [234].

The first clinical evidence for involvement of gabaergic systems in seizures came with the demonstration that severe dietary deficiency of B_6 vitamins result in seizures which can be controlled by B_6 supplements [235-239]. It has been suggested [184, 240] that the explanation for these seizures in B_6 deficiency relates to the function of vitamin B_6 in the form of pyridoxal $5'$-phosphate as coenzyme for GAD. Lott et al [241] recently demonstrated decreased GABA content in frontal and occipital cortex with normal GAD activity in a patient who had pyridoxine-dependent seizures. Unfortunately the GABA and GAD content of deep structures were not determined and four of five patients used for control values of GABA and GAD had severe primary CNS disease. There are a number of other enzyme systems in brain which utilize pyridoxal $5'$-phosphate as a coenzyme. Thus the conclusion that GAD alone is involved in B_6 deficient and dependent seizures may be erroneous. Initial reports of decreased GABA content in biopsy specimens of human epileptic foci [242] have been refuted [243]. CSF GABA has been reported to be significantly decreased in seizure patients [244, 245].

A variety of therapeutic modalities addressed to correcting a presumed GABA deficiency in seizure disorders have been attempted. An early report of successful treatment of seizures with GABA [246] has not been duplicated. Cerebellar stimulation has been used in seizure disorders [247-252] based on the following rationale: (1) cerebellar mechanisms may be involved in experimental seizures [253-255]; (2) some anticonvulsants produce an increase in firing rate of cerebellar Purkinje cells [256-258]; and (3) cerebellar stimulation would be expected to cause GABA to be released with increased Purkinje cell firing [14, 37]. However, recent evidence disproved the latter thesis. Transfolial cerebellar stimulation in fact is associated with suppression of cerebellar Purkinje cell activity [259] and a decrease in CSF GABA concentration [260, 261] associated with no change or deterioration in seizure control [260].

Another mode of therapy ostensibly aimed at gabaergic systems is the anticonvulsant drug sodium valproate. This drug has definite but complex actions on GABA metabolism. It inhibits GABA-T and SSDH competitively but produces a stronger, noncompetitive inhibition of NADPH-dependent aldehyde reductase, the enzyme presumably responsible for the formation of GHB in brain [22]. Indeed there is serious doubt that sodium valproate acts by increasing GABA concentrations in brain because it is a relatively weak inhibitor of GABA-T [227, 231, 232]. Furthermore oral sodium valproate is not associated with elevations in CSF GABA levels [262].

Thus, on the whole, the experimental and clinical evidence would seem to favor some involvement of gabaergic systems in seizure disorders; however, this is a complex issue and one must define the clinical type of seizure in which a role for GABA is claimed. Illustrative of this point is the fact that GHB, a GABA metabolite, has the propensity to produce experimental petit mal seizure activity [263-265] (figure 4-4). Although the evidence for this activity being due to gabaergic mechanisms is contradictory [266-268], at least one author proposed that *hyperactive* gabaergic systems may be involved in petit mal epilepsy [269].

Another factor to take into account when considering treating seizures with gabaergic drugs [270] is that other neurotransmitters such as monoaminergic [271-273] or serotonergic [274-276] systems may be involved in various human epileptic disease states. Therefore a purely unitary approach to therapy of seizures would not seem to have much chance of success.

Other Diseases

There are a number of other diseases such as hypothalamic dysfunction, hyperactivity, and visual problems in which a role for gabaergic systems has been postulated [41]. However, there is scarce experimental evidence to support such a role to date. There has been recent evidence of possible gabaergic involvement in Alzheimer's disease which is a neurologic disorder characterized by dementia and severe cerebral cortical degeneration [277]. CSF GABA was found to be significantly low in these patients [78]. In addition GAD is decreased in the temporal lobes of patients with senile dementia, a more nonspecific type of dementia [278, 279]. The fact that dementia and GABA deficiency are common to both Huntington's and Alzheimer's disease raises the possibility that gabaergic systems or a deficiency thereof may be involved in the pathogenesis of memory loss and intellectual dysfunction. Bowen et al. [279] suggested that GAD deficiency may be a marker to distinguish senile from vascular dementias.

There is some experimental data that link gabaergic systems to opiate analgesia, not surprising in view of the involvement of enkephalinergic neuronal circuitry in a number of brain pathways [42] (figure 4-3). Naloxone (an opiate antagonist) blocks GABA receptors in high doses [280]; furthermore muscimol (a GABA agonist) and aminooxyacetic acid (a GABA-T inhibitor) both potentiate morphine analgesia and enhance development of tolerance and physical dependence [281, 282]. The ratio of GABA to

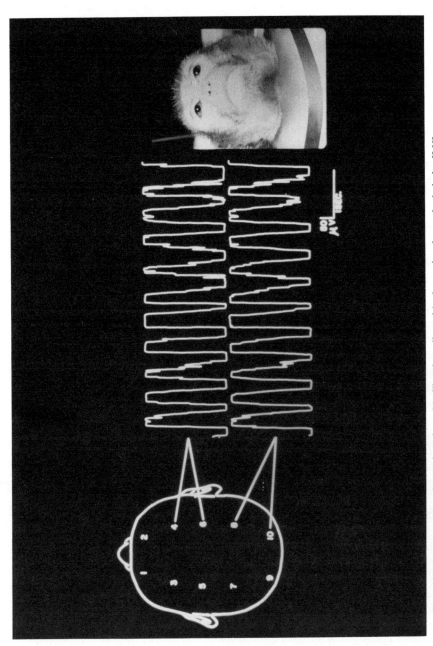

Note: The animal was unresponsive and staring with dilated pupils and had occasional myoclonic jerks [265].

Figure 4-4. Prepubescent Rhesus Monkey That Received 400 mg/kg of the GABA Metabolite (figure 4-1) GHB

glutamate is felt to be a reliable characteristic of the exposure of mice to ex-perimentally induced pain and can serve as a neurochemical indicant of this pain. The ratio increases following pain and can be used to assess analgestic effects of drugs [283, 284]. Biggio et al. [281] postulated that GABA receptor activation may inhibit a neuronal system that normally counteracts morphine analgesia. To date there are no clinical data [285] to support or refute the hypothesis that gabaergic mechanisms might be involved in anal-gesia or addiction.

A final aspect of gabaergic function worthy of mention concerns the rapidly growing area of the chemistry and pharmacology of the ben-zodiazepines. The relation between GABA and these antianxiety agents has been recognized for several years [286-292]; however, the precise nature of this relationship still eludes us. Specific receptors for benzodiazepines have been demonstrated in mammalian CNS using ^{3}H-diazepam as an exogenous ligand [293-297]. GABA and GABA-mimetic drugs potentiate the binding of benzodiazepines to this receptor [298, 299]. Conversely benzodiazepines enhance the binding of GABA to GABA receptors possibly by displacing an endogenous protein inhibitor of GABA binding. This protein inhibitor may represent the endogenous ligand for the benzodiazepine receptor [300-302].

Whether the benzodiazepines exert their anxiolytic actions via direct stimulation of the benzodiazepine receptor or by their potentiation of gabaergic effects is not known [286, 302-304]. There is little human data regarding GABA, the benzodiazepines, and their interaction in disease states. The benzodiazepine receptor has it highest density in human brain in cortical areas. A decrease in benzodiazepine receptor binding has been found in Huntington's chorea in caudate and putamen but this may be a nonspecific reflection of neuronal degeneration [305]. It is tempting to draw an analog between morphine, enkephalins, endorphins, the opiate receptor, and pain mechanisms [306-308] and the benzodiazepines, the en-dogenous protein inhibitor of the GABA receptor, the benzodiazepine receptor, and affective and anxiety states. Such an analogy is sheer specula-tion at this point since there is currently no clinical data concerning ben-zoidazepines comparable to the endogenous opiate data [309, 310].

Future Research Strategies

We reviewed the human and animal data that support a role for gabaergic systems in a variety of psychiatric and neurologic disease processes. A number of elegant and detailed animal studies provided us with a plethora of animal models, wiring diagrams, and neurochemical hypotheses concern-ing pathogenesis of these disease states. However, the human data, limited by imprecision of available techniques, provided only a few tantalizing clues as to what role GABA might play in these disorders. Exciting research strategies at an animal level that might elucidate more detailed mechanisms of disease include elaborate turnover studies to follow the activity of gabaergic neurons and their response to various drug treatments [164-166, 311-313], immunocytohistochemical techniques to further map out gabaergic pathways in brain [40], radioactive binding and lesioning studies, and kindling techniques to assess electrical and behavioral results of gabaergic neuronal stimulation or blockade [221]. At the human level further postmortem studies of GAD and GABA receptor may be helpful and if the nonspecific nature of any change is taken into account, CSF GABA levels could continue to be a broad screening device for the presence of gabaergic involvement in a specific disease state being helpful in that regard only if they were decreased. Finally, positron emission tomography, a noninvasive imaging technique that utilizes radiolabeled agents [315-319] with very short half-lives, may provide an opportunity to visualize GABA binding sites in human brain and illustrate mechanisms of interactions of drugs used in neurologic and psychiatric disorders with gabaergic and other neuronal systems.

References

1. Schötten, C. 1883. Uber die oxydation des piperidins. *Ber dt Chem* 16: 643-647.
2. Awapara, A.; Landua, A.J.; Fuerst, R.; Seale, B. 1950. Free γ-aminobutyric acid in brain. *J Biol Chem* 187:35-39.
3. Roberts, E., and Frankel, S. 1950. γ-aminobutyric acid in brain: Its formation from glutamic acid. *J Biol Chem* 187:55-63.
4. Udenfriend, S. 1950. Identification of γ-aminobutyric acid in brain by isotope derivative method. *J Biol Chem* 187:65-69.
5. Hayashi, T., and Nagai, K. 1956. Action of ω-amino acids on the motor cortex of higher animals, especially γ-amino-β-oxybutyric acid as the real inhibitory principle in brain. 20th Int. Physiol. Congr., Brussels, Abstracts of Communications, p. 410.
6. Hayashi, I., and Suhara, R. 1956. Substances which produce epileptic seizures when applied on the motor cortex of dogs, and substances which inhibit the seizure directly. 20th Int. Physiol. Congr., Brussels, Abstracts of Communications, p. 410.
7. Killam, K.F., and Bain, J.A. 1957. Convulsant hydrazides 1: In vitro and in vivo inhibition of vitamin B_6 enzymes by convulsant hydrazides. *J Pharmacol Exp Ther* 119:255-262.

8. Killam, K.F. 1957. Convulsant hydrazides 2: Comparison of electrical changes and enzyme inhibition induced by the administration of thiosemicarbazide. *J Pharmacol Exp Ther* 119:263-271.

9. Altman, H.; Bruggencate, G.; Sonnhof, U.; and Steinberg, R. 1973. Action of γ-aminobutyric acid and glycine on red nucleus neurons. *PFlügers Arch ges Physiol* 342:283-289.

10. Hill, R.G., and Simmonds, M.A. 1973. A method for comparing the potencies of γ-aminobutyric acid antagonists on single cortical neurons using micro-iontophoretic techniques. *Br J Pharmacol* 48:1-11.

11. Curtis, D.R., and Johnston, G.A.R. 1974. Amino acid transmitters in the mammalian central nervous system. *Rev Physiol* 65:97-125.

12. Levy, R.A. 1974. GABA: A direct depolarizing action at the mammalian primary afferent terminal. *Brain Res* 76:155-161.

13. Krnjevic, K., and Schwartz, S. 1967. The action of γ-aminobutyric acid on cortical neurons. *Exp Brain Res* 3:320-327.

14. Obata, K.; Ito, M.; Ochi, R.; and Sato, N. 1967. Pharmacological properties of the postsynaptic inhibition of Purkinje cell axons and the action of γ-aminobutyric acid on Deiters neurons. *Exp Brain Res* 4:43-57.

15. Sytinsky, I.A.; Soldatenkov, A.T.; and Lajtha, A. 1978. Neurochemical basis of the therapeutic effect of γ-aminobutyric acid and its derivatives. *Prog Neurobiol* 10:89-133.

16. Roberts, E. 1974. γ-aminobutyric acid and nervous system function: A perspective. *Biochem Pharmacol* 23:2637-2649.

17. Costa, E. Some recent advances in the biochemical pharmacology of γ-aminobutyric acid. In *Neuroregulators and psychiatric disorders*. Usdin, E.; Hamberg, D.A.; and Barchas, J.D., eds. New York: Oxford Univ. Press, pp. 372-380.

18. Krnjevic, K. 1970. Glutamate and γ-aminobutyric acid in brain. *Nature* 228:119-124.

19. Cooper, J.R.; Bloom, F.E.; and Roth, R.H. 1974. *The biochemical basis of neuropharmacology*. New York: Oxford Univ. Press, pp. 223-247.

20. Roberts, E., and Hammerschlag, R. 1976. Amino acid transmitters. In *Basic Neurochemistry*. Siegel, G.J.; Albers, R.W.; Katzman, R.; and Agranoff, R.W., eds. Boston: Little, Brown and Co., pp. 218-245.

21. Anderson, R.A.; Ritzmann, R.F.; and Tabakoff, B. 1977. Formation of γ-hydroxybutyrate in brain. *J Neurochem* 28:633-639.

22. Whittle, S.R., and Turner, A.J. 1978. Effects of the anticonvulsant sodium valproate on γ-aminobutyrate and aldehyde metabolism in ox brain. *J Neurochem* 31:1453-1459.

23. Doherty, J.D.; Hattox, S.E.; Snead, O.C.; and Roth, R.H. 1978. Identification of endogenous γ-hydroxybutyrate in human and bovine brain and its regional distribution in human, guinea pig, and rhesus monkey brain. *J Pharmacol Exp Ther* 207:130-139.
24. Fahn, S. 1976. Regional distribution studies of GABA and other putative neurotransmitters and their enzymes. In *GABA in nervous system function*. Roberts, E.; Chase, T.N.; and Tower, D.B., eds. New York: Raven Press, pp. 169-186.
25. Fahn, S., and Coté, L.J. 1968. Regional distribution of gamma aminobutyric acid (GABA) in brain of the rhesus monkey. *J Neurochem* 15:209-213.
26. Miller, A.L., and Pitts, F.N., Jr. 1967. Brain succinate semialdehyde dehydrogenase. 3: Activities in 24 regions of human brain. *J Neurochem* 14:579-584.
27. Kanazawa, I.; Miyata, Y.; Toyokura, Y.; and Otsuka, M. 1973. The distribution of gamma aminobutyric acid (GABA) in the human substantia nigra. *Brain Res* 51:363-365.
28. Fonnum, F.; Grofová, I.; Rinvik, E.; Storm-Mathisen, J.; and Walberg, F. 1974. Origin and distribution of glutamate decarboxylase in substantia nigra of the cat. *Brain Res* 71:77-92.
29. Gottesfeld, Z., and Jacobowitz, D.M. 1978. Neurochemical and anatomical studies of GABAergic neurons. In *Interactions between putative neurotransmitters in the brain*. Garattini, S.; Pujol, J.F.; and Samanin, R., eds. New York: Raven Press, pp. 109-126.
30. Roberts, E. 1978. Interrelationships of GABA neurons explored by immunocytochemical techniques. In *Interactions between putative neurotransmitters in the brain*. Garattini, S.; Pujol, J.F.; and Samanin, R., eds. New York: Raven Press, pp. 89-107.
31. Cooper, J.R.; Bloom, F.E.; and Roth, R.H. 1974. *The biochemical basis of neuropharmacology*. New York: Oxford Univ. Press, pp. 102-122.
32. Eccles, J.C.; Ito, M.; and Szentagothai, J. 1967. *The cerebellum as a neuronal machine*. New York: Springer-Verlag.
33. Curtis, D.R.; Duggan, A.W.; and Felix, D. 1970. GABA and inhibition of Deiters' neurones. *Brain Res* 23:117-120.
34. Ito, M., and Yoshida, M. 1964. The cerebellar-evoked monosynaptic inhibition of Deiters' neurones. *Experientia* 20:515-516.
35. Ito, M.; Yoshida, M.; and Obata, K.: Monosynaptic inhibition of the intracerebellar nuclei induced from the cerebellar cortex. *Experientia* 20:575-576.
36. Ten-Bruggencate, G., and Engberg, I. 1971. Iontophoretic studies in Deiters' nucleus of the inhibitory actions of GABA and related amino

acids and the interactions of strychnine and picrotoxin. *Brain Res* 25:431-448.

37. Obata, K., and Takeda, K. 1969. Release of γ-aminobutyric acid into the fourth ventricle induced by stimulation of the cat's cerebellum. *J Neurochem* 16:1043-1047.

38. Gale, K.; Hong, J.; and Guidotti, A. 1977. Presence of substance P and GABA in separate striatonigral neurons. *Brain Res* 136:371-375.

39. Hattori, T.; McGeer, P.L.; Fibiger, H.C.; and McGeer, E.G. 1973. On the source of GABA-containing terminals in the substantia nigra: Electron microscopic autoradiographic and biochemical studies. *Brain Res* 54:103-114.

40. Roberts, E. 1976. Immunocytochemistry of the GABA system: A novel approach to an old transmitter. In *Neuroscience symposia. vol 1: Neurotransmitters, hormones, and receptors: Novel approaches*. Ferrendelli, J.; McEwen, B.S.; and Snyder, S.H., eds. Society for Neuroscience, Bethesda, Md., pp. 123-138.

41. Roberts, E. 1976. Disinhibition as an organizing principle in the nervous system: The role of the GABA system: Application to neurologic and psychiatric disorders. In *GABA in nervous system function*. New York: Raven Press, pp. 515-540.

42. Costa, E.; Fuatta, W.; Hong, J.S.; Moroni, F.; and Yang, H.U.T. 1978. Interactions between enkephalinergic and other neuronal systems. *Adv Biochem Psychopharmacol* 18:207-226.

43. Costa, E.; Cheney, D.L.; Mao, C.C.; and Moroni, F. 1978. Action of antischizophrenic drugs on the metabolism of γ-aminobutyric acid and acetylcholine in globus pallidus, striatum, and N. accumbens. *Fed Proc* 37:2408-2414.

44. Cheramy, A.; Nieoullon, A.; and Glowinski, J. 1978. In vivo changes in dopamine release in cat caudate nucleus and substantia nigra induced by nigral application of various drugs including GABAergic agonists and antagonists. In *Interactions between putative neurotransmitters*. Garattini, S.; Pujol, J.F.; and Samanin, R., eds. New York: Raven Press, pp. 175-190.

45. Scheel-Krüger, J.; Arnt, J.; Braestrup, C.; Christensen, A.V.; Cools, A.R.; and Magelund, G. 1978. GABA-dopamine interaction in substantia nigra and nucleus accumbens—Relevance to behavioral stimulation and stereotyped behavior. *Adv Biochem Psychopharmacol* 19:343-346.

46. Dray, A.; Fowler, L.J.; Oakley, N.R.; Simmonds, M.A.; and Tanner, T. 1977. Regulation of nigro-striatal dopaminergic neurotransmission in the rat. *Neuropharmacology* 16:511-518.

47. Racagni, G.; Bruno, F.; Cattabeni, F.; Maggi, A.; Di Giulio, A.M.; Parenti, M.; and Grupetti, A. 1977. Functional interaction between rat substantia nigra and striatum: GABA and dopamine interrelation. *Brain Res* 134:353-358.

48. Reubi, J.C.; Iversen, L.L.; and Jessell, T.M. 1978. Regulation of GABA release by dopamine in the rat substantia nigra. *Adv Biochem Psychopharmacol* 19:401-404.

49. Fuxe, K.; Hokfelt, T.; Ljungdahl, A.; Agnatri, L.; Johansson, O.; and de la Mora, M.P. 1977. Evidence for an inhibitory GABAergic control of the mesolimbic dopamine neurons: Possibility of improving treatment of schizophrenia by combined treatment with neuroleptics and GABAergic drugs. *Med Biol* 53:177-183.

50. Hokfelt, T.; Ljungdahl, A.; Fuxe, K.; Johansson, O.; de la Mora, M.P.; and Agnati, L. 1977. Some attempts to explore possible central GABAergic mechanisms with special reference to control of dopamine neurons. In *Neuroregulators and psychiatric disorders*. Usdin, E.; Hamburg, D.A.; and Barchas, J.D., eds. New York: Oxford Univ. Press, pp. 358-371.

51. Fonnum, F.; Walaas, I.; and Iversen, E. 1977. Localization of GABAergic, cholinergic and aminergic structures in the mesolimbic system. *J Neurochem* 29:221-230.

52. Fonnum, F.; Iversen, E.; and Walaas, I. 1977. Localization of glutamic decarboxylase, choline acetyltransferase, and DOPA decarboxylase in mesolimbic structures. *Adv Biochem Psychopharmacol* 16:417-421.

53. Makara, G.B., and Stark, E. 1978. Role of GABA in the hypothalamic control of the pituitary gland. In *Interactions between putative neurotransmitters in the brain*. Garattini, S.; Pujol, J.F.; and Samanin, R., eds. New York: Raven Press pp. 263-283.

54. Guidotti, A.; Gale, K.; Hong, J.; and Toffano, G. 1978. Models to study drug effects on the integrated function of GABAergic, peptidergic (substance P), and dopaminergic neurons. In *Interactions between putative neurotransmitters in the brain*. Garattini, S.; Pujol, J.F.; and Samanin, R., eds. New York: Raven Press, pp. 217-229.

55. Simler, S.; Ciesielski, L.; Maitre, M.; Randrianarssoa, H.; and Mandel, P. 1973. Effect of sodium N-dipropylacetate on audiogenic seizures and brain γ-aminobutyric acid level. *Biochem Pharmacol* 22:1701-1708.

56. Kupferberg, H.J.; Lust, W.D.; and Penry, J.K. 1975. Anticonvulsant activity of dipropylacetic acid (DPA) in relation to GABA and cGMP brain levels in mice. *Fed Proc* 34:283.

57. Simon, D., and Penry, K.J. 1975. Sodium di-n-propylacetate (DPA) in the treatment of epilepsy. *Epilepsia* 16:549-573.

58. Lovell, R.A.; Elliott, S.J.; and Elliott, K.A.C. 1963. The GABA and factor 1 content of brain. *J Neurochem* 10:479-488.

59. Aldermann, J.L., and Shellenberger, M.K. 1974. Gamma aminobutyric acid in the rat brain: Reevaluation of sampling procedures and the post mortem increase. *J Neurochem* 22:937-940.

60. Wood, J.H.; Hanes, T.A.; Glaeser, B.S.; and Post, R.M. 1979. Cerebrospinal fluid GABA reductions in seizure patients. *Neurology* 29:601.

61. Heathfield, K.W.G. 1973. Huntington's chorea: A centenary review. *Post Grad Med J* 49:32-45.

62. Perry, T.L.; Hansen, S.; and Kloster, M. 1973. Huntington's chorea: Deficiency of gamma-aminobutyric acid in brain. *N Eng J Med* 288: 337-342.

63. McGeer, P.L.; McGeer, E.G.; and Fibiger, H.C. 1973. Choline acetylase and glutamic acid decarboxylase in Huntington's chorea. *Lancet* 1:1090-1092.

64. Bird, E.D.; Mackay, A.V.P.; Ragner, C.N.; and Iversen, L.L. 1973. Reduced glutamic acid decarboxylase activity of post-mortem brain in Huntington's chorea. *Lancet* 1:1090-1092.

65. Bird, E.D., and Iversen, L.L. 1974. Huntington's chorea: Post mortem measurement of glutamic acid decarboxylase, choline acetyltransferase, and dopamine in basal ganglia. *Brain* 97:457-472.

66. Stahl, W.L., and Swanson, P.D. 1974. Biochemical abnormalities in Huntington's chorea. *Neurology* 24:813-819.

67. McGeer, P.L. and McGeer, E.G. 1976. The GABA system and function of the basal ganglia: Huntington's disease. In *GABA in nervous system function*. Roberts, E.; Chase, T.N.; and Tower, D.B., eds. New York: Raven Press, pp. 487-495.

68. McGeer, P.L., and McGeer, E.G. 1976. Enzymes associated with the metabolism of catecholamines, acetylcholine, and GABA in human controls and patients with Parkinson's disease and Huntington's chorea. *J Neurochem* 26:65-76.

69. Lloyd, K.G.; Dreksler, S.; and Bird, E.D. 1977. Alterations in ^{3}H-GABA binding in Huntington's chorea. *Life Sci* 21:747-754.

70. Lloyd, K.G., and Dreksler, S. 1979. An analysis of (^{3}H) gamma aminobutyric acid binding in the human brain. *Brain Res* 163:77-87.

71. Enna, S.J.; Bird, E.D.; Bennett, J.P.; Bylund, D.B.; Yamamura, H.I.; Iversen, L.L.; and Snyder, S.H. 1976. Huntington's chorea: Changes in neurotransmitter receptors in brain. *N Eng J Med* 284: 1305-1309.

72. Enna, S.J.; Bennett, J.P.; Bylund, D.B.; Snyder, S.H.; Bird, E.D.; and Iversen, L.L. 1976. Alterations of brain neurotransmitter receptor binding in Huntington's chorea. *Brain Res* 116:531-537.

73. Ando, N.; Gold, B.I.; Bird, E.D.; and Roth, R.H. 1979. Regional brain levels of γ-hydroxybutyrate in Huntington's disease. *J Neurochem* 32:617-622.

74. Doherty, J.D., and Roth, R.H. 1978. Metabolism of γ-hydroxy-$(1-^{14}C)$ butyrate by rat brain: Relationship to the Krebs cycle and

metabolic compartmentation of amino acids. *J Neurochem* 30:1305-1309.

75. Doherty, J.D.; Stout, R.W.; and Roth, R.H. 1975. Metabolism of $(1 - {}^{14}C)$ γ-hydroxybutyric acid by rat brain after intraventricular injection. *Biochem Pharmacol* 24:469-474.

76. Bala Manjam, N.V.; Hane, T.A.; Katz, C.; and Glaeser, B.S. 1978. Huntington's disease: Cerebrospinal fluid GABA levels in at-risk individuals. *Arch Neurol* 35:728-730.

77. Glaeser, B.S.; Vogel, W.H.; and Oleweiler, D.B. 1975. GABA levels in cerebrospinal fluid of patients with Huntington's chorea: A preliminary report. *Biochem Med* 12:380-385.

78. Enna, S.J.; Stern, L.Z.; Wastek, G.J.; and Yamamura, H.I. 1977. Cerebrospinal fluid γ-aminobutyric acid variations in neurological disorders. *Arch Neurol* 34:683-685.

79. Coyle, J.T., and Schwarcz, R. 1976. Lesion of striatal neurons with kainic acid provides a model for Huntington's chorea. *Nature* 263:244-246.

80. Coyle, J.T.; McGeer, E.G.; McGeer, P.L.; and Schwarcz, R. 1978. Neostriatal injections: A model for Huntington's chorea. In *Kainic acid as a tool in neurobiology*. McGeer, E.; Olney, J.W.; and McGeer, P.L., eds. New York: Raven Press, pp. 139-159.

81. Fibiger, H.C. Kainic acid lesions of the striatum: A pharmacological and behavioral model of Huntington's disease. In *Kainic acid as a tool in neurobiology*. McGeer, E.; Olney, J.W.; and McGeer, P.L., eds. New York: Raven Press, pp. 161-176.

82. Kizer, J.S.; Nemeroff, C.B.; and Youngblood, W.W. 1978. Neurotoxic amino acids and structurally related analogs. *Pharmacol Rev* 29:301-318.

83. Nadler, J.V. 1979. Kainic acid: Neurophysiological and neurotoxic actions. *Life Sci* 24:289-300.

84. Zaazek, L.; Schwarcz, R.; and Coyle, J.T. 1978. Long term sequelae of striatal kainate lesion. *Brain Res* 152:626-632.

85. Mason, S.T.; Sanberg, P.R.; and Fibiger, H.C. 1978. Kainic acid lesions of the striatum dissociate amphetamine and apomorphine stereotypy: Similarities to Huntington's chorea. *Science* 20:352-355.

86. Mason, S.T.; Sandberg, P.R.; and Fibiger, H.C. 1978. Amphetamine-induced locomotor activity and stereotypy after kainic acid lesions of the striatum. *Life Sci* 22:451-460.

87. Mason, S.T., and Fibiger, H.C. 1978. Kainic acid lesions of the striatum: Behavioral sequelae similar to Huntington's chorea. *Brain Res* 155:313-329.

88. Mason, S.T., and Fibiger, H.C. 1979. Kainic acid lesions of the

striatum in rats mimic the spontaneous motor abnormalities of Huntington's disease. *Neuropharmacology* 18:403-407.

89. Ando, N.; Simon, J.R.; and Roth, R.H. 1979. Inverse relationship between GABA and γ-hydroxybutyrate levels in striatum of rat injected with kainic acid. *J Neurochem* 32:623-625.

90. Beaumont, K.; Maurin, Y.; Reisine, T.D.; Fields, J.Z.; Spokes, E.; Bird, E.D.; and Yamamura, H.I. 1979. Huntington's disease and its animal model: Alterations in kainic acid binding. *Life Sci* 24:809-816.

91. Resine, I.D.; Fields, J.Z.; Stern, C.Z.; Johnson, P.C.; Bird, E.D.; and Yamamura, H.I. 1977. Alterations in dopaminergic receptors in Huntington's disease. *Life Sci* 21:1123-1128.

92. Roberts, E., and Kuriyama, K. 1968. Biochemical-physiological correlations in studies of the γ-aminobutyric acid system. *Brain Res* 8:1-35.

93. Chase, T.N., and Walters, J.R. 1976. Pharmacologic approaches to the manipulation of GABA-mediated synaptic function in man. In *GABA in nervous system function*. Roberts, E.; Chase, T.N.; and Tower, D.B., eds. New York: Raven Press, pp. 487-496.

94. Shoulson, I.; Chase, T.N.; and Roberts, E. 1975. Huntington's disease: Treatment with imidazole-4-acetic acid. *N Eng J Med* 293:504-505.

95. Shoulson, I.; Kartzinel, R.; and Chase, T.N. 1976. Huntington's disease: Treatment with dipropyl acetic acid and gamma-aminobutyric acid. *Neurology* 26:61-63.

96. Pearce, I.; Heathfield, K.W.G.; and Rearce, J.M.S. 1977. Valproate sodium in Huntington's chorea. *Arch Neurol* 34:308-309.

97. Bachman, D.S.; Butler, I.J.; and McKhann, G.M. 1977. Long-term treatment of juvenile Huntington's chorea with dipropyl acetic acid. *Neurology* 27:193-197.

98. Lenman, J.A.R.; Ferguson, I.T.; and Fleming, A.M. 1976. Sodium valproate in chorea. *Br Med J* 2:1107-1108.

99. Perry, T.L.; Wright, J.M.; Hansen, S.; and MacLeod, P. 1970. Isoniazid therapy of Huntington disease. *Neurology* 29:370-375.

100. Perry, T.L.; Macleod P.M.; and Hansen, S. 1977. Treatment of Huntington's chorea with isoniazid. *N Engl J Med* 297:840.

101. Wood, J.D., and Peesker, S.J. 1972. The effect on GABA metabolism in brain of isonicotinic acid hydiazide and pyridoxine as a function of time after administration. *J Neurochem* 19:1526-1537.

102. Berry, H.K., and Steiner, J.C. 1979. L-glutamine increases cerebrospinal fluid (CSF) gamma-aminobutyric acid (GABA) in a patient with Huntington's disease. *Neurology* 29:535.

103. Schwarz, R.; Bennett, J.P.; and Coyle, J.T. 1977. Inhibitors of GABA metabolism: Implications for Huntington's disease. *Ann Neurol* 2:299-303.

104. Snead, O.C. Unpublished data.

105. Snead, O.C.; Bearden, L.J.; and Pegram, V. 1979. Effect of anticonvulsant drugs on endogenous levels of γ-hydroxybutyrate in brain. *Neurology* 29:602.

106. Martin, W.E.; Loewenson, R.B.; Resch, J.A.; and Baker, A.B. 1973. Parkinson's disease: Clinical analysis of 100 patients. *Neurology* 23: 783-790.

107. Hoen, M.M., and Yahr, M.D. 1967. Parkinsonism: Onset, progression, and mortality. *Neurology* 17:427-435.

108. Barbeau, A. 1960. Preliminary observations on abnormal catecholamine metabolism in basal ganglia diseases. *Neurology* 10:446-451.

109. Carlsson, A. 1959. The occurrence, distribution and physiologic role of catecholamines in the nervous system. *Pharmacol Rev* 11:490-493.

110. Marsden, C.D.; Duvoisin, R.C.; Jenner, P.; Parkes, J.D.; Pycock, C.; and Tarsy, D. 1975. Relationship between animal models and clinical Parkinsonism. *Adv Neurol* 9:165-175.

111. Hornykiewicz, O. 1966. Dopamine (3-hydroxytryamine) and train function. *Pharmacol Rev* 18:925-964.

112. Barbeau, A.; Murphy, C.F.; and Sourkes, T.L. 1961. Excretion of dopamine in diseases of basal ganglia. *Science* 133:1706-1707.

113. Bischoff, F., and Tones, A. 1962. Determination of urine dopamine. *Clin Chem* 8:370-377.

114. Ehringer, H., and Hornykiewicz, O. 1960. Verteilung von Noradrenalin und Dopamin (3-Hydroxytryamin) im Gehirn des menschen und ihr verhalten bei Erkrankungen des extrapyramidalen systems. *Klin Wochenschr* 38:1236-1239.

115. Bernheimier, H., and Hornykiewicz, O. 1962. Das verhalten einiger enzyme im Gehirn normaler und Parkinson-Kranker Menschem. *Arch Exp Path Pharmak* 243:295.

116. Hornykiewicz, O. 1972. Neurochemistry of parkinsonism. In *Handbook of neurochemistry*, vol. 7. Lajtha, A., ed. New York: Plenum Press, pp. 465-501.

117. Rinne, U.K.; Laakonen, H.; Reikinen, P.; and Sonninem, V. 1974. Brain glutamic acid decarboxylase activity in Parkinson's disease. *Eur Neurol* 12:13-19.

118. McGeer, P.; McGeer, E.G.; and Wada, J.A. 1971. Glutamic acid decarboxylase in Parkinson's disease and epilepsy. *Neurology* 21: 1000-1007.

119. Hornykiewicz, O.; Lloyd, K.G.; and Davidson, L. 1976. The GABA system, function of the basal ganglia, and Parkinson's disease. In *GABA in nervous system function*. Roberts, E.; Chase, T.N.; and Tower, D.B., eds. New York: Raven Press, pp. 479-485.

120. Lloyd, K.G.; Davidson, L.; and Hornykiewicz, O. 1973. Metabolism of levodopa in the human brain. *Adv Neurol* 3:173-188.

121. Rinne, U.K.; Koskinon, V.; Laaksonen, H.; Lonnberg, P.; and Son-

ninen, V. 1978. GABA receptor binding in the Parkinsonian brain. *Life Sci* 22:2225-2228.

122. Barbeau, A. 1969. L-DOPA therapy in Parkinson's disease: A critical review of nine years experience. *Can Med Assoc J* 101:791-800.

123. Barbeau, A., and Roy, M. 1976. Six year results of treatment with levodopa plus benzerazide in Parkinson's disease. *Neurology* 26:399-404.

124. Barbeau, A. 1975. Long term assessment of levodopa therapy in Parkinson's disease. *Can Med Assoc J* 112:1379-1380.

125. Calne, D.B. 1977. Developments in the pharmacology and therapeutics of Parkinsonism. *Ann Neurol* 2:111-119.

126. Rinne, U.K., and Marttila, R. 1978. Brain dopamine receptor stimulation and the relief of Parkinsonism: Relationship between bromocriptine and levodopa. *Ann Neurol* 4:263-267.

127. Spehlmann, R., and Stahl, S.M. 1976. Dopamine acetylcholine imbalance in Parkinson's disease. *Lancet* 1:724-725.

128. Lloyd, K.G., and Hornykiewicz, O. 1973. L-Glutamic acid decarboxylase in Parkinson's disease: Effect of L-DOPA therapy. *Nature* 243:521-523.

129. Thudichum, J.L.W. 1884. Treatise on the chemical composition of the brain. London: Balliere, Tindall, and Cox.

130. Bradley, R.J., and Smythies, J.R. 1976. The biochemistry of schizophrenia. In *Biological foundations of psychiatry*. Greyell, R.G., and Gabay, S., eds. New York: Raven Press, pp. 653-682.

131. Baldessarini, R.J. 1977. Schizophrenia. *N Engl J Med* 297:988-997.

132. Matthysse, S., and Lipinski, J. 1975. Biochemical aspects of schizophrenia. *Ann Rev Med* 26:551-565.

133. Kety, S.S. 1959. Biochemical theories of schizophrenia: A two-part critical review of current theories and of the evidence used to support them. *Science* 129:1528-1532, 1590-1596.

134. Weil-Malherbe, H., and Szara, S.I. 1971. *The biochemistry of functional and experimental psychoses*. Springfield, Ill.: Charles C. Thomas.

135. Carlsson, A. 1978. Antipsychotic drugs, neurotransmitters, and schizophrenia. *Am J Psychiatry* 135:164-173.

136. Van Kammen, D.P. 1977. γ-aminobutyric acid (GABA) and the dopamine hypothesis of schizophrenia. *Am J. Psychiatry* 134:138-143.

137. Crow, T.J.; Johnstone, E.C.; Longden, A.; and Owen, F. 1978. Dopamine and schizophrenia. *Adv Biochem Psychopharmacol* 19:301-309.

138. Horrobin, D.F. 1979. Schizophrenia: Reconciliation of the dopamine,

prostaglandin, and opioid concepts and the role of the pineal. *Lancet* 1:529.

139. Lidsky, T.I.; Weimhold, P.M.; and Levine, F.M. 1979. Implications of basal ganglionic dysfunction for schizophrenia. *Biol Psychiatry* 14:3-12.

140. Iversen, L.L. 1975. Dopamine receptors in brain. *Science* 188:1084-1089.

141. Snyder, S.H. 1976. The dopamine hypothesis of schizophrenia: Focus on the dopamine receptor. *Am J Psychiatry* 133:197-202.

142. Meltzer, H.Y., and Stahl, S.M. 1976. The dopamine hypothesis of schizophrenia. *Schizophr Bull* 2:19-76.

143. Angrist, B.; Sathanamthan, G.; Wilk, S.; and Gershon, S. 1974. Amphetamine psychosis: Behavioral and biochemical aspects. *J Psychiatr Res* 11:13-23.

144. Ellinwood, E.H. 1967. Amphetamine psychosis: I. Description of the individuals and process. *J Nerv Ment Dis* 144:274-283.

145. Griffith, J.D.; Cavanaugh, J.; Held, J.; and Oates, J.A. 1972. Dextroamphetamine: Evaluation of psychotomimetic properties in man. *Arch Gen Psychiatry* 26:97-100.

146. Connell, P.H. 1958. *Amphetamine psychosis*. London: Chapman and Hall.

147. Janowksy, D.S.; El-Yousef, M.K.; and Davis, J.M. 1973. Provocation of schizophrenic symptoms by intravenous administration of methylphenidate. *Arch Gen Psychiatry* 28:185-191.

148. Angrist, B.; Sathananthan, G.; and Gershon, S. 1973. Behavioral effects of L-DOPA in schizophrenic patients. *Psychopharmacologia* (Berlin) 31:1-12.

149. Yaryura-Tobias, J.A.; Diamond, B.; and Merlis, S. 1970. The action of L-DOPA on schizophrenic patients. *Curr Ther Res* 12:528-531.

150. Bianchine, J.R.; Shaw, G.M.; Greenwald, J.E.; and Dandalides, S.M. 1978. Clinical aspects of dopamine agonists and antagonists. *Fed Proc* 37:2434-2439.

151. Seeman, P.; Tedesco, J.L.; Lee, T.; Chau-Wong, M.; Muller, P.; Bowles, J.; Whitaker, P.M.; McManus, C.; Tittler, M.; Weinreich, P.; Friend, W.C.; and Brown, G.M. 1978. Dopamine receptor in the central nervous system. *Fed Proc* 37:130-136.

152. Titeler, M.; Weinreich, P.; Sinclair, D.; and Seeman, P. 1978. Multiple receptors for brain dopamine. *Proc Natl Acad Sci* (USA) 75:1153-1156.

153. Creese, I.; Burt, D.R.; and Snyder, S.H. 1976. Dopamine receptor binding predicts clinical and pharmacological potencies of antischizophrenic drugs. *Science* 192:491-483.

154. Stevens, J.R., and Livermore, A. 1978. Kindling of the mesolimbic dopamine system: Animal model of psychosis. *Neurology* 28:36-46.

155. Bird, E.D.; Barnes, J.; Iversen, L.L.; Spokes, E.G.; Mackay, A.V.P.; and Shepherd, M. 1977. Increased brain dopamine and reduced glutamic acid decarboxylase and choline acetyl transferase activity in schizophrenia and related psychoses. *Lancet* 2:1157.

156. Klawans, H.L.; Goetz, C.; and Westheimer, R. 1976. The pharmacology of schizophrenia. *Clinical neuropharmacology* 1:1-28.

157. Snyder, S.H.; Banerjee, S.P.; Yamamura, H.I.; and Greenberg, D. 1974. Drugs, neurotransmitters, and schizophrenia. *Science* 184:1243-1247.

158. Stevens, J.R. 1973. An anatomy of schizophrenia? *Arch Gen Psychiatry* 29:177-189.

159. Bowers, M.B. 1974. Central dopamine turnover in schizophrenic syndromes. *Arch Gen Psychiatry* 31:50-54.

160. Post, R.M.; Fink, E.; Carpenter, W.T.; and Goodwin, F.K. Cerebrospinal fluid amine metabolites in acute schizophrenia. *Arch Gen Psychiatry* 32:1013-1069.

161. Gershorn, S.; Hekimian, L.H.; Floyd, A., Jr.; and Hollister, L.E. 1967. Alpha-methyl-p-tyrosine (AMT) in schizophrenia. *Psychopharmacologia* 11:189-194.

162. Crow, T.J.; Johnstone, E.C.; and McClelland, H.A. 1976. The coincidence of schizophrenia and Parkinsonism: Some neurochemical implications. *Psychol Med* 6:227-233.

163. Roberts, E. 1972. A hypothesis suggesting that there is a defect in the GABA system in schizophrenia. *Neurosci Res Program Bull* 10:468-481.

164. Costa, E.; Cheney, D.L.; Mao, C.C.; and Moroni, F. 1978. Action of antischizophrenic drugs on the metabolism of γ-aminobutyric acid and acetylcholine in globus pallidus, striatum, and n. accumbens. *Fed Proc* 37:2408-2414.

165. Marco, E.; Mao, C.C.; Revuelta, A.; Peralta, E.; and Costa, E. 1978. Turnover rates of γ-aminobutyric acid in substantia nigra, n. caudatus, globus pallidus, and n. accumbens of rats injected with cataleptogenic and non-cataleptogenic antipsychotics. *Neuropharmacology* 17:589-596.

166. Cheney, D.L.; Zsilla, G.; and Costa, E. 1977. Acetylcholine turnover rate in n. accumbens, n. caudatus, globus pallidus, and substantia nigra: Action of cataleptogenic and non-cataleptogenic antipsychotics. *Adv Biochem Psychopharmacol* 16:179-192.

167. Collins. G.G.S. 1973. Effect of aminooxyacetic acid, thiosemicarbazide, and haloperidol on the metabolism and half-lives of glutamate and GABA in rat brain. *Biochem Pharmacol* 22:101-111.

168. Lloyd, K.G., and Hornykiewicz, O. 1977. Effect of chronic neuroleptic or L-DOPA administration on GABA levels in rat substantia nigra. *Life Sci* 21:1489-1496.
169. Kim, J., and Hassler, R. 1975. Effects of acute haloperidol on the gamma-aminobutyric acid system in rat striatum and substantia nigra. *Brain Res* 88:150-153.
170. Stevens, J.; Wilson, K.; and Foote, W. 1974. GABA blockade, dopamine, and schizophrenia: Experimental studies in the cat. *Psychopharmacologia* (Berl.) 39:105-119.
171. Stevens, J. 1975. GABA blockade: Dopamine and schizophrenia: Experimental activation of the mesolimbic system. *Int J Neurol* 10:115-127.
172. Roberts, E. 1977. The γ-aminobutyric acid system and schizophrenia. In *Neuroregulators and psychiatric disorders*. Usdin, E.; Hamberg, D.A.; and Barchas, J.D. eds. New York: Oxford Univ. Press, pp. 372-380.
173. Perry, T.L.; Buchanan, J.; Kish, S.J.; and Hansen, S. 1979. γ-aminobutyric acid deficiency in brain of schizophrenic patients. *Lancet* 1:237-239.
174. Cross, A.J.; Crow, T.J.; and Owen, F. 1979. Gamma aminobutyric acid in the brain in schizophrenia. *Lancet* 1:560-561.
175. Lichtshtein, D.; Dobkin, J.; Ebstein, R.B.; Biederman, J.; Rimon, R.; and Belmaker, R.H. 1978. Gamma-aminobutyric acid (GABA) in the CSF of schizophrenic patients before and after neuroleptic treatment. *Br J Psychiatry* 132:145-148.
176. Perlow, M.J.; Enna, S.J.; O'Brien, P.J.; Hoffman, H.J.; and Wyatt, R.J. 1979. Cerebrospinal fluid gamma-aminobutyric acid: Daily pattern and response to haloperidol. *J Neurochem* 32:265-268.
177. Frederiksen, P.K. 1975. Baklofen vid behandling AV schizofreniett preliminärt meddeland. *Läkartid Nigen* 72:456-458.
178. Simpson, G.N.; Lee, J.H.; Shrivastava, S.; and Branchey, M.M. 1978. Baclofen in the treatment of tardive dyskinesia and schizophrenia. *Psychopharmacol Bull* 14:16-19.
179. Fredericksen, P.K. 1975. Baclofen in the treatment of schizophrenia. *Lancet* 1:702-704.
180. Tamminga, C.A.; Crayton, J.W.; and Chase, T.N. 1978. Muscimol: GABA agonist therapy in schizophrenia. *Am J Psychiatry* 135:746-747.
181. Schmidt, J., and Wilder, B.J. 1968. *Epilepsy*. Philadelphia: F.A. Davis & Co.
182. Prince, D.A. 1978. Neurophysiology of epilepsy. *Ann Rev Neurosci* 1:395-415.
183. Wood, J.D. 1975. The role of γ-aminobutyric acid in the mechanism of seizures. In *Progress in neurobiology*, vol. 15, part 1. Kerkut, G.A.; and Phillis, J.W., eds. New York: Pergamon Press, pp. 79-95.
184. Tower, D.B. 1976. GABA and seizures: Clinical correlates in man. In

GABA in nervous system function. New York: Raven Press, pp. 461-476.

185. Maynert, E.W.; Marczynski, B.; and Browning, R.A. 1975. The role of the neurotransmitters in the epilepsies. *Adv Neurol* 13:79-147.

186. Meldrum, B.S. 1975. Epilepsy and γ-aminobutyric acid-mediated inhibition. *Int Rev Neurobiol* 17:1-36.

187. Emson, P.C. 1975. Neurochemistry of focal epilepsy. *Int J Biochem* 6:689-694.

188. Brazier, M.A.B. 1974. The search for the neuronal mechanism in epilepsy: An overview. *Neurology* 24:903-911.

189. Carlsson, A. 1974. Some aspects of central neurohumoral transmission in relation to epilepsy. In *Epilepsy.* Harris, P., and Mawdsky, C., eds. Edinburgh: Churchill Livingston, pp. 1-4.

190. Tower, D.B. 1969. Neurochemical mechanisms. In *Basic mechanisms of the epilepsies.* Jasper, H.H.; Ward, A.A.; and Pope, A., eds. Boston: Little, Brown & Co., pp. 611-638.

191. Lovell, R.A. 1971. Some neurochemical aspects of convulsions. In *Handbook of neurochemistry,* vol. 2. Lajtha, A., ed. New York: Plenum Press, pp. 63-102.

192. Symonds, C. 1959. Excitation and inhibition in epilepsy. *Brain* 82:133-146.

193. Goldensohn, E.S., and Ward, A.A. 1975. Pathogenesis of epileptic seizures. In *The nervous system. Vol. 2: The clinical neurosciences.* New York: Raven Press, pp. 249-265.

194. Wiechert, P., and Herbst, A. 1966. Provocation of cerebral seizures by derangement of the natural balance between glutamic and γ-aminobutyric acid. *J Neurochem* 13:59-64.

195. Kubrin, S., and Seifter, J. 1966. ω-amino acids and various biogenic amines as antagonists to pentylenetetrazol. *J Pharmacol Exp Ther* 154:646-651.

196. Berl, S.; Purpura, D.P.; Girado, M.; and Waelch, H. 1959. Amino acid metabolism in epileptogenic and nonepileptogenic lesions of the neocortex (cat). *J Neurochem* 4:311-317.

197. Berl, S.; Takagaki, G.; and Purpura, D.P. 1961. Metabolic and pharmacological effects of injected amino acids and ammonia on cortical epileptogenic lesions. *J Neurochem* 7:198-209.

198. Wood, J.D.; Watson, W.J.; and Clydesdale, F.M. 1963. γ-aminobutyric acid and oxygen poisoning. *J Neurochem* 10:625-633.

199. Ballantine, E. 1963. Effect of γ-aminobutyric acid on audiogenic seizure. *Colloq Intern Centre Natl Rech Sci* (Paris) 112:447-451.

200. Feher, O.; Halasz, P.; and Mechler, F. 1965. The influence of γ-aminobutyric acid (GABA) on seizure potentials. *Epilepsia* 6:47-53.

201. Guerrero-Figueroa, R.; De Balbain Verster, F.; Barros, A.; and Heath, R.G. 1964. Cholinergic mechanism in subcortical mirror focus and effects of topical application of γ-aminobutyric acid and acetylcholine. *Epilepsia* 5:140-155.
202. Crighel, E. 1966. The effects of GABA and strychnine on neocortical structures involved in the onset mechanism of epileptic activity. *Epilepsia* 7:283-290.
203. Horton, R.W.; Chapman, A.G.; and Meldrum, B.S. 1978. Regional changes in cerebral GABA concentration and convulsions produced by D and by L-allylglycine. *J Neurochem* 30:1501-1504.
204. Maynert, E.W., and Kaji, H. 1962. On the relationship of brain γ-aminobutyric acid to convulsions. *J Pharmacol Exp Ther* 137:114-121.
205. Wood, J.P.; Watson, W.J.; and Murray, G.W. 1969. Correlation between decreases in brain γ-aminobutyric acid levels and susceptibility to convulsions induced by hyperbaric oxygen. *J Neurochem* 16:281-287.
206. Stansky, Z. 1969. Time course of rat brain GABA levels following methionine sulphoximine treatment. *Nature* 224:612-613.
207. Roa, P.D.; Tews, J.K.; and Stone, W.E. 1964. A neurochemical study of thiosemicarbazide seizures and their inhibition by aminooxyacetic acid. *Biochem Pharmacol* 13:477-487.
208. Wood, J.D., and Peesker, S.J. 1974. Development of an expression which relates the excitable state of the brain to the level of GAD activity and GABA content, with particular reference to the action of hydriazine and its derivatives. *J Neurochem* 23:703-712.
209. Utley, J.D. 1963. The effects of anthranilic hydroxamic acid on rat behavior and rat brain γ-aminobutyric acid, norepinephrine, and 5-hydroxytryptamine concentrations. *J Neurochem* 10:423-432.
210. Saito, S., and Tokunga, Y. 1967. Some correlations between picrotoxin-induced seizures and γ-aminobutyric acid in animal brain. *J Pharmacol Exp Ther* 157:546-554.
211. Sytinskii, I.A., and ThiThin, N. 1964. The distribution of γ-aminobutyric acid in the monkey brain during picrotoxin-induced seizures. *J Neurochem* 11:551-556.
212. Beart, P.M., and Khalidah, B. 1979. Allylglycine: Intranigral effects and reappraisal of actions on the GABA system. *Biochem Pharmacol* 28:449-454.
213. Curtis, D.R.; Duggan, A.W.; Felix, D.; and Johnston, G.A.R. 1970. GABA, bicuculline, and central inhibition. *Nature* 226:1222-1230.
214. Curtis, D.R.; Duggan, A.W.; Felix, D.; and Johnston, G.A.R. 1971. Bicuculine an antagonist of GABA and synaptic inhibition in the spinal cord of the cat. *Brain Res* 32:69-96.

215. Nicoll, R.A., and Padjen, A. 1976. Pentylenetetrazol: An antagonist of GABA at primary afferents of the isolated frog spinal cord. *Neuropharmacology* 15:69-71.
216. Macdonald, R.L., and Barker, J.L. 1977. Studies of the mechanisms of action of convulsants and anticonvulsants in cultured mammalian neurons. *Ann Neurol* 2:264.
217. Macdonald, R.L., and Barker, J.L. 1977. Pentylenetetrazol and penicillin are selective antagonists of GABA mediated postsynaptic inhibition in cultured mammalian neurons. *Nature* 267:720-721.
218. Macdonald, R.L., and Barker, J.C. 1978. Specific antagonism of GABA-mediated postsynaptic inhibition in cultured mammalian spinal cord neurons: A common mode of convulsant action. *Neurology* 28:325-330.
219. Worms, P., and Lloyd, K.G. 1978. Differential blockade of bicuculline convulsions by neuroleptics. *Eur J Pharmacol* 51:55-88.
220. Olsen, R.W.; Ticku, M.K.; Van Ness, P.C.; and Greenlee, D. 1978. Effects of drugs on γ-aminobutyric acid receptors, uptake, release, and synthesis in vitro. *Brain Res* 139:277-294.
221. Wasterlain, C.G.; Morin, A.M.; Jones, V.; and Brillawalla, T. 1979. Kindling with blockers of inhibitory synapses. *Neurology* 29:582.
222. Murakami, Y.; Abe, M.; and Murakami, K. 1976. Anticonvulsant activity of aminooxyacetic acid on convulsions induced by thiosemicarbazide. *J Neurochem* 26:655-656.
223. Anlezark, G.; Horton, R.W.; Meldrum, B.S.; and Sawaya, A.C.B. 1976. Anticonvulsant action of ethanolamine-o-sulphate and di-n-propylacetate and the metabolism of γ-aminobutyric acid (GABA) in mice with audiogenic seizures. *Biochem Pharmacol* 25:413-417.
224. Schecter, P.J.; Tranier, Y.; and Grove, J. 1978. Effect of n-dipropyl acetate on amino acid concentrations in mouse brain: Correlations with anticonvulsant activity. *J Neurochem* 31:1325-1327.
225. Simler, S.; Ciesielski, L.; Maitre, M.; Randrianarisoa, H.; and Nandel, P. 1973. Effect of sodium-n-dipropylacetate on audiogenic seizures and brain γ-aminobutyric acid level. *Biochem Pharmacol* 22:1701-1708.
226. Schechter, P.J.; Tranier, Y.; Jung, M.; and Sjoerdsma, A. 1977. Antiseizure activity of γ-acetylenic γ-aminobutyric acid: Catalytic irreversible inhibitor of γ-amino acid transaminase. *J Parmacol Exp Ther* 201:606-612.
227. Schechter, P.J.; Tranier, Y.; Jung, M.; and Sjoerdsma, A. 1977. Audiogenic seizure protection by elevated GABA concentration in mice: Effects of γ-acetylenic GABA and γ-vinyl GABA, two irreversible GABA-T inhibitors. *Eur J Pharmacol* 45:319-328.

228. Anlezark, G.; Collins, J.; and Meldrum, B. 1978. GABA agonists and audiogenic seizures. *Neurosci Lett* 7:337-340.
229. Meldrum, B., and Horton, R. 1978. Blockade of epileptic responses in the photosensitive baboon, Papio Papio, by two irreversible inhibitors of GABA transaminase, γ-acetylenic GABA (4-amino-hex-5-enoic acid) and γ-vinyl GABA (4-amino-hex-5-enoic acid). *Psychopharmacology* 59:47-50.
230. Horton, R.W.; Anlezark, G.M.; Sawaya, C.B.; and Meldrum, B.S. 1977. Monoamine and GABA metabolism and the anticonvulsant action of di-n-propylacetate and ethanolamine-o-sulphate. *Eur J Pharmacol* 41:387-397.
231. Emson, P.C. 1976. Effects of chronic treatment with aminooxyacetic acid on sodium n-dipropyl acetate on brain GABA levels and the development and regression of cobalt epileptic foci in rats. *J Neurochem* 27:1489-1494.
232. Perry, T.L., and Hansen, S.H. 1978. Biochemical effects in man and rat of three drugs which can increase brain GABA content. *J Neurochem* 30:679-684.
233. Löscher, W., and Frey, H. 1978. Aminooxyacetic acid: Correlation between biochemical effects, anticonvulsant action and toxicity in mice. *Biochem Pharmacol* 27:103-108.
234. Collins, R.C. 1979. Anticonvulsant effects of muscimol, a GABA agonist. *Neurology* 29:603.
235. Snyderman, S.E.; Holt, L.E.; Carretero, R.; and Jacobs, K. 1953. Pyridoxine deficiency in the human infant. *J Clin Nutr* 1:200-207.
236. Coursin, D.B. 1954. Convulsive seizures in infants with pyridoxine-deficient diet. *JAMA* 154:406-408.
237. Coursin, D.B. 1955. Vitamin B_6 deficiency in infants: A followup study. *Am J Dis Child* 90:344-348.
238. Scriver, C.R. 1976. Vitamin B_6 deficiency and dependency in man. *Am J Dis Child* 113:109-114.
239. Hunt, A.D.; Stokes, J.; McCrory, W.W.; and Stroud, H.H. 1954. Pyridoxine dependency: Report of a case of intractable convulsions in an infant controlled by pyridoxine. *Pediatrics* 13:140-145.
240. Tower, D.G. 1956. Neurochemical aspects of pyridoxine metabolism and function. *Am J Clin Nutr* 4:329-345.
241. Lott, I.T.; Couloumbe, T.; DiPaolo, R.V.; Richardson, E.P.; and Levy, H.L. 1978. Vitamin B_6-dependent seizures: Pathology and chemical findings in brain. *Neurology* 28:47-54.
242. Van Gelder, N.M.; Sherwin, A.L.; and Rasmussen, T. 1972. Amino acid content of epileptogenic human brain; Focus versus surrounding regions. *Brain Res* 40:385-397.

243. Perry, T.L.; Hansen, S.; Kennedy, J.; Wada, J.A.; and Thompson, G.B. 1975. Amino acids in human epileptogenic foci. *Arch Neurol* 32:752-754.

244. Enna, S.J.; Wood, J.H.; and Snyder, S.H. 1977. γ-aminobutyric acid (GABA) in human cerebrospinal fluid: Radioreceptor assay. *J Neurochem* 28:1121-1124.

245. Wood, J.H.; Hare, T.A.; Glaeser, B.S.; and Post, R.M. 1979. Cerebrospinal fluid GABA reductions in seizure patients. *Neurology* 29:601.

246. Tower, D.B. 1960. The administration of gamma-aminobutyric acid to man: Systemic effects and anticonvulsant action. In *Inhibition in the nervous system and gamma aminobutyric acid*. Roberts, E., ed. New York: Pergamon Press, pp. 562-578.

247. Cooper, I.S. 1973. Effect of chronic stimulation of anterior cerebellum on neurologic disease. *Lancet* 1:206.

248. Cooper, I.S.; Amin, I.; and Gilman, S. 1973. The effect of chronic cerebellar stimulation upon epilepsy in man. *Trans Am Neurol Assoc* 98:192-196.

249. Cooper, I.S.; Amin, I.; Upton, A.; Ricklan, M.; Watkins, S.; and McLellan, L. 1978. Safety and efficacy of chronic cerebellar stimulation. *Appl Neurophysiol* 40:124-134.

250. Cooper, I.S., and Gilman, S. 1973. Chronic stimulation of the cerebellar cortex in the therapy of epilepsy in humans. In *Neural organization and its relevance to prosthetics*. Fields, W., ed. New York: Intercontinental Publishing Company, pp. 371-375.

251. Cooper, I.S.; Amin, I.; Riklan, M.; Walter, J.M.; and Poon, T.P. 1976. Chronic cerebellar stimulation in epilepsy. *Arch Neurol* 33:559-570.

252. Grabow, J.D.; Ekersold, M.J.; Albers, J.W.; and Schima, E.M. 1974. Cerebellar stimulation for control of seizures. *Mayo Clin Proc* 49:759-774.

253. Julien, R.M., and Laxer, K.D. 1974. Cerebellar responses to penicillin-induced cortical cerebral epileptiform discharge. *Electroencephalogr Clin Neurophysiol* 37:123-132.

254. Dow, R.S.; Fernandez-Guardiola, A.; and Manni, E. 1962. The influence of the cerebellum on experimental epilepsy. *Electroencephalogr Clin Neurophysiol* 14:383-398.

255. Reiner, G.R.; Grimm, R.J.; and Dow, R.S. 1967. Effects of cerebellar stimulation on cobalt-induced epilepsy in cat. *Electroencephalogr Clin Neurophysiol* 23:456-462.

256. Halpern, L., and Julian, R. 1972. Augmentation of cerebellar Purkinje cell discharge rate after diphenylhydantoin. *Epilepsia* 13:377-385.

257. Halpern, L., and Julian, R. 1972. Effects of diphenylhydantoin and other antiepileptic drugs on epileptiform activity and Purkinje cell discharge rates. *Epilepsia* 13:387-400.

258. Puro, D.G., and Woodward, D.J. 1973. Effects of diphenylhydantoin on activity of rat cerebellar Purkinje cells. *Neuropharmacology* 12:433-440.

259. Dauth, G.W.; Dell, S.; and Gilman, S. 1978. Alteration of Purkinje cell activity from transfolial stimulation of the cerebellum in the cat. *Neurology* 28:654-660.

260. Wood, J.H.; Glaeser, B.S.; Hanes, T.A.; Sode, J.; Brooks, B.R.; and Van Buren, J.M. 1977. Cerebrospinal fluid GABA reductions in seizure patients evoked by cerebellar surface stimulation. *J Neurosurg* 47:502-589.

261. Van Buren, J.M.; Wood, J.H.; Oakley, J.; and Hanbrecht, J. 1978. Preliminary evaluation of cerebellar stimulation by double-blind stimulation and biological criteria in the treatment of epilepsy. *J Neurosurg* 48:407-416.

262. Neophytides, A.N.; Suria, A.; and Chase, T.N. 1978. Cerebrospinal fluid GABA in neurologic disease. *Neurology* 28:359.

263. Snead, O.C.; Yu, R.K.; and Huttenlocher, P.R. 1976. Gamma hydroxybutyrate: Correlation of serum and cerebrospinal fluid levels with electroencephalographic and behavioral effects. *Neurology* 26:51-56.

264. Godschalk, M.; Dzoljic, M.R.; and Bonta, I.L. 1977. Slow wave sleep and a state resembling absence epilepsy induced in the rat by gamma-hydroxybutyrate. *Eur J Pharmacol* 44:105-111.

265. Snead, O.C. 1978. Gamma-hydroxybutyrate in the monkey. I: Electroencephalographic, behavioral, and pharmacokinetic studies. *Neurology* 7:636-648.

266. Roth, R.H., and Nowycky, M.C. 1977. Dopaminergic neurons: Effects elicited by γ-hydroxybutyrate are reversed by picrotoxin. *Biochem Pharmacol* 26:2079-2082.

267. De Carolis, A.S., and Massotti, M. 1978. Electroencephalographic and behavioral observations on "GABAergic" drugs, muscimol, baclofen, and sodium γ-hydroxybutyrate: Implications on human epileptic studies. *Prog Neuropsychopharmacol* 2:431-442.

268. Olpe, H., and Koella, W.P. 1979. Inhibition of nigral and neocortical cells by γ-hydroxybutyrate: A microiontophoretic investigation. *Eur J Pharmacol* 53:359-364.

269. King, G.A. 1979. Effects of systemically applied GABA agonists and antagonists on wave-spike ECoG activity in rat. *Neuropharmacology* 18:47-55.

270. Meldrum, B.S. 1978. Gamma-aminobutyric acid and the search for new anticonvulsant drugs. *Lancet* 2:304-306.

271. Brooks, B.R.; Wood, J.H.; Post, R.M.; Ekert, M.; Goodwin, F.K.; and Van Buren, J.M. 1979. Cerebrospinal fluid (CSF) 5-hydroxy-indoleacetic acid (5-HIAA) and homovanillic acid (HVA) metabolism in anticonvulsant treated seizure disorders in man. *Neurology* 29: 603.
272. Shagwitz, B.A.; Cohen, D.J.; and Bowers, M.D. 1975. Reduced cerebrospinal fluid 5-hydroxyindoleacetic acid and homovanillic acid in children with epilepsy. *Neurology* 25:72-79.
273. Papeschi, R.; Molina-Negro, P.; and Sourkes, T.L. 1972. The concentration of homovanillic and 5-hydroxyindoleacetic acids in ventricular and lumbar CSF: Studies in patients with extrapyramidal disorders, epilepsy, and other diseases. *Neurology* 22:1151-1159.
274. Chadwick, D.; Hallett, M.; Harris, R.; Jenner, P.; Reynold, E.H.; and Marsden, C.D. 1977. Clinical biochemical and physiological features distinguishing myoclonus responsive to 5-hydroxytryptophan with a monoamine oxidase inhibitor, and clonazepam. *Brain* 100: 455-488
275. Chadwick, D.; Jenner, P.; and Reynolds, E.H. 1975. Amines, anti-convulsants, and epilepsy. *Lancet* 1:473-476.
276. Chadwick, D.; Jenner, P.; and Reynolds, E.H. 1977. Serotonin metabolism in human epilepsy: The influence of anticonvulsant drugs. *Ann Neurol* 1:218-224.
277. DeJong, R.N., and Pope, A. 1975. Dementia. In *The Nervous System: The Clinical Neurosciences*. Chase, T.N., ed. New York: Raven Press, Vol. 2, pp. 449-456.
278. Bowen, D.B.; Smith, C.B.; White, P.; Flack, H.A.; Carrasco, L.H.; Gedge, J.L.; and Davison, A.N. 1977. Chemical pathology of the organic dementias. I: Validity of biochemical measurements on human postmortem brain specimens. *Brain* 100:397-426.
279. Bowen, D.M.; Smith, C.B.; White, P.; Flack, R.H.F.; Carrasco, L.H.; Gedge, J.L.; and Davison, A.M. 1977. Chemical pathology of the organic dementias. II: Quantitative estimation of cellular changes in postmortem brains. *Brain* 100:427-453.
280. Dingledine, R.; Iversen, L.L.; and Breuker, E. 1978. Naloxone as a GABA antagonist: Evidence from iontophoretic, receptor binding and convulsant studies. *Eur J Pharmacol* 47:19-27.
281. Biggio, G.; Della Bella, D.; Frigeni, V.; and Guidotti, A. 1977. Potentiation of morphine analgesia by muscimol. *Neuropharmacology* 16:149-150.
282. Ho, I.L.; Loh, H.H.; and Way, E.L. 1976. Pharmacological manipulation of gamma-aminobutyric acid (GABA) in morphine analgesia, tolerance, and physical dependence. *Life Sci* 18:1111-1124.

283. Sherman, A., and Gebhart, G.F. 1974. Regional levels of GABA and glutamate in mouse brain following exposure to pain. *Neuropharmacology* 13:673-677.

284. Sherman, A., and Gebhart, G.F. 1975. An evaluation of the analgesia induced by morphine and gamma-hydroxybutyrate. *Arch Int Pharmacodyn Ther* 213:195-199.

285. Basbaum, A.I., and Fields, H.L. 1978. Endogenous pain control mechanisms: Review and hypothesis. *Ann Neurol* 4:451-462.

286. Haefely, W.; Kulcsar, A.; Möhler, H.; Pieri, L.; Pola, P.; and Schaffuer, R. 1975. Possible involvement of GABA in the central actions of benzodiazepines. *Adv Biochem Psychopharmacol* 14:131-151.

287. Costa, E.; Guidotti, A.; and Mao, C.C. 1975. Evidence for involvement of GABA in the action of benzodiazepines: Studies on rat cerebellum. *Adv Biochem Psychopharmacol* 14:131-151.

288. Costa, E.A.; Guidotti, Al; Mao, C.C.; and Sura, A. 1975. New concepts on the mechanisms of action of benzodiazepines. *Life Sci* 17:167-174.

289. Waddington, J.L. 1978. Behavioral evidence for GABAergic activity of the benzodiazepine flurazepam. *Eur J Pharmacol* 51:417-422.

290. Montarolo, P.G.; Raschi, F.; and Strata, P. 1979. Interactions between benzodiazepines and GABA in the cerebellar cortex. *Brain Res* 162:358-362.

291. Guidotti, A. 1978. Synaptic mechanisms in the action of benzodiazepines. In *Psychopharmacology: A generation of progress*. Lipton, M.A.; DiMascio, A.; and Killam, K.G., eds. New York: Raven Press, pp. 1359-1357.

292. Haefely, W.E. 1978. Behavioral and neuropharmacological aspects of drugs used in anxiety and related states. In *Psychopharmacology: A generation of progress*. Lipton, M.A.; DiMascio, A.; and Killam, K.G., eds. New York: Raven Press, pp. 1359-1374.

293. Squires, R., and Broestrup, C. 1977. Benzodiazepine receptors in rat brain. *Nature* 266:732-734.

294. Möhler, Okada, T. 1977. Benzodiazepine receptor demonstration in the central nervous system. *Science* 198:849-851.

295. Broestrup, C.R.; Albrechtsen, R.; and Squires, R.F. 1977. High densities of benzodiazepine receptors in human cortical areas. *Nature* 269:702-704.

296. Broestrup, C.R., and Squires, R. 1977. Brain specific benzodiazepine receptors in rats characterized by high affinity ^{3}H-diazepam receptor binding. *Proc Natl Acad Sci* (USA) 74:3805-3809.

297. Broestrup, C.R., and Squires, R. 1978. Pharmacological characterization of benzodiazepine receptors in the brain. *Eur J Pharmacol* 48:263-270.

298. Martin, I.L., and Candy, J.M. 1978. Facilitation of benzodiazepine binding by sodium chloride and GABA. *Neuropharmacology* 17:993-998.

299. Williams, M., and Risley, E.A. 1979. Enhancement of the binding of ³H-diazepam to rat brain membranes in vitro by S Q 20009, a novel anxiolytic, γ-aminobutyric acid (GABA) and muscimol. *Life Sci* 24: 833-844.

300. Costa, E.; Guidotti, A.; and Toffano, G. 1978. Molecular mechanisms mediating the action of diazepam on GABA receptors. *Br J Psychiatry* 133:239-242.

301. Toffano, G.; Guidotti, A.; and Costa, E. 1978. Purification of an endogenous protein inhibitor of the high affinity binding of γ-aminobutyric acid to synaptic membranes of rat brain. *Proc Natl Acad Sci* (USA) 75:4024-4028.

302. Guidotti, A.; Toffano, G.; and Costa, E. 1978. An endogenous protein modulates the affinity of GABA and benzodiazepine receptors in rat brain. *Nature* 275:553-555.

303. Macdonald, R. 1978. Benzodiazepines specifically modulate GABA-mediated postsynaptic inhibition in cultured mammalian neurons. *Nature* 271-563-564.

304. Kozhechkin, S.N., and Ostrovskaga, R.U. 1977. Are benzodiazepines GABA antagonists? *Nature* 269:72-73.

305. Haefely, W.E. 1978. Central actions of benzodiazepines: General introduction. *Br J Psychiatry* 133:231-238.

306. Kosterlitz, H.W., and Hughes, J. 1978. Development of the concepts of opiate receptors and their ligands. *Adv Biochem Psychopharmacol* 18:31-44.

307. Bloom, F.C.; Rosser, J.; Battenberg, E.L.F.; Bayon, A.; French, E.; Henrikson, S.J.; Siggins, G.R.; Segal, D.; Browne, R.; Ling, N.; and Guillemin, R. 1978. β-endorphin: Cellular localization, electrophysiological and behavioral effects. *Adv Biochem Psychopharmacol* 18:89-110.

308. Lord, J.A.H.; Waterfield, A.A.; Hughes, J.; and Kosterlitz, H.W. 1977. Endogenous opioid peptides: Multiple agonists and receptors. *Nature* 267:495-499.

309. Jeffcoate, W.J.; McLoughtin, L.; Hope, J.; Rees, C.H.; Ratter, S.J.; Lowry, P.J.; and Besser, G.M. 1978. β-endorphin in human cerebrospinal fluid. *Lancet* 1:119-121.

310. Terenius, L. 1978. Significance of endorphins in endogenous antinociception. *Adv Biochem Psychopharmacol* 18:321-332.

311. Bertilsson, L., and Costa, E. 1976. Mass fragmentographic quantitation of glutamic acid and γ-aminobutyric acid in cerebellar nuclei and sympathetic ganglia of rats. *J Chromatogr* 18:395-402.

312. Bertilsson, L.; Mao, C.C.; and Costa, E. 1977. Application of principles of steady state kinetics to the estimation of γ-aminobutyric acid turnover rate in nuclei of rat brain. *J Pharmacol Exp Ther* 200:277-284.

313. Mao, C.C.; Marco, E.; Reuvelt, A.; Bertilsson, L.; and Costa, E. 1977. The turnover rate of γ-aminobutyric acid in the nuclei of telencephalon: Implications in the pharmacology of antipsychotics and of a minor tranquilizer. *Biol Psychiatry* 12:359-371.

314. Adamec, R. 1976 Behavioral and epileptic determinants of predatory attack behavior in the cat. In *Kindling*. Wada, J., ed. New York: Raven Press, pp. 135-154.

315. Ell, P.J.; Deach, J.; Jarritt, P.H.; Brown, N.J.G.; and Williams, E.S. 1978. Emission computerized tomography. *Lancet* 1:608-609.

316. Pinching, A.J.; Travers, R.C.; and Hughes, G.R.V. 1978. Oxygen-15 brain scanning for detection of cerebral involvement in systemic lupus erythematosus. *Lancet* 1:898-900.

317. Lenzi, G.L.; Jones, T.; Reid, J.; and Moss, S. 1977. Noninvasive study of the metabolism-to-blood flow relationship in Parkinson's disease. *Acta Neurol Scand Suppl* 64:184-185.

318. 1975. *Noninvasive brain imaging: Computed tomography and radionuclides*. DeBlanc, H.J., Jr., and Sorenson, J.A., eds. New York: Society of Nuclear Medicine, Inc.

319. Raichle, M.E.; Welch, M.J.; Grubb, R.L. 1978. Higgins, C.S.; Ter-Pogossian, M.M.; and Larson, K.B. 1978. Measurement of regional substrate utilization rates by emission tomography. *Science* 199:986-987.

5 The Neurology of Violence

James R. Merikangas

In the fourth chapter of the Book of Genesis, Cain and Abel, the sons of Adam and Eve, offer a sacrifice to God. For reasons not explained in the text, God was pleased with Abel's gift but was dissatisfied with Cain's. Learning this, Cain became very angry and downcast. While in this depressed and angry mood he invited Abel out into the fields where he turned upon him and killed him. In this first report in the Western literature of a premeditated murder we are given the suggestion that disappointment, envy, anger, and striking out in violence are as old as the human race. How can we understand this murder? Cain had nothing to gain from Abel's death; Abel had done nothing to offend him. Fear of punishment was no deterrent, for Cain surely knew that his father, Adam, was severely punished by God for the much lesser offense of stealing an apple. There is no suggestion that Cain was intoxicated, or that he had a psychomotor seizure, or that he was suffering from any form of brain damage. Perhaps Cain was a paranoid schizophrenic; the voice of God disapproving of his gift could have been an hallucination consistent with his delusional frame of reference. Could he then be excused on a plea of insanity? In fact, Cain was punished by exile (significantly not by capital punishment). I doubt if Cain himself could explain why he killed his brother. If questioned he would probably reply, "I don't know why I did it."

In this prototypic tale of murder we see some of the dilemmas which face us today. In our country over 400,000 people are currently imprisoned, about 79 percent for violent crimes [1]. Despite this statistic there is still no evidence to suggest that punishment will reform violent people [2]. We frequently hear of convicted criminals who are released from prison only to rape, murder, or steal again. The human tendency to violent crime and murder has persisted despite taboo, culture, and religion. We are all capable of violence; it would be a mistake to assume that violent acts are perpetrated by sociopaths, criminals, or antisocial personalities only. Much violence is domestic; child abuse and spouse abuse are now popular topics for public discussion. Execution, corporal punishment, and maiming are prominent features of the political life of entire cultures of people. No further introduction is required to justify violent aggression as a topic. It is necessary, however, to examine why this should be a topic for clinical discussion.

Violence is not a diagnosis; aggression is not a disease. Violence implies fury, intensity, and injury, but some aggressive acts require only squeezing a trigger or pushing a button. Some violence is quite deliberate, performed with utmost control and premeditation, and some is really out of the control of the person performing the act. Much legal debate has gone into knowing right from wrong, being able to conform one's actions to the idea of right and wrong, and understanding the consequences of one's actions [3-6]. Practically every discipline dealing with humans has elaborated theories and explanations for violent behavior, from anthropology to zoology. The American Psychiatric Association (APA) task force on violence states that we do not have a satisfactory classification for violent behavior [7]. Yet at the same time, it is quite clear to both the lay person and the criminologist that some forms of violent aggression are pathological. Aside from evil people or those motivated by lust, greed, hunger, or love, there are persons who commit acts of violent aggression which by the type of act they perform or the manner in which they behave suggest that they are set apart from the norms of human behavior. An individual defending his person or home may kill in a most savage manner and be considered no worse than unfortunate. But a Charles Manson or a Richard Speck is recognized by almost everyone as savage and barbaric. It is the pathological aspect of behavior then which explains why some of these people are the proper subject of neuropsychiatric investigation.

Aggression is defined by Konrad Lorenz as the fighting instinct in animals and humans which is directed against members of the same species [8]. It is important to note that for the ethologist this behavior is shared by all animal species. Aggression is one of the fundamental and instinctual behaviors of all animals. Instinctual behaviors, including the sexual urge, food seeking, and defense territory, are important to the survival of species. Killing other species for food is not considered aggression. Aggression in large carnivores is almost exclusively directed against animals of other species. When it is expressed against animals of like species, as tiger against tiger or wolf against wolf, it is seldom a struggle to the death but rather an elaborately controlled dominance struggle which results in territorial demarcation and mate selection.

There are brain mechanisms not only for hunger, thirst, and reproduction but also for aggression. Anger, rage, and violent behavior in cats, dogs, and primates require the integrity of the hypothalamus. This has been demonstrated by numerous experiments which show that the brain mechanisms for the execution of the fixed-action patterns of rage cease function only with ablation of the hypothalamus. The expression of rage is inhibited by mechanisms in the rhinencephalon including the amygdala on both sides. The inhibitory influences of the forebrain which emanate from the amygdala and the neocortex become dominant when the neocortex is removed. If the neocortex of a cat is removed except for the limbic cortex, the animal is rendered placid. Therefore the neocortex normally lowers the threshold of rage reactions. However, if the amygdala is removed, rage reactions can be set off by a variety of stimuli, including high-pitched sounds. In the absence of cortex such attacks are stereotyped and poorly directed [9]. Electrical stimulation of the lateral hypothalamus in the monkey produces the reaction pattern characteristic of rage [10]. Defensive, aggressive, and fearful reactions can also be elicited by stimulation of the proper areas. Unlike the behavior produced by animals with brain lesions, the behaviors produced by electrical stimulation are well-organized, skillfully performed, and properly directed. In the case when the cortex is intact, therefore, stimulation induces "drive behavior." No electrical discharge suggestive of an epileptic phenomenon is associated with this behavior. Aggressive behavior so induced is not stereotypic motor response and is not a seizure. Destruction of a small part of the posterior hypothalamus renders the animal incapable of rage under any type of stimulation [11].

Given that such programs of behavior exist in the brain and that they can be set off by electrical stimulation and eliminated by destruction of a small part of the posterior hypothalamus, it becomes our task to examine those factors which inhibit, release, and modify these behaviors in the natural state.

It may be argued that human behavior is much more complex than the aggressive reactions seen in lower animals subjected to neurosurgical lesions or driven by electrical stimulation [12]. There are, however, numerous examples of analogous situations described by a number of investigators, including Mark and Ervin in their treatise *Violence and the Brain* [13], and the behaviors observed in certain brain-damaged patients [14, 15], epileptics [16-19], dements, stress reactors [20], the mentally retarded [21], and others [22] which are well-known to neurologists and psychiatrists. It is not behavior in response to a clear stimulus which presents a problem. Behavior which is apparently spontaneous or which occurs without a clear stimulus-response relationship requires explanation. A digression into the nature of instinctual behavior is necessary at this point in order to explain the theoretical scheme used to classify and treat our violent patients.

Eric Kandel defines behavior as all observable processes by which an animal responds to perceived changes in the internal state of its body or the environment [23]. We stated earlier that aggression is an instinctual behavior. Instinctive behavior refers to fixed-action patterns released in certain circumstances. Certainly labeling a particular behavior instinctual does not add much to our understanding of it without some further elucidation of the neuromechanisms and releasing factors involved. Instinctual behaviors are in general just those which require no learning; they are by their very nature genetic. Darwin pointed out that behavior is as specific to species as any other physical characteristic [24]. It is certainly well-known and generally accepted that insects such as honeybees, for instance, have instinctual behavior. This allows them to fly, to seek pollen, to make honey, and to construct hives without any form of learning. Communication between honeybees is also instinctual; it appears to be a ritual of patterned motor activity common to the species. Similar behavior patterns of a much more complex nature are familiar in humans. For example, a newborn baby has the ability to cry for food and suck at the breast. Both these factors serve to induce mothering behavior and lactation. I might go as far as to say that smiling at a baby is so universal and difficult to repress that it too is probably instinctual.

The naturalistic study of instinctual behavior in animals and humans quickly corrects the erroneous view that behavior is primarily reactive or learned. Animals are not like slates upon which the environment writes. Culture is not necessarily some acquired trait which is passed on by learning and experience in a traditional sense to future generations [25]. The universality of the essentials of human behavior may make a more convincing argument for the fundamental biological unity of the human race than the comparisons of bone structure and skin color which divide and unify the species.

Instinctive behavior is described by ethologists as *highly stereotypic* movements (fixed-action patterns) released by specific stimuli [23]. There are lower-order behaviors which consist of elementary and complex types, and higher-order behaviors. The elementary behaviors are further subdivided into reflex acts and fixed acts, while complex is divided into reflex patterns and fixed-action patterns. Higher-order behaviors include courtship, nest building, and communication. If we recall Kandel's definition of behavior as response both to changes in the internal state and to the external world, the situation becomes very complex. Biological rhythms and other changes in the internal state occur normally. Disease states such as depressive psychosis, periodic catatonia, narcolepsy, and depressions may represent exaggerations in naturally occurring homeostatic rhythms [26]. Much confusion has arisen in the study of human behavior because scientists, particularly in America, have historically looked at the modifiable components of behavior while taking for granted or overlooking the invariant stereotypic (and therefore biologically determined) behaviors.

The simpler behaviors, such as reflex patterns, have responses which are smoothly graded to relatively nonspecific stimuli. On the other hand, more complex fixed-action patterns have a form, sequence, and intensity which are relatively independent of the pattern and intensity of the stimulus. Kandel illustrates this by the analogy of the control which the driver of an automobile has over the speed of the car with the gas pedal. The car speed is like a reflex which responds smoothly to the intensity of the stimulus. Pressing the gas pedal makes it go faster, whereas a fixed-action pattern is more like the ringing of a telephone which has the same intensity no matter how urgent the call [23].

Reflex patterns and fixed-action patterns are behaviors which require central programs in the nervous system for their execution. These may be very simple like the monosynaptic arc of a stretch reflex, or they may be quite complex like the mechanisms for locomotion. It has been shown, for instance, that in the cat, the spinal cord contains all the neuromechanisms for coordinated walking movements in response to stimulation. Transecting the spinal cord removes brain control over the cord, but the reflexes and coordinated movements for walking remain at spinal levels [27].

It is not clear at what stage of complexity a reflex pattern becomes a fixed-action pattern, or if there is a fundamental difference other than complexity. Programs no doubt exist in the brain for very complex behaviors. Noam Chomsky states (comparing animals to humans) that "as far as we know, possession of human languages is associated with a specific *type* of mental organization, not simply a higher degree of intelligence" [28]. The mechanism for language may exist in the brain in much the same manner as the well-known visual systems for the perception of lines, angles, and motions reside in the occipital cortex [28]. The profound similarities of human beings of every race and culture in most of the fundamental aspects of behavior and intellectual life suggest that innate programs have a foundation in human anatomy. This does not minimize the contribution of various types of learning, including classical and instrumental conditioning, imprinting, latent learning, and sensory presensitization. It does indicate, however, that human behavior is not entirely malleable.

In general, instinctual behaviors are inhibited by neuromechanisms and then released by stimuli of varying complexity. An important observation by such ethologists as Lorenz and others is that complex behavior sequences can be further broken down into steering or appetitive components, which are followed by a consummatory component [8]. The steering and orienting appetitive components can be changed by learning and conditioning, but the fixed-action pattern components are relatively unchangeable by experience. The fact that there is a genetic basis for much behavior does not imply that everything can be reduced to stimulus response, or that there is no such thing as motivation and free will. The dissection of behavior, however, into those components modifiable by learning and those that are invariant (and genetic) leads to logical maneuvers for control. Again according to Lorenz, "the first prerequisite for rational control over an instinctive behavior pattern is a knowledge of the stimulus situation which releases it" [8].

It is not enough just to examine a particular act of violence. We must examine the internal state of the organism, including aberrations from normal physiology over time, with normal changes in time secondary to biological rhythms. We must look at the meaning of the stimulus in the context of learning and culture, in both group and personal relationships. We must compare an intended result with the actual result of the given aggressive act. We must examine the performance itself for evidence of ritual, fixed-action patterns, or reflex behavior. A human behavior can have so many different meanings (or even multiple etiologies) that cases which appear to be similar have on deeper inspection fundamental differences calling for entirely different remedies.

Aggressive behavior must be analyzed in the same manner that all human behavior is approached in the medical setting. This requires examination of mood, movement, sensation, cognition, and consciousness [29]. In the case of children and adolescents, the problems are more complex because of the educational and developmental issues involved. The interplay of environment, constitution, and development are only the background for the further effects of organic brain disease or psychopathology. In the words of B.F. Skinner, quoted by Kandel, "What is generally not understood by those interested in establishing a neurological basis [of behavior] is that a rigorous description at the level of behavior is necessary for the demonstration of a neurological correlate" [30].

The fundamental problem with most classification schemes of human beings in regard to violent behavior is the use of outcome as a variable. The outcome classifications are not useful for the study of neuromechanisms. Violence is not a diagnosis. In the diagnostic and statistical manual of the APA, DSM-II, explosive personality is described as "behavior pattern characterized by gross outbursts of rage or verbal or physical aggressiveness. These outbursts are strikingly different from the patient's usual behavior and he may be regretful or repentant for them. These patients are generally considered excitable, aggressive, and overresponsive to environmental pressure. It is the intensity of the outbursts and the individual's inability to control them which distinguish this group" [31]. The DSM-II appears to have no classification for people whose behavior is *always* aggressive, violent, and excitable or for the aggressive behavior of the suspicious paranoid person or the driven behavior of the sex criminal. The episodic dyscontrol syndrome as described by Monroe [32] and Bachy-Rita et al. [33] amounts to much the same thing. In European neuropsychiatry the behavior disorders of children are divided into syndromes due to (1) disturbances of psychological development; and (2) frustration-induced disturbances [34]. This classification is useful but is too vague for the interpretation of neuromechanisms. Tupin [35] suggested another diagnostic breakdown which is behaviorally manifested in the following ways.

1. Extreme stimulus sensitivity, such as a hair trigger
2. Inability to reflect on the meaning or intent of the stimulus, that is, lack of introspection to assess accidental or purposeful attack
3. Maximal response with little capacity to modulate the expression of anger

This classification has the virtue of addressing threshold (stimulus sensitivity), intervening variables, and lack of response inhibition.

This chapter now presents a conceptualization scheme and a method of analysis of violent individuals. For population studies of criminal and antisocial behavior, see the reviews of Mednick and Christiansen [36], Reid [37], and Smith [38]. In general, when examining violent behavior, one must keep in mind that the mainstream of thought in current psychiatry and neurology recognizes that the mind is an expression of the functioning of the brain [39] and that the basic mechanisms of learning are being elucidated at the level of single neurons [40] and brain systems [41]. For the rational treatment of violent behavior, one must be aware that psychopharmacology has advanced to the point where precise diagnosis is required.

I propose performing what ethologists call a motivation analysis. This analysis examines stimuli of different significance in each situation and then looks at the component parts of an observed reaction in order to finally evaluate the behavior patterns which follow. If we assume that rage reactions and aggressive behavior depend upon fixed-action patterns which, for their expression, require structures in the lateral hypothalamus which are normally inhibited by the amygdala and disinhibited or released by structures in the forebrain under a variety of stimuli, we may proceed to a different classification. Given the additional assumptions that the steering or appetitive components of the complex behavioral sequences of instinctual behavior can be modified by learning, we may allow for educational and cultural influences, which may have modifying effects on behavior without undermining our ability to dissect and analyze the genetic and more invariant components of a particular violent act. The analysis of any given act of violence would then require examination of at least six components: (1) the stimulus; (2) the stimulus threshold; (3) the steering component; (4) the drive level; (5) the fixed action pattern; and (6) the nature of response inhibition.

Stimuli may be internal or external to the organism and may be modified by a variety of factors. Drive level may be high for one instinctual behavior and low for another, as the drive for sex may take precedence over the drive for food or vice versa. Response inhibition may be high, as in the case of fear induced by a superior force, or low, as in the case of disinhibition produced by intoxication with alcohol or drugs. Each of these variables may change independently in time so that dangerousness may be a moment-to-moment result, not a stable characteristic attached to each individual. Mood, cognition, and brain damage may vary the effect of our six components on different branches in the program and must be evaluated in each individual case at each point in time. If the stimulus threshold, drive level, and response inhibition could each be reduced to a differential equation indicating their value at any given time, the entire ensemble might be expressed as a complex variable of an arbitrary number of dimensions that would predict at any given instant the potential for violence. We are a long way from that degree of precision; however, it is not out of the question to work toward such a goal.

Figure 5-1 presents a binary branching schematic diagram devised to segregate violent patients into groups according to three characteristics. These correspond to the brain mechanisms discussed in the preceding outline of the neurophysiology of aggression. The first branch is the measure of drive level; the second is the stimulus threshold; and the third is response inhibition. Drive level is divided into high or normal, depending upon the physician's estimate in relation to his own experience. When greater degrees of precision are available and uniform scales are devised, perhaps each of the branches may be further elaborated. Stimulus threshold is divided into low and high, based upon the clinician's estimate, as is response inhibition. A stimulus is not specified because it is unique to each case and its meaning will be different to each individual. The steering component of the fixed-action pattern is not categorized because that in general corresponds to the social, environmental, and learning factors which we acknowledge to be extremely important but very difficult to observe and to measure. The drive level, stimulus threshold, and response inhibition are therefore all derived from the historical evaluation of the patient's general responses to specific situations, especially the particular act of violence in question.

The branching program of drive level, stimulus threshold, and response inhibition results in eight categories of violent patients. This is useful for the analysis of any given individual in terms of motivation and criminal responsibility as well as for the planning of therapeutic intervention. Individuals in each of the eight categories will require different treatment regimens. High-drive states may be treated with Medroxyprogesterone acetate (depo-provera) [42], carbamazepine (tegretol) [43, 44, 46], or lithium (lithane) [35-48]. Disorders of inhibition may be treated with carbamazepine, phenothiazines, or behavior therapy [34]. Organic brain syndromes, resulting in low-stimulus threshold or low-response inhibition, may be treated with specific remedies dependent upon their etiology [49].

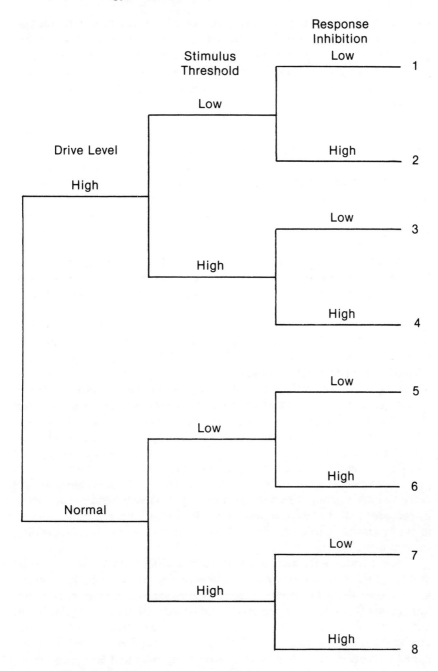

Figure 5-1. Scheme for the Categorization of Violent Patients

Conventional psychiatric disorders such as psychosis and depression also will fall in one of these eight categories and may be treated with their appropriate remedies. Extraordinary external stresses may be treated with social engineering, behavior modification, or sedation with minor tranquilizers or propranolol. In general, minor tranquilizers make impulse disorders worse if they are secondary to some abnormality of the organism [50]. The mechanism of action of lithium carbonate or carbamazepine in impulsive-aggressive behavior is not known. Previous diagnostic criteria have not been useful in the selection of a therapeutic agent.

Selection of subjects for the study of violence deserves some comment, particularly in view of the lack of standard diagnostic criteria. In the case of murder, rape, or assault, we at least have an easily recognizable marker of behavior. The prevalence of violent aggression in our society, however, makes a complete sampling very difficult. Apparently many acts of violence escape the attention of any authority. This leaves us with a bias toward people who are apprehended, in the case of referrals from the legal system, or those who are motivated for change, as 'n the case of self-referred people for whom violence and aggression are in some way dysphoric or egodystonic.

I shall present descriptive data on 128 patients who have in common a history of having performed an act of violent aggression. These patients were referred to the author at the Behavioral Neurology program of the Western Psychiatric Institute and Clinic, University of Pittsburgh School of Medicine. Some were referred from juvenile authorities for evaluation and advice in management. Some were referred by either defense or prosecution attorneys for questions of competence or an insanity defense. Some were sent by penal authorities because they were clearly in need of psychiatric or neurologic attention. Many were self-referred because of feelings or knowledge that self-control was a problem, either as a chief complaint or as part of complaints of depression, paranoia, irritability, or seizures. In any case, we have a group which shares a history of violence and the suspicion by someone that the violence was the result of a pathological process which might be amenable to medical evaluation for the purpose of understanding or treatment.

Each person underwent a complete neurologic examination, one or more psychiatric interviews, psychological testing including IQ assessment, and a Halstead-Reitan battery. Electroencephalograms, computerized axial tomograms (CAT scan) of the brain, and routine laboratory tests of blood and urine were also obtained. Social and developmental histories and behavioral observations from collaterals or custodial authorities were obtained in most cases. These patients were then evaluated according to the above schema and each was assigned to the appropriate group. Clinical and demographic data are presented in tables 5-1 through 5-8.

Group I

Group I is characterized by high-drive level, low-stimulus threshold, and low-response inhibition. There are forty-one patients in this group: fourteen females and twenty-seven males. Three are murderers (7 percent), four sex criminals (10 percent), seven thieves (17 percent), and six drug-abusers (15 percent). Fourteen have a clinical diagnosis of epilepsy, four of the epileptics having normal EEGs and eight of the nonepileptics having abnormal EEGs. Fifteen patients have a diagnosis of brain damage, six of whom are also epileptic. Fourteen patients are psychotic, of whom four are also epileptic; fourteen are mentally retarded. Metabolic disorders include both hypothyroidism and hyperthyroidism, diabetes, and one case of Prader Willi syndrome.

Case Reports

A 27-year-old single white female had an unhappy love affair with an alcoholic psychopath. When she attempted to leave him, he took revenge on her through a series of harassing maneuvers including midnight phone calls, threats against her life, damage to her automobile, and a public beating. She left town to avoid him but he announced publicly that he had taken out a contract on her life. She began to suffer from extreme anxiety, sleep loss, depression, and feelings of hopelessness. She pretended to have a reconciliation with the man and while he slept shot him in the head, killing him. Following that she shot his girlfriend, wounding her, and then took an overdose of sleep medication in a motel room. When a maid noted that the "Do Not Disturb" sign had not been moved in two days, she opened the room with a passkey and found the patient comatose and near death. After medical treatment, the patient was examined and noted to be suffering from an agitated psychotic depression. Treatment with tricyclic antidepressants and hospitalization greatly helped her mental state. She was tried and convicted of first-degree murder.

A 22-year-old female had a lifelong history of poor adaptation and violent aggressive episodes. Despite this, she succeeded in completing school and getting married. She also suffered from dissociative episodes and attacks of extreme fear and anxiety which she described as worse than death. During one of these episodes, she severely cut her upper arm and required surgical attention. This resulted in neuropsychiatric evaluation which revealed a left posterior temporal lobe spike and wave discharge on the EEG. A computed tomogram of the brain was normal, as was her neurologic examination. Treatment with carbamazepine eliminated the dissociative episodes and rage attacks but left her quite depressed. The addi-

Table 5-1
Violent Patients with High Drive Level, Low Stimulus Threshold, and Low Response Inhibition

Group I	L.M.	M.F.	T.G.	L.H.	J.J.	M.J.	S.W.	A.F.	M.D.	A.B.	R.B.	A.B.	K.F.	P.K.	K.F.	T.M.	R.M.	D.T.	C.W.	L.M.	D.C.
Age	9	16	15	15	18	14	17	10	16	18	15	16	17	22	43	10	22	18	18	12	28
Sex	F	M	M	M	M	F	M	M	M	F	M	M	F	F	F	M	M	M	M	M	M
Epilepsy	x		x	x	x		x		x	x			x	x	x	x	x		x		x
Psychosis			x	x	x		x			x							x		x	x	x
Psychopathy						x						x									
EEG abnormal			x		x	x	x	x	x	x			x	x	x		x		x		x
Metabolic abn.					x	x	x								x		x				
Depression							x							x							x
Mania																	x				
Neuro. abn.	x	x						x	x	x			x								
CAT scan abn.		x					x						x								x
Mental retardation		x		x		x					x							x	x		
Assault	x	x	x	x	x	x	x	x	x	x	x	x	x	x	x	x	x	x	x	x	x
Murder				x																	
Sex crime										x											
Vandalism								x			x										
Stealing		x				x		x	x					x							
Drug abuse			x						x	x		x				x					
Brain damage	x						x									x	x	x	x		x

Group I	R.S.	C.P.	K.S.	R.K.	S.P.	M.W.	T.L.	J.S.	G.W.	R.D.	J.C.	R.B.	G.B.	G.C.	J.C.	B.F.	V.N.	S.P.	W.P.	H.S.
Age	27	35	25	18	38	14	17	27	16	33	23	20	28	12	34	72	32	43	25	13
Sex	F	F	F	M	M	M	M	M	M	M	M	M	F	M	M	F	F	F	M	F
Epilepsy			x						x			x		x	x				x	
Psychosis	x				x		x			x						x	x	x		
Psychopathy		x						x												x
EEG abnormal				x		x				x	x	x			x					
Metabolic abn.									x							x				
Depression	x	x						x												
Mania																				
Neuro. abn.				x					x			x	x	x	x					
CAT scan abn.							x			x	x									
Mental retardation	x	x	x	x	x	x	x	x	x	x	x	x	x	x	x	x	x	x		x
Assault	x	x	x	x	x	x	x	x	x	x	x	x	x	x	x	x	x	x		x
Murder	x								x				x	x						
Sex crime						x			x											
Vandalism								x												
Stealing						x									x					
Drug abuse		x																		
Brain damage	x			x	x	x	x	x	x		x	x		x			x	x	x	

Table 5-2
Violent Patients with High Drive Level, Low Stimulus Threshold, and High Response Inhibition

Group II	E.P.	C.C.	J.K.	D.S.	M.D.	R.P.	J.H.	D.M.
Age	30	14	14	30	39	17	22	23
Sex	F	M	M	M	F	M	M	M
Epilepsy		x						
Psychosis				x		x		
Psychopathy					x			
EEG abnormal	x	x	x					
Metabolic abn.			x					
Depression	x						x	
Mania	x							
Neuro. abn.			x					x
CAT scan abn.								
Mental retardation								
Assault	x	x	x	x	x	x		
Murder								
Sex crime							x	x
Vandalism								
Stealing								
Drug abuse								x
Brain damage								

Table 5-3
Violent Patients with High Drive Level, High Stimulus Threshold, and Low Response Inhibition

Group III	R.L.	K.M.	M.S.	L.W.	J.D.	A.D.	T.D.	R.D.	R.W.	J.W.	W.P.	D.N.	A.K.	J.H.	P.C.	M.B.	R.K.	J.M.	L.S.
Age	15	17	15	16	16	18	12	28	26	84	17	16	15	17	23	23	26	25	22
Sex	M	F	M	M	M	M	M	M	M	F	M	M	M	M	F	M	M	M	F
Epilepsy		x						x	x			x			x		x	x	x
Psychosis						x				x						x			
Psychopathy													x						
EEG abnormal		x	x			x		x	x			x					x	x	x
Metabolic abn.					x			x											x
Depression																x			x
Mania																			
Neuro. abn.	x	x	x				x	x	x	x	x								
CAT scan abn.																			
Mental retardation	x	x	x	x											x				
Assault	x	x	x			x	x	x	x	x	x	x		x	x	x	x	x	x
Murder														x					
Sex crime	x		x	x	x	x													
Vandalism						x													
Stealing			x		x	x													
Drug abuse	x	x						x		x	x	x				x	x		
Brain damage							x	x		x	x				x				

Table 5-3 *(continued)*

	E.S.W.	M.E.	R.L.K.	J.B.	T.P.	W.M.	D.M.	J.V.
Age	29	18	17	21	15	54	29	30
Sex	M	M	M	M	M	M	M	M
Epilepsy	x	x						
Psychosis	x		x	x	x	x	x	
Psychopathy	x		x					
EEG abnormal				x		x	x	x
Metabolic abn.								
Depression								x
Mania								
Neuro. abn.	x	x						
CAT scan abn.		x						
Mental retardation		x	x		x			
Assault	x	x	x	x	x			x
Murder	x			x		x	x	
Sex crime					x			
Vandalism							x	
Stealing								
Drug abuse			x			x		x
Brain damage	x	x						

Table 5-4
Violent Patients with High Drive Level, High Stimulus Threshold, and High Response Inhibition

Group IV	M.S.	C.M.	E.M.
Age	23	41	41
Sex	F	M	F
Epilepsy	x		
Psychosis			x
Psychopathy			
EEG abnormal		x	x
Metabolic abn.			
Depression			
Mania			
Neuro. abn.		x	
CAT scan abn.			
Mental retardation			
Assault	x		
Murder	x	x	x
Sex crime			
Vandalism			
Stealing			
Drug abuse	x		
Brain damage	x	x	

Table 5-5
Violent Patients with Normal Drive Level, Low Stimulus Threshold, and Low Response Inhibition

Group V	D.H.	O.J.	E.H.	M.M.	D.S.	W.L.	C.Y.	L.O.	B.M.	B.G.	C.D.	M.J.D.	D.A.	E.B.	D.C.	M.M.	J.N.	B.S.	C.V.
Age	16	13	14	30	26	15	16	38	16	16	26	23	50	31	26	14	22	15	28
Sex	M	M	F	F	M	M	F	M	F	M	F	F	M	M	M	M	M	M	M
Epilepsy			x	x					x	x		x		x	x	x		x	
Psychosis			x	x				x											
Psychopathy																			
EEG abnormal	x		x	x	x	x			x			x		x	x	x		x	
Metabolic abn.												x							
Depression					x														
Mania																			x
Neuro. abn.			x												x				
CAT scan abn.															x				
Mental retardation	x	x		x	x		x	x	x	x		x		x	x	x	x		
Assault	x	x	x	x	x		x	x	x	x	x	x	x	x	x	x	x	x	x
Murder						x													
Sex crime										x									
Vandalism							x		x										
Stealing		x											x						
Drug abuse													x						x
Brain damage	x		x	x		x							x	x	x	x			x

Group I	L.C.	C.A.	D.S.	E.B.	D.P.	L.W.	G.L.	R.C.	W.M.
Age	15	43	21	14	15	16	14	15	41
Sex	M	M	M	M	F	M	M	M	M
Epilepsy									
Psychosis		x							
Psychopathy	x		x		x				x
EEG abnormal							x	x	
Metabolic abn.									
Depression									
Mania									
Neuro. abn.									
CAT scan abn.									
Mental retardation									x
Assault	x				x		x	x	
Murder		x		x					x
Sex crime			x						
Vandalism									
Stealing									
Drug abuse		x				x			x
Brain damage									

Table 5-6
Violent Patients with Normal Drive Level, Low Stimulus Threshold, and High Response Inhibition

Group VI	R.G.	J.B.
Age	16	17
Sex	M	M
Epilepsy		
Psychosis		
Psychopathy		
EEG abnormal		
Metabolic abn.		
Depression		
Mania		
Neuro. abn.		
CAT scan abn.		
Mental retardation		
Assault	x	x
Murder		
Sex crime		
Vandalism		
Stealing	x	
Drug abuse	x	
Brain damage		

Table 5-7
Violent Patients with Normal Drive Level, High Stimulus Threshold, and Low Response Inhibition

Group VII	L.P.	T.T.	J.C.	C.C.	J.L.	A.M.F.	M.A.Z.	D.H.	R.G.	R.F.	G.C.	A.M.	G.T.	B.A.C.	G.F.	R.G.
Age	17	15	14	13	14	37	22	15	57	9	27	45	28	19	18	33
Sex	F	M	M	M	M	F	F	M	M	M	M	M	M	F	M	M
Epilepsy						x				x	x		x			
Psychosis							x							x		
Psychopathy																x
EEG abnormal					x	x	x			x	x	x	x	x		
Metabolic abn.											x	x				
Depression																
Mania																
Neuro. abn.					x	x	x		x	x	x	x	x			
CAT scan abn.									x	x	x	x	x			
Mental retardation																
Assault	x	x	x		x	x	x	x	x	x	x	x	x	x	x	
Murder																x
Sex crime	x		x	x				x								
Vandalism					x					x						
Stealing		x		x	x											
Drug abuse	x			x			x						x		x	
Brain damage		x				x	x		x							

Table 5-8
Violent Patients with Normal Drive Level, High Stimulus Threshold, and High Response Inhibition

Group VIII	S.W.	R.B.	W.S.
Age	15	16	15
Sex	M	M	M
Epilepsy			
Psychosis			
Psychopathy			
EEG abnormal			
Metabolic abn.			
Depression	x		
Mania			
Neuro. abn.			x
CAT scan abn.			
Mental retardation			x
Assault			
Murder			x
Sex crime	x		
Vandalism			
Stealing			
Drug abuse			x
Brain damage			

tion of lithium resulted in improvement in her mood and she has had a good treatment result.

Group II

Group II is characterized by high-drive level, low-stimulus threshold, and high inhibition. There are eight members: six males and two females. There are no murderers, and only one epileptic (12.5 percent).

Case Reports

This 22-year-old male student was referred by his defense attorney after being charged with rape and assault with a deadly weapon. Following a series of arguments, the patient had moved out of his girlfriend's apartment where he had been living for the previous six months. The core of their disagreement was his desire for clarity, finality, and security in their living together arrangement, but he was frustrated by his girlfriend's ambivalent, vague, and arbitrary manner of relating. The patient came from a macho culture and a rather sheltered and naive upbringing. This girlfriend was his first, but she was a rather experienced older woman. During their separation, he decided to settle the matter by arriving at her apartment with a loaded pistol. He gave the gun to his girlfriend with the instructions that she should either promise to love him or she should kill him. She put the gun aside, and they proceeded to have sexual intercourse. The following day, while at a local hospital with a bout of gastroenteritis, the girlfriend reported that she had been raped. The patient was examined in jail, where he appeared to be depressed and distraught. No evidence was found for either a psychiatric disorder or a neurologic disease. The rape charge was dropped in return for a guilty plea on a charge of carrying a dangerous weapon without a permit.

A 26-year-old married graduate student was referred by a marriage counselor because of violent aggressive behavior toward his wife. These were characterized by episodes of violent rage lasting for only several seconds. They appeared to be relatively unprovoked. Often the patient would have a feeling of "butterflies in the stomach" prior to the episode. After the rage, the patient would feel tired and would have buzzing in his ears and appear to be depressed and remorseful. He also suffered from episodes of depression lasting up to six hours which appeared to be unrelated to external events. He had medicated himself with alcohol and marijuana, reporting that these helped his functioning. He denied blackouts, seizures, fainting, or unconsciousness of any kind. An EEG, neurologic examination, and CAT scan of the brain were all normal. The patient was treated with carbamazepine, 200 mg twice a day, resulting in a blood level in the therapeutic range. He reported that his mood was improved, his thinking was more organized, and he was no longer interrupted by extraneous rapid shifts of mood or anger.

Group III

Group III is characterized by high-drive level, high-stimulus threshold, and low-response inhibition. There are twenty-seven members: twenty-three males and four females. Five are murderers (18.5 percent) and ten are epileptic (37 percent), including one of the murderers.

Case Reports

A 29-year-old prison inmate was accused of stabbing a fellow prisoner with a table knife in front of a large number of witnesses. The attack was described as savage and mutilating. Following the killing, he stood apparently in a daze and refused to drop the knife for several seconds afterward. When apprehended by guards, the knife fell from his hand and he was led quietly away.

On examination, he was noted to be a short man with scoliosis and a congenital deformity of the lower extremities resulting in a several inch difference in leg length. On mental status and interview, he revealed an elaborate delusional paranoid system involving the black Muslim religion, food and drug idiosyncracies, and direct communication with Allah. He was rambling, vague, circumstantial, tangential, and demonstrated an inappropriate effect. His history revealed epileptic seizures treated with Dilantin. An EEG, on Dilantin, was read as equivocal, without clear epileptic discharge. The patient was diagnosed as suffering from a psychotic organic brain syndrome with epilepsy. Treatment with phenothiazines and anticonvulsants was recommended. He was convicted of murder.

A 30-year old male was neuropsychiatrically evaluated following being charged with communicating threats of murder to his wife, her family, and members of the city government and police force. On examination, a history of kidney stones and synthetic narcotic and analgesic abuse was obtained. He was taking minor tranquilizers and sedatives for sleep. The patient related a series of financial and legal difficulties complicated by his increasing frustration and depression. The patient appeared to be clinically depressed, but he refused to be withdrawn from psychotropic medication for evaluation and treatment.

Group IV

Group IV is characterized by high-drive level, high-stimulus threshold, and high-response inhibition. There are three members: two females and a male. One is psychotic and two are brain-damaged. There are two murderers (66.7 percent) and one epileptic.

Case Report

A 30-year-old woman with a history of auditory hallucinations of distant voices talking to each other was charged with a stabbing death of her common-law husband. On the day of the killing, she was drinking her usual beer with her landlady in the kitchen. Her common-law husband went into the bedroom and when he returned, she grabbed a kitchen knife, stabbed him, and fled the house. On subsequent questioning, she reported that she suddenly had the thought that he had gone to the bedroom for a gun and that he was going to kill her. She claimed that she was merely trying to escape when he got in the way and was stabbed. Subsequent psychiatric examination revealed an IQ of 80 and a history of psychotic episodes under stress. She was convicted of murder and sentenced to continued psychiatric treatment.

Group V

Group V is characterized by normal-drive level, low-stimulus threshold, and low-response inhibition. There are twenty-eight members: twenty-one males and seven females. Four are murderers (14.3 percent), nine have epilepsy (32 percent), and thirteen have abnormal EEGs.

Case Reports

A 28-year-old policeman suffered from headaches and anxiety attacks accompanied by aggressive outbursts so severe that he had to be restrained by fellow police officers on one occasion. Physical and neurological examinations were normal but the EEG was noted to be low voltage and fast, without the presence of alpha activity. Further history revealed a pattern of migraine and hyperventilation. Treatment with propranolol was instituted, resulting in a remission of all symptoms.

A 15-year-old boy was referred because of aggressive behavior and school difficulties. His history included fire setting, cruelty to animals, and somnambulism, but no enuresis. Medical history revealed the usual childhood diseases and one episode of unconsciousness following a head injury, caused by a blow to the occiput with a brick. A trial of carbamazepine was ineffective. After being placed on a therapeutic dose of lithium, his school performance and reports of behavior showed a dramatic improvement.

Group VI

Group VI is characterized by normal-drive level, low-stimulus threshold, and high-response inhibition. There are two members, neither being a murderer or an epileptic.

Case Report

A 16-year-old male was referred for evaluation of an impulse control disorder characterized by excessive reactivity to ordinary situations. Neurologic examination was unremarkable. The EEG was abnormally slow and disorganized for age, a finding described as "immaturity." The patient was sent to a juvenile institution before treatment could be initiated, and he was lost to follow-up.

Group VII

Group VII is characterized by normal-drive level, high-stimulus threshold, and low-response inhibition. There are sixteen members: twelve males and four females. One is a murderer (6 percent), four are epileptics (25 percent), and eight have abnormal EEGs (50 percent).

Case Reports

A 37-year-old white female high school teacher was sent from the state hospital for evaluation of episodes of regressive psychotic violent behavior which were apparently exacerbated by or at least not ameliorated by treatment with phenothiazines or antidepressants. Her neurologic examination and EEG were normal. Psychologic testing revealed a verbal IQ of 118 and performance IQ of only 92. No evidence of peculiar ideation, delusions, idiosyncratic responses, or any other evidence of a thought disorder was elicited. When she was hospitalized for observation it was noted on one occasion that she was staring off to the right, smacking her lips, and opening and closing her right hand in an apparent automatic manner. Treatment with Dilantin resulted in marked improvement followed by a return to her normal activities. Six subsequent EEGs were normal prior to demonstrating a temporal lobe spike and wave discharge on the seventh.

A 28-year-old white male was seen twelve years after a severe head injury suffered in a motorcycle accident. He had made a good recovery from hemiplegia and slight aphasia, but over the past few years had suffered from violent outbursts and increasing paranoid ideation with delusions about a supposed sexual affair between his mother and his sister. During that period, his physical condition was also deteriorating. On the assumption that this might represent Dilantin toxicity, his medication was changed to carbamazepine. The patient's mood improved, but the gait difficulty and paranoid ideation persisted. Computerized tomography and isotope cisternography documented the presence of communicating hydrocephalus. This was treated with ventriculoperitoneal shunting. Following the surgery, the patient's gait was remarkably improved and some clearing in his mental state was noted, but a depressive component became more noticeable. Treatment with a monoamine oxidase inhibitor, tranylcypromine (Parnate), 20 mg twice a day was followed by a disappearance of paranoia and improvement in mood.

Group VIII

Group VIII is characterized by normal-drive level, high-stimulus threshold, and high-response inhibition. There are three males in this group, one murderer (33 percent), but no epileptics.

Case Report

A 16-year-old male with a long history of poor adaptation and unsuccessful treatment by a Child Guidance Clinic was charged with attempting to strangle a female classmate. The patient claimed to have been invited into the home of the young girl in question while soliciting door-to-door for a charity. He claimed that nothing other than conversation transpired. Later that day, the girl's father came home and discovered that she had been beaten about the head and shoulders, leaving severe bruises. The girl claimed that the patient had attempted to rape and strangle her. The patient claimed that the girl had had a fight with her boyfriend and falsely accused him to prevent suspicion from falling upon her boyfriend. Psychiatric examination, psychologic testing, neurologic examination, and EEG showed no abnormality but subsequent investigation revealed that the patient had a previous charge of assault and rape which had been dropped for lack of evidence. No treatment was undertaken.

In the sample of 128 assaultive patients there are 7 vandals, 20 sex criminals, 16 murderers. Three of the murderers were epileptic, but two of the epileptics had normal EEGs at the time of testing, and four not diagnosed as epileptic had nonfocal abnormal EEGs. Five of the murderers had abnormal neurologic examinations, including all three epileptics. Four individuals were brain-damaged and four were retarded. Three of the psychotic murderers had EEG abnormalities, and nine were psychotic. Five killers were diagnosed as psychopathic. All the groups contained killers except groups II and VI, which are characterized by high-response inhibition.

Summary

There are no large studies of the epidemiology of violent behavior which include a thorough neuropsychiatric evaluation. Because the patients in this study were referred to a medical setting, it is not surprising that 30 percent of them were found to be epileptic and that 45.3 percent had EEG abnormalities. This statistic and the finding of 23.4 percent with neurological abnormalities and 9.4 percent with abnormalities demonstrable on the CAT scan is higher than that found in other studies [22]. A diagnosis of brain damage was found in 29.7 percent, mental retardation in 25 percent, and metabolic abnormalities in 10.9 percent. One-quarter of the sample was diagnosed as psychotic. It may be predicted that a thorough evaluation of all the inhabitants of a prison would reveal similar findings.

We have no treatment for psychopathy or criminality at present; therefore, offenders with this diagnosis are best kept in prison or in some other form of structured behavior-modification setting. It is clear that many of the psychiatrically and neurologically disordered offenders do not meet the various contradictory requirements for a court finding of innocence by reason of insanity, but they nevertheless require appropriate medical treatment. On the other hand, many of the patients who may be innocent by reason of insanity also require confinement and treatment to prevent harm to themselves or to other members of society.

The current trend in progressive legal circles is to separate the legal finding of guilt or innocence of a particular act from the psychiatric and neurologic determination of criminal responsibility and motivation. The question, then, is not which dangerous person should be punished and which should be released, but rather which form of treatment and social restraint may be applied for the benefit of both the individual and society around him [51].

The data here presented suggest that large numbers of aggressive people suffer from fairly specific disorders which may be related to known brain pathology or psychiatric syndromes. The fallacy that crime is caused by slums or poverty or oppression of minority groups is exposed as a fraud when the individual violent person is closely examined [52]. A rational system of criminal justice must take into account the real causes of aggressive behavior which will not disappear, even if a social utopia were realized. This should not discourage social reformers from improving living conditions and working for economic justice, but rather it should allow them to discern that point at which human nature rather than human mismanagement is to blame for the ills of society.

References

1. Chinlund, S. 1980. Myths about prisons. *The New York Times*, 10 February, p. 21.
2. Price, H.B. 1980. Let the punishment fit the criminal. *The New York Times*, 19 June, p. 18.
3. Footlick, J.K.; Monroe, S.; Kasindorf, M.; Reese, M.; and Camper, D. 1978. Insanity on trial. *Newsweek*, 8 May, pp. 109-112.
4. Greenspan, E.L. 1978. The role of the psychiatrist in the criminal justice system. *Can Psychiatr Assoc J* 23:137-142.
5. Steadman, H.J. 1980. Insanity acquittals in New York State, 1965-1978. *Am J Psychiatry* 137:321-326.
6. Peszke, M.A. 1980. Competency to stand trial: An abridgement of due process. *Hosp Community Psychiatry* 31:132-133.
7. APA Task Force Report. 1974. *Clinical aspects of the violent individual.* American Psychiatric Association.
8. Lorenz, K. 1977. *On aggression.* New York: Bantam Books.
9. Bard, P. The hypothalamus. In Mountcastle, V.B., ed. *Medical physiology*, vol. 2. St Louis: C.V. Mosby, pp. 1847-1851.
10. Hofstatter, L., and Girgis, M. 1973. Depth electrode investigations of the limbic system with radiostimulation, electrolytic lesions, and histochemical techniques. In Laitinen C.V. and Livingston, K.E. *Surgical approaches in psychiatry.* Baltimore: Univ. Park Press, pp. 224-236.
11. Nadvornik, P.; Pogady, J.; and Sramka, M. 1973. The results of stereotactic treatment of the aggressive syndrome. In Laitinen, L.V. and Livingston, K.E. *Surgical approaches in psychiatry.* Baltimore: Univ. Park Press. pp. 125-128.
12. Pinel, J.P.J.; Treit, D.; and Rovner, L.I. 1977. Temporal lobe aggression in rats. *Science* 197:1088-1089.
13. Mark, V.H. and Ervin, F.R. 1970. *Violence and the brain.* New York: Harper & Row.

14. Elliott, F.A. 1977. Propranolol for the control of belligerent behavior following acute brain damage. *Ann Neurol* 1:489-491.
15. Krynicki, V.E. 1978. Cerebral dysfunction in repetitively assaultive adolescents. *J Nerv Ment Dis* 166:59-67.
16. Gunn, J. 1978. Epileptic homicide: A case report. *Br J Psychiatry* 132: 511-513.
17. Cope, R.V., and Donovan, W.M. 1979. A case of insane automatism? *Br J Psychiatry* 135:574-575.
18. Lewis, D.O. 1976. Delinquency, psychomotor epileptic symptoms, and paranoid ideation: A triad. *Am J Psychiatry* 133:1395-1398.
19. Marsh, G.G. 1978. Neuropsychological syndrome in a patient with episodic howling and violent motor behavior. *J Neurol Neurosurg Psychiatry* 41:366-369.
20. Arnold, L.; Fleming, R.; and Bell, V. 1979. The man who became angry once: A study of overcontrolled hostility. *Can J Psychiatry* 24: 762-766.
21. Goetzl, U.; Grunberg, F.; and Berkowitz, B. Lithium carbonate in the management of hyperactive aggressive behavior of the mentally retarded. *Compr Psychiatry* 18:599-606.
22. Washbrook, R.A.H. 1977. The psychiatrically ill prisoner. *Lancet* pp. 1302-1303.
23. Kandel, E.R. 1976. *Cellular basis of behavior: An introduction to behavioral neurobiology.* San Francisco: W.H. Freeman.
24. Darwin, C. 1860. *On the origin of species by means of natural selection.* New York: Appleton.
25. Fabrega, H. 1977. Culture, behavior and the nervous system. *Ann Rev Anthropol* 6:419-455.
26. National Institute of Mental Health. 1940. *Biological rhythms in psychiatry and medicine.* Washington, D.C.: U.S. Government Printing Office.
27. Mountcastle, V.E., ed. 1968. *Medical physiology*, vol. 2. Saint Louis: C.V. Mosby, p. 1745.
28. Chomsky, N. 1972. *Lanuage and mind.* New York: Harcourt Brace Jovanovich.
29. Merikangas, J.R. 1977. Common neurologic syndromes in medical practice. *Med Clin N Am* 61:723-736.
30. Skinner, B.F. 1938. *The behavior of organisms: An experimental analysis.* New York: Appleton-Century.
31. American Psychiatric Association. 1968. Diagnostic and statistical manual of mental disorders (DSM-II).
32. Monroe, R.R. 1975. Anticonvulsants in the treatment of aggression. *J Nerv Ment Dis* 160:119-126.
33. Bach-y-Rita G.; Lion, J.R.; Climent, C.E.; and Ervin, F.R. 1971. Episodic dyscontrol: A study of 130 violent patients. *Am J Psychiatry* 127:1473-1478.

34. Nissen, G. 1976. Behavioral disorders in children and the possibilities offered by drugs in their treatment. In Birkmayer, W., ed. *Epileptic seizures, behavior and pain*. Baltimore: Univ. Park Press, pp. 230-242.
35. Tupin, J.P. 1978. Usefulness of lithium for aggressiveness. *Am J Psychiatry* 135:1118.
36. Mednick, S.A. and Christiansen, K.O. 1977. *Biosocial bases of criminal behavior*. New York: Gardner.
37. Reid, W.H. 1978. *The psychopath*. New York: Brunner/Mazel.
38. Smith, R.J. 1978. *The psychopath in society*. New York: Academic Press.
39. Kandell, E.R. 1979. Psychotherapy and the single synapse. *N Engl J Med* 301:1028-1037.
40. Castellucci, V., and Kandel, E.R. 1976. Presynaptic facilitation as a mechanism for behavioral sensitization. *Aplysia Sci* 19:1176-1178.
41. Edelman, G.M., and Mountcastle, V.B. 1978. *The mindful brain*. Cambridge: MIT.
42. Blumer, D., and Migeon, C. 1976. Hormone and hormonal agents in the treatment of aggression. *J Nerv Ment Dis* 160:127-137.
43. Puente, R.M. 1976. The use of carbamazepine in the treatment of behavioral disorders in children. In Birkmayer, W., ed. *Epileptic seizures, behavior and pain*. Baltimore: Univ. Park Press, 243-252.
44. VanKrevelen, D.A.; Maresca, A.; and Dijkstra, M.S. 1970. Evaluation of tegretol in the treatment of behavior disorders in children. *Acta Paedopsychiatr* 37:222-234.
45. Remschmidt, H. 1976. The psychotropic effect of carbamazepine in nonepileptic patients with particular reference to problems posed by clinical studies in children with behavioral disorders. In Birkmayer, W., ed. *Epileptic seizures, behavior and pain*. Baltimore: Univ. Park Press, pp. 253-258.
46. Tunks, E.R., and Dermer, S.W. 1977. Carbamazepine in the dyscontrol syndrome associated with limbic system dysfunction. *J Nerv Ment Dis* 164:56-63.
47. Marini, J.L., and Sheard, M.H. 1977. Antiaggressive effect of lithium ion in man. *Acta Psychiatry Scand* 55:269-286.
48. Sheard, M.H.; Marini, J.L.; Bridges, M.A.; and Wagner, E. 1976. The effect of lithium on impulsive aggressive behavior in man. *Am J Psychiatry* 133:1409-1413.
49. Lishman, W.A. 1978. *Organic psychiatry*. Oxford: Blackwell.
50. Lion, J. 1979. Benzodiazepines in the treatment of aggressive patients. *J Clin Psychiatry* 40:70-71.
51. Gaylin, W. 1977. Up the river, but why? *The New York Times*, 18 December, p. 8.
52. Adams, V. 1977. Causes of crime, maybe. *The New York Times*, 8 December, p. 8.

6 Neurology of Nonverbal and Emotional Behavior

Robert E. Miller

You are standing on a subway platform late at night. The handful of passengers from an arriving train have hurried on their way to the street as though they feared to linger in this isolated place. Suddenly, you see a young man staggering down the platform toward you, muttering and laughing as he approaches. What are you going to do? Well, most of us will feel rather apprehensive, alert, and aroused. We would not know just what to expect from the stranger but we would be sure that we would rather have nothing to do with him at all. Is he drunk? Will he demand money and perhaps threaten us if we do not give it to him? Is he apt to pass out and fall near the tracks so that we will have to accept responsibility for his safety? Or is he the victim of a progressive and disabling disease which makes it impossible for him to control his gait or his euphoria and who is deserving of our compassion and considerate help? Most people in this situation, I suspect, would not wait to find out just what the trouble might be. They would seek to avoid contact with the stranger at all costs, moving away as he approached so that a safe distance was maintained, access to an escape route to the street preserved, and with movement toward any other individuals who might arrive on the scene. We might relate this incident to others at a later time with the acknowledgment that we were scared.

One of the essential features of a society is that its members can make reliable predictions about the expectable behaviors of others in the group. It is vital that we have confidence that our associates will treat us with familiarity and warmth, that strangers whom we pass on the street will not suddenly turn and assault us, and that those with whom we deal in our everyday commerce will observe the common courtesies of social intercourse. It is upsetting and alarming when an individual behaves in unpredictable ways and we cannot determine what his next action might be. We are annoyed and discomfited when a drunk staggers up to us on the street and attempts to initiate a conversation with us. A secretary who bursts into tears and rushes from the room leaves her employer with a feeling of acute embarrassment and helplessness. The guest in a restaurant who gets into a loud and angry argument with the waiter may spoil the meal for all the other diners and elicit a determination not to dine again at that place in the future.

The individual in the social group must understand and conform to the rules of appropriate social conduct so that others will know what to expect

187

from him and, conversely, he must behave in a manner that permits others to recognize that he expects certain behaviors from them. How are these complex and dynamic relationships conveyed from one individual to the other? In the most obvious way, we acquire the accoutrements of a social role which help to define our position in the social fabric in ways that are immediately obvious to others. The uniform is a clear example. The police officer wears a uniform so that he is instantly recognizable as an authority figure and that he may take actions which would be impermissible for the ordinary citizen. In fact, the police officer's uniform is so identifiable that it may become a detriment to the investigation and apprehension of criminals, so the officer may have to adopt the guise of an ordinary citizen (plainclothes) to perform effectively. It is, of course, obvious that there are many kinds of "uniform" that facilitate predictions about the behaviors which may be expected from the wearer; physicians, business executives, society matrons, Krishnas, and motorcycle gangs wear apparel which identifies them to strangers and which conditions the kinds of social interactions that can be expected to be forthcoming. Other kinds of visible accoutrements can alter expected social relationships. Casts, braces, slings, crutches, wheelchairs, white canes and dark glasses, hearing aids, and the like are announcements that the individual is to some extent suffering from a disability and may be expected to behave differently than do normals. Special considerations may have to be extended to accommodate the pace and limitations of the afflicted person and the potential social partners will be expected to behave in an especially solicitous and compassionate manner, whether the afflicted person desires it or not.

While the external appearance of an individual provides some clues about the person and what we may reasonably expect from him, it is not enough information to be certain that a satisfactory social relationship will ensue. We need to know much more about him. Is he ill or well? What is his current mood state? Is he intellectually competent or dull? Does he feel friendly or antagonistic toward us? Is his present behavior compatible with his past performances or are there subtle signs that he has changed in some important way?

Much of the information relevant to the prediction of another's behavior in a social situation is communicated through nonverbal channels which accompany and modify verbal productions. Movements, gestures, gait, gazes, smiles, head nods, and the like provide the subtle cues which reveal that partners recognize a social relationship, have a commitment to it, are attending to the content of the interaction, and have some emotional reactions to the exchange. In 1927 Sapir described nonverbal communication as "an elaborate and secret code that is written nowhere, known by none, and understood by all" [40]. That description still applies today though social scientists have begun to identify some behaviors that are critical to the development and maintenance of social relationships. Most of us, fortunately, perform the subtle and delicate behavioral actions that facilitate and coordinate social exchanges with others without conscious or continual self-monitoring and, similarly, we are exquisitely sensitive to the nonverbal nuances of others even though we may not be able to specify exactly what actions have led to alterations in our own perceptions of the course of the exchange.

The importance of nonverbal behavior is most obvious in the breach. When a partner fails to meet our gaze and consistently looks over our shoulder, we may conclude that he is not interested in the current relationship and will terminate the conversation shortly, and we may feel decidedly miffed by his inattention. Similarly, it is uncomfortable when someone moves too close to us during a conversation or stares at us for too long a period of time. Frequently, one makes the attribution that a nonverbal deviant is queer, rude, crazy, or possibly dangerous [14].

Scientific evidence reveals that acceptable interpersonal behaviors are rather closely prescribed and that they must occur within specific temporal patterns of action and reaction for both parties in a social interaction to feel comfortable and easy with each other [2, 47]. It is also recognized that fluency in this behavioral "language" consists of two mutually imperative skills: the ability to transmit clear and appropriate expressive messages and sensitivity in decoding the subtle behaviors of the social partner. A deficit in either element will produce a social deficit in the individual.

What has nonverbal behavior to do with neurology? The very subtle and complex interchange of behavioral nuance which subserves successful social function depends in large measure on an intact and integrated central nervous system (CNS). Even minor disturbances such as ingestion of a few ounces of ethanol, excessive fatigue, or mental preoccupation can elicit noticeable deficits in nonverbal performance while more serious neurological disease may result in permanent and catastrophic impairment. The changes may be of three types: failure of expression such that adequate behaviors are either obscured by behavioral "noise" or are altogether absent as in the case of paralyses; failure of reception where the individual may be unable to detect the expressions of social partners; and basic changes in the affective responses of subjects which are reflected as amplified, damped, or inappropriate nonverbal expressions. Changes in any of these spheres of behavioral performance will be disruptive to the individual's social relationships within the family and the community at large and, additionally, may provide important data for an early differential diagnosis of a neurological deficit. One would want to determine the specifics of the behavioral deficit, the duration of the disturbance, and the stimulus conditions which affect the presentation of the symptom. Clearly, these data are extremely useful to the clinical neurologist and are often noted in neurology texts as vital diagnostic signs. Disorders of the CNS often distort the expression or reception of nonverbal communications and in some cases produce affect disturbances which are manifested in inappropriate expressive displays. The neurologist must be keenly attuned to the shading and pacing of expression which betray damage and dysfunction to the intricate social signals which flow from the patient throughout the examination. He must be a nonverbal expert.

The problem for the patient does not resolve simply because the neurologist has identified a pathophysiological process which provides a reasonable explanation for the aberrant behavior. Even though it is manifestly demonstrable that the individual is in no way responsible for the flaws in his performance, there is a persisting social cost for behavioral deviance. Goffman [18] discussed the concept of stigmatization of the person who is perceived to have either a moral or physical affliction. He analyzes the situation of the "discredited" individual who has a present and visible defect, as would be the case of a stroke victim, and that of the discreditable person, who has a secret liability which may become known to others under the right set of circumstances (for example, epilepsy). The discredited individual elicits a variety of nonnormal social behaviors from others according to the kind and extent of his perceived handicap. If the flaw is interpreted as a moral failure (alcoholism or criminality), the individual is likely to be treated with coldness and contempt by his normal peers; but if the affliction is seen as a physical malady, the person will be regarded with considerable ambivalence by the social group. In our society there is a strong social norm to treat the crippled or ill individual with special compassion and sympathetic help but we feel so uncomfortable and uneasy in the presence of disorder that we cannot admit the afflicted into the normal social group. Goffman also points out that the social stigmatization which accrues to the deviate is often generalized to intact individuals who are in the social presence of the individual. Thus the person who pushes the wheelchair of a palsied patient or guides a blind individual to his seat at a concert may perceive that he himself attracts unusual attention and unwelcome solicitation. This guilt-by-association phenomenon may make the normal individual somewhat reluctant to accompany a defective person in public places and may strain friendships.

There has been some interesting research on the reactions of intact individuals to the physically disabled. Richardson et al. [37] asked groups of 10-to-11-year-olds to rank their preferences for a set of standardized pictures. The pictures were of (1) a child with no physical handicap, (2) a child with crutches and a leg brace, (3) a child in a wheelchair, (4) a child with the left hand amputated, (5) a child with a facial disfigurement, and (6) an obese child. In every group of children that ranked the pictures the order of preference was exactly the same ($p < .001$). The preference was identical for subjects of various racial groups, socioeconomic status, and urban versus rural background. In all groups the order of preference agreed with the listed order, that is, the normal picture was preferred above all others and the picture of the obese child was least preferred. Even samples of crippled children obtained from a summer camp for the handicapped conformed to the same rank ordering. To determine the subjects' own explanations for their preference rankings, one group of twenty children were asked to explain why they had chosen as they did. Although they initially denied that they had weighted the physical appearances of the children in the pictures, when pressed they admitted that they were "uncomfortable" and "didn't know what to say" to a handicapped person.

Robert Kleck and colleagues at Dartmouth reported a series of clever experiments on the social effects of a physical handicap. In the first experiment undergraduates were recruited to serve in an opinion survey [26]. For the interview session they were presented with either a nonhandicapped interviewer or one seated in a wheelchair. The interviewer was an intact student who played the role of normal and handicapped for half of the subjects. Contrary to expectations, the subjects talked longer to the handicapped interviewer than to the normal one ($p < .02$). The investigators had anticipated that the subjects would terminate the conversation with the handicapped interviewer sooner because of social anxiety or discomfort, but in retrospect they hypothesized that subjects had tried to give the crippled confederate a good interview and thus prolonged the session. It was found that, relative to those subjects interviewed by the normal person, subjects in the handicap situation tended to report that they had fewer friends, went to fewer parties, and claimed that appearance, sports, and dating were less important to them. Finally, subjects who believed that the interviewer was crippled rated him as more liked than did subjects in the control group ($p < .01$). This study revealed that there was a systematic bias in the revealed behaviors and attitudes of subjects who were attempting to be kind to a handicapped person. In a second experiment the disability of the interviewer was augmented by the use of a special wheelchair which made it appear that the interviewer was a left-leg amputee [26]. In this study the subject was attached through a pair of electrodes on the hand to a psychogalvanometer to obtain a measure of general physiological arousal during the interview. Subjects were interviewed by the confederate appearing either as intact or as an amputee. The interview schedule consisted of questions on how the subject formed impressions of others, how he felt about the importance of academic achievement, attitudes toward sports and religion, and how important he believed physical appearance was in his judgments of others. Subjects in the handicap interview were much more physiologically aroused than those in the control condition when they were introduced to the interviewer. Those exposed to the amputee condition also displayed consistent distortion in their expressed attitudes in the direction of giving answers which would seem to make the crippled interviewer more comfortable ($p < .01$). Finally, a relationship was found between the discomfort felt in the interview situation and the length of the interview, with the most uncomfortable subjects giving the shortest interview.

Kleck [24] extended his studies to determine precisely which behaviors exhibited by subjects interacting with a handicapped person differed from those in the normal social interaction. Using the wheelchair to simulate an amputee, subjects were interviewed about themselves and their attitudes toward academics and sports. In a second session they were interviewed by a nonhandicapped individual. Each interview was filmed. Once again the hypothesis that subjects would attempt to minimize anxiety in the interpersonal situation by systematically distorting their verbalized attitudes toward sports and academic achievement was confirmed ($p < .01$ for sports). In additional important findings, subjects displayed significant motoric inhibition when listening to the handicapped interviewer speak ($p < .02$) and showed longer durations of mutual eye contact when listening to the disabled as compared with the nonhandicapped interviewer ($p < .02$). Subjects had a decidedly positive bias in their postinterview ratings of the interviewer in the handicapped as compared with the control situation. The handicapped interviewer was rated as more friendly, intelligent, and warm than the nonhandicapped ($p < .02$). This result was found even though the study had been carefully designed to ensure that the two confederates played the roles of normal and handicapped for exactly half of the subjects in a counterbalanced order. This finding presumably reflects the general norm in our culture that we are to be especially kind and considerate to the handicapped. Finally, however, the subjects reported significantly more emotional discomfort when interacting with the disabled interviewer than with the normal one [23].

Some handicaps are only sporadically visible to others, such as epilepsy. These are the discreditable persons which Goffman considered. They are placed in an extremely discomfortable situation with strangers, not knowing whether they should "pass" as normals or delicately disclose their infirmity before it manifests itself. These afflictions may pass unnoticed for some time and the subject enjoy normal social relationships but on disclosure of the stigma, impairment in social interactions may be great. In a study of the effect of various social stigmas on the physical distance between interactants, Kleck and colleagues [25] asked subjects to place a figure on a scale to represent the distance that they would use in interaction with a liked professor, a friend, a blind person, a black, a stranger, an amputee, an epileptic, a mental patient, and a disliked professor. The results indicated that students were very discriminating, ranking the targets in the order listed above and with highly significant differences between categories. The rankings demonstrated that the visible defects of blindness and amputation were more tolerable in terms of physical approach than were the less visible defects of epilepsy and mental illness. In a second phase of this study subjects were placed in a social situation with a person identified as an epileptic or in a control situation where the disease was not mentioned. Subjects with an epileptic partner placed their chairs at a greater distance from the person than in the control situation ($p < .02$). There were no significant differences in the amount of eye contact in the epileptic and control dyads.

These studies demonstrate that certain kinds of diseases invoke a social penalty above and beyond the physical pain and suffering of the disorder. While patients with ulcers, hypertension, diabetes, and coronary disease certainly have physical problems, they are at least treated socially as normal persons. But the neurological patient not only must cope with the direct sequelae of his disease but also suffers from the embarrassment and social discomfort attendant upon his affliction. Abnormal movements, facial expressions, and disorders of gait may elicit unwanted attention and social avoidance, especially in public places where strangers are encountered. The presence of visible abnormality of behavior does affect the relationships with others by making the nonverbal messages more obscure and less predictable and by imposing upon the viewer the requirement that he not pay too obvious attention to the defect. It is considered rude and socially inappropriate to look at or comment on the handicap of another, particularly a stranger. The social partner who observes an impropriety in the performer is constrained to "civil inattention" of the lapse, pretending that it never happened or was not noticed [17]. Most parents are acutely discomforted when their child comments openly on the physical appearance or the behavioral faux pas of a guest. There is just no way to paper over such a lack of civil inattention and the parties must accommodate to an embarrassing situation as best they can. The neurological patient may be so afflicted that the constraints upon social partners become intolerable, and they then may simply avoid further interactions with the patient. It is easy to see how the patient, conscious of the discomfort of normals and their unease in relationships with him, might progressively constrict his excursions into their world, becoming more and more isolated from the community at large. Despite the fact that many seriously handicapped individuals, through hard work and great ability, have achieved much in accomplishment and recognition, it cannot be denied that the road to occupational and social success is extraordinarily difficult for the person with a visible and stigmatizing defect.

Before we turn our attention to the varieties of nonverbal deficit which may be encountered in a neurological patient, let us consider briefly the results of controlled experiments in animals. The human has a unique advantage over other animals in that the nonverbal channel of communication is supplemented, though not supplanted, by a rich and flexible verbal capacity. Usually, it is only during the first months of life that the human subject is restricted exclusively to nonverbal modes of communication. But behavioral cues continue to play an indispensable role in the modulation and augmentation of spoken exchange throughout the lifetime of the individual, especially in conveying emotional tones (warmth, friendship, and antipathy), which characterize continuing social contacts.

Animals are obviously restricted to nonverbal means of communication. Ethologists have provided detailed descriptions of the elaborate and elegant systems and structures which have evolved to permit individuals to locate suitable mates and to determine their current receptivity; to establish, delineate, and defend feeding and nesting sites; to signal aggressive or submissive intent; and to respond to their offspring in appropriately parenting ways. The animal that fails to perform in a fashion which is consistent with the group's expectations of social behavior is not admitted as a social partner and may indeed be forced to live a solitary life. A well-known example is that of imprinting in the precocial fowl [28]. The young bird that is not exposed to a member of its species within the first few hours of hatching does not acquire the essential affiliative following response, upon which the full repertoire of social interaction seems to depend. Instead, it may learn to follow the representative of another species, such as humans. Thereafter, for the remainder of the individual's life, it is incapable of social and sexual relationships with its conspecifics because it does not "recognize" the appropriate behavioral patterns displayed by others and fails to display the proper behaviors which together regulate and control the social behaviors of that species.

Neurological Deficit and Nonverbal Behavior in the Monkey

The infrahuman primates are excellent models for the study of communication and social behavior because they have both elaborate and stable patterns of social organization and maintain this social structure exclusively through the exchange of nonverbal behaviors. Field and laboratory studies over the past several decades identified some of the major variables which impact on social organization, and specified the particular behaviors which serve to control aggression, coordinate intragroup cohesion and defense, and promote sexual and maternal behaviors [1, 7]. Furthermore, study of infrahuman primates permits intensive investigation of neurological, pharmacological, and environmental manipulations which could not be attempted in humans.

One of the most significant series of studies was the work of Harlow and associates on the arrest of social development in monkeys deprived of maternal and peer contact during the first months of life [34]. These experiments are so well-known that they need not be detailed here except to point out that the socially deprived infants show normal physical growth, development of adequate neuromuscular coordination, and virtually unimpaired cognitive ability [20]. However, they display a profound and persistent social pathology consisting of hyperaggressive behavior, asexuality, and asociality [19]. Our own studies [31] demonstrated that the social isolate is totally incapable of either sending adequate expressive signals to another monkey or correctly interpreting such social cues from others. Thus though the necessary neuromuscular apparatus is intact, the isolate has not learned when to display the appropriate facial or gestural expression or what to make of the signal behaviors of their normal partners. The Harlow experiments reveal that the social significance of nonverbal behaviors is acquired during the first months of life and suggests that there is a critical period for such learning to take place. There are two important implications of these studies: that learning plays an important role in the appropriate utilization of social expression despite the innate capacity for expression, and that the essential groundwork for interpersonal communication begins early in life when the infant is quite helpless and dependent.

One of the ways that a researcher can alter expressive behavior and thereby social functioning is through the administration of drugs which affect the CNS. We are all familiar with the behavioral changes that occur in people after ingesting too much alcohol: the staggering gait, the loud voice, the annoying decrease in social distancing, and the increase in touching behaviors. Fortunately, these changes are reversible within a few hours and appropriate social expressiveness is restored to within normal limits. There has been a considerable interest in examination of the effects of various psychoactive drugs on social communication and social interaction in primates. The term *social pharmacology* was coined [10] to describe these efforts to determine the effect on the social group process of the administration of a drug to one or more of its members. The literature in this field is large and expanding rapidly. While an exhaustive review is not possible in this chapter, suffice it to say that careful studies have been reported on the social effects of alcohol [6, 8, 10]; delta-9-THC [32, 41, 42]; opiates [9, 10]; stimulants [22, 43]; and neuroleptics [29].

These studies revealed that the psychoactive compounds have significant and differential effects on social interactions and that the influence of the drugs is manifest not only in the treated subject but in the untreated social partners which are faced with unexpected and unpredictable behaviors from the drugged members. A specific study was designed to examine the communication of affect via facial expression in monkeys given small dosages of chlorpromazine, phencyclidine, or amphetamine and to relate expressive deficits with the alterations in social behaviors observed

in the larger social group [33]. Amphetamine, which sharpened and inten-
sified facial expressiveness in the communication experiments, was found to
enhance the prosocial activities within the group and to heighten the social
attractiveness of the treated monkey. Phencyclidine reduced the effectiveness of expression somewhat without diminishing the monkey's ability to
receive social messages from others. It had a devastating effect on social
behavior in the group, with markedly increased levels of aggression and
overall diminished levels of social behavior. The untreated animals were extremely wary of the drugged subject who continually violated the taboo of
looking directly into the eyes of his partners. Chlorpromazine impaired
both the sending and the receiving of nonverbal signals, and in the social
situation the treated subject was simply ignored by the untreated partners
who refused all interactions with the tranquilized monkey. The drug effects
were temporary and all communication and social interaction scores were
restored to normal levels within twenty-four hours.

The social pharmacological studies provide convincing evidence that
even minor and transient disturbances in CNS function may reflect in the
subtle and intricate communication systems upon which social relationships
are dependent. One would anticipate that more intrusive and irreversible
damage to neurological integrity might have even more serious effects on
the individual's ability to form and maintain a position within a social
group. A number of studies have shown that, generally speaking, this is indeed the case.

Perhaps in response to human clinical observations, studies were initiated by Brody and Rosvold [4] on the effects of prefrontal lobotomy on
social performance in the rhesus monkey. Over a period of several months
three monkeys in a group of six were successively subjected to lobotomy,
and after a short period for recovery were reintroduced into the group. It
was found that all the operated monkeys were more active motorically
following lobotomy, that they showed diminished response to the aggressive
threat behaviors of their partners, and that two of the three operatees were
unable to maintain their social dominance status within the group and
showed unusual and inappropriate aggressive behavior toward animals
above them in the dominance hierarchy, thus drawing retaliatory attacks
upon themselves. In a related study Franzen and Myers [15] examined the
social deficits of monkeys subjected to prefrontal lesions at various
developmental ages. Prefrontal lobectomies were performed on infants and
on 1-to-3-year-old juveniles which were members of established social
groups. The operated infants were immediately reattached to their mothers
when reintroduced into their social groups and showed no major social impairments during the four months of postsurgical observation. The lobectomized yearling increased submissive kinds of behaviors and social grooming activities but in most respects was reintegrated into his group and seemed

to function adequately. The 2-year-olds and 3-year-olds were more seriously impaired by lobectomy. They were hyperactive, attracted aggressive attack by comembers, decreased the important affiliative behavior of social grooming, and vocalized less frequently than they had prior to surgery. The 3-year-olds manifested considerable increases of submissiveness. The number of operated subjects was small in this experiment (N = 6) so that the results should be viewed as suggestive rather than conclusive regarding the age effect of cortical damage.

Deets et al. [11] studied the effects on social behavior of bilateral prefrontal lobectomy and bilateral frontal topectomy. The topectomy series included a group operated at age 2 and a second group at age 1. Unfortunately, in this study there were some possible confounds with infant-rearing variables: the lobectomized animals had been reared in partial isolation during the first year of life, the 2-year-old topectomies had had social interaction with peers after the third month of life, and the 1-year-old topectomies were mother- and peer-reared. As Harlow demonstrated, social experiences during the first year of life have a profound effect on subsequent social adjustment [19]. However, in mitigation of the rearing differences, there was an appropriate, similarly reared, unoperated control for each of the frontal animals. In the analysis of data there was no distinction between lobectomy and topectomy; both procedures were lumped under the title *frontal*.

Each experimental and control subject was tested with twelve normal stimulus monkeys of which two were adult males, two adult females, two subadult males, two subadult females, two juvenile males, and two juvenile females. During the test sessions a subject animal was placed into an enclosure with one stimulus animal and behavior was observed and coded over a twenty-minute period. The study results revealed that damage to frontal granular cortex does affect social interaction in systematic ways. The operated animals displayed inappropriate threatening to male stimulus monkeys with reduced frequencies of threat to females. Control subjects showed exactly the opposite behavior; they threatened females more often than males. Frontal animals spent less time in spatial proximity to social partners than did their controls and had high levels of disturbance behaviors during the testing situation as reflected in stereotypy, fear grimacing, and self-aggressing. They were less exploratory of the physical features of the environment than their intact controls. The behavior of stimulus monkeys was also interesting in that they reacted to lesioned animals quite differently than to nonoperated subjects in several respects. They both approached and withdrew from frontals more frequently than with normals, indicating a high frequency of very brief contacts with the operatees. They showed lower levels of sexual behavior toward frontals than controls and they also engaged in less environment and self-manipulatory behavior when paired with frontals, suggesting that they were more wary of the operated animals. These data indicate that damage to frontal areas is not only reflected in behavioral aberrations on the part of the operated subjects, but is detectable and responded to by intact strangers in the social situation. In an interesting companion study from the University of Wisconsin laboratory, a group of monkeys subjected to bilateral frontal lobectomy was compared with a sham-operated group of controls with respect to their social preferences in the Sackett Self-Selection Circus, a device in which the monkey is simultaneously exposed to several social stimuli which he can approach but not contact physically [44]. The results indicated that frontal animals preferred other frontal animals of the opposite sex but showed no consistent choice between frontal and intact animals of the same sex. Similarly, intact monkeys chose other intact monkeys of the opposite sex but, curiously, preferred frontal animals of their own sex. The authors concluded that there were perceptible differences in behavior of frontal and intact monkeys which translated into these social choices and speculated that they might be facial, postural, activity, or auditory cues which were detectable by the animals.

Miller [30] investigated the effect of dorsal lateral lesions of frontal cortex on social behavior in rhesus monkeys. This procedure markedly increased aggression within the social group, both on the part of the operatees and their intact partners. The investigator noted that the frontal animals failed to show appropriate threatening expressions prior to or during an attack, manifesting masklike faces even during aggression. In fact, the decrease in threats with a simultaneous increase in aggressiveness was the major finding in this study. Interestingly, the overall dominance structure of the group and the social grooming pattern were not disturbed by the operations.

Another area of the brain that has been studied vis-a-vis social behavior is the anterior temporal cortex. Franzen and Myers [16] examined the effects of lesions of the prefrontal cortex, the anterior temporal area, the cingulate, and the visual association area. Animals with bilateral damage to the cingulate or visual association area suffered no social impairment postsurgically. They were accepted back into their former social groups immediately and behaved normally in their relationships with other monkeys. Both the prefrontal and the anterior temporal animals, on the other hand, suffered profound and persistent social deficits upon restoration to the social situation. The female operatees with infants showed disinterest in or active rejection of their offspring. The prefrontals diminished both vocal and facial expressive behaviors toward other animals, they were less aggressive and less affiliative than they had been prior to surgery, and they engaged in stereotyped, hyperactive pacing. The anterior temporals were also less expressive vocally and facially postsurgically, they failed to rejoin their former social companions and lost dominance positions within the group, and they were less aggressive. The anterior temporals displayed a curious behavior of approaching and sniffing the head and face of the other animals in the group. The intact animals at first attacked both prefrontal and anterior temporal operatees but this active aggressive behavior decreased over time, and the normals simply withdrew from social relationships with these monkeys which no longer were behaving with appropriate or predictable behavioral responses.

There has also been a considerable amount of experimental investigation on the social effects of amygdalectomy in the infrahuman primate. The most prevalent effect of amygdalectomy is the development of social fear and inability to retain a dominant position in the social hierarchy [38, 45, 46]. Interestingly, intact monkeys seemed to prefer amygdalectomized partners to intact animals as judged by the number of social approaches and invitations to play [45]. The operated monkeys were capable of performing appropriate facial and postural expressions of both fear and aggression but they seemed less sensitive to photographs of affective facial expressions of other monkeys.

The preceding has been only a limited examination of the many experiments which have been conducted on the effects of chemical, electrical, and surgical interventions in the CNS on social relationships of infrahuman primates. However, I hope that it has been sufficient to illustrate the impact of neurological insult on those important social and maternal relationships which are essential in these species, just as they are in humans. The studies were all conducted in laboratory settings where the animals were confined during their confrontation with social partners. Before we leave the animal literature, it will be instructive to consider situations where the damaged subject has the option of interacting with his conspecifics or of leaving the social group entirely.

Myers and his group at the National Institute of Neurological Disease and Stroke Laboratories in San Juan, Puerto Rico, reported a series of studies on the free-ranging monkeys of Cayo Santiago. The animals in this colony live in well-established and stable groups which are free to roam a forty-acre island without significant predation and with adequate human provisioning. Some 700 monkeys, all descended from a group imported in 1938, organized themselves in seven social groups with recognizable structure and territories. Myers captured specific individuals from these groups and subjected them to experimental surgical procedures and then released them in the vicinity of their home group. In their first report, two young adult males were lesioned in amygdala and uncus [13]. They were confined for seven days postsurgically to allow recovery and then were released in the presence of their social group. They failed to rejoin their group but instead attempted to join an alien group. They were savagely attacked by the strangers and driven off into the bush. Although later sighted by the investigators and observed to be severely wounded, they never rejoined a group and actively avoided contacts with other monkeys. One animal was found dead within four days of release (presumably from wounding) and the other lived a solitary life for at least three weeks when he disappeared and was presumed dead. In the second series of operations four males were amygdalectomized without encroachment upon uncus while a fifth was sham-operated as a control. The younger animals (2-to-3-year-olds) ultimately rejoined the social group upon release after a brief period of social isolation and appeared to behave quite normally at the conclusion of the observations. The two older operatees (4-year-old and 9-year-old) failed to rejoin their group and both died within three weeks after release.

In a second experiment three females and two males received bilateral removals of anterior temporal neocortex [35]. Eight animals were trapped and subjected to various control procedures which ranged from simply shaving the head to craniotomies and removal of the pineal. Upon release all control animals quickly rejoined the social group and were accepted without difficulty. None of the temporal animals even attempted to make contact with its group but melted into the underbrush and lived as a solitary animal thereafter. Not a single instance was observed of a temporal animal acting within a social group of monkeys. They were never seen to exhibit aggressive behavior toward other monkeys. The oldest operatees survived longest, only five months.

Finally, Myers, Swett, and Miller [36] examined the effects of prefrontal lesions on the social behaviors of the Cayo Santiago monkeys. Two males and three females were subjected to resection of all prefrontal cortex anterior to the frontal eye fields including the orbitofrontal cortex. Four other animals (two males and two females) received removals of cingulate gyrus and ten others were subjected to various control procedures including craniotomy and pinealectomy. All control subjects rejoined the social group immediately upon release without any difficulty. Similarly, three of the four animals with cingulate lesions were accepted back into the group despite some motor deficit in one subject. The fourth animal with cingulectomy, an adult male, simply passed through the social group and disappeared. He was found dead within three days. Of the prefrontal animals only the youngest, a 1-year-old, rejoined the group even though its mother, also operated, rapidly disappeared to a solitary life. Another female prefrontal with a 10-month-old infant not only left the group but abandoned her offspring which was subsequently cared for by the adult males of the parent group. The prefrontal animals were so reclusive that they were rarely spotted by observers in the field or were their deaths recorded.

These studies provide convincing evidence that neurological damage produces profound and permanent impairment of social capacity when lesions are in specific areas of the neocortex and, further, that these animals forced into leading a solitary life do not survive well in the wild. One could easily imagine that in the truly natural habitat the solitary animal would be especially vulnerable to predation since it would lack the warning and protection afforded by group membership. The field studies offer dramatic proof of the essential importance of social affiliation and the fragility of social competence in the event of neurological damage.

The sequelae of neurological disorder on the social behavior and adjustment in humans are no less devastating than those of other primates. While we may not allow a damaged individual to starve alone in the wilderness, he may perceive that he is not welcome in the social group, that others are uncomfortable around him, and that he is treated differently than are others. In modern Western societies it is not unusual for persons to elect expensive and painful remediation for even simple cosmetic defects such as a small bust or a large nose or a balding pate so that others will more readily accept them into social relationships. How much more difficult it must be for the individual who cannot control his movements and his facial expressions.

Let us consider some kinds of deficit which might be encountered in a neurological practice. Certainly the neurologist is confronted often with the many varieties of bizarre expressiveness which provide crucial data regarding the nature of disorder. Hopefully, he is also sensitive to the trauma in social relationships which may affect the patient and his family as a result of these expressive impairments. The shame and embarrassment of these dysfunctions may produce profound social and emotional consequences quite as important as the direct effects of the disorder itself.

Disorders of Production

In some respects, effector disorders are the most tragic of the neurological nonverbal disorders because the individual may be entirely competent in every other respect (intellectually and emotionally) but incapable of controlling those muscle groups which subserve the subtle nuances of expression. The defects can be of two kinds: overexaggerated movement or lack of movement. An example of exaggerated expressive movement is the extreme and distorted facial, locomotor, and gestural behavior of the individual with cerebral palsy (CP). The palsied person displays nonverbally in dyssynchronous and contorted gestures, frequently with associated speech defects that interfere with the important paralinguistic features of speech—timbre, volume, and phrasing—which convey affective cues to social partners. These expressive flaws burden social interactions in two ways: the delicate shadings of expression are obliterated, and the viewer is constrained by social convention from attending too closely to the face of a palsied partner.

The consequence is social embarrassment for both parties. The palsied individual is subjected to an unusually high level of surreptitious and distance scrutiny but a dearth of eye contact and gaze at social distances. While over time close associates and friends may accommodate to the differences in expression, the palsy victim is likely to continue to suffer socially in business and casual contacts. Social relationships may be more difficult to establish and the patient is likely to have a relatively meager social network.

CP is only one example of the several dyskinesias which may obstruct nonverbal production. Another example of increasing importance is the tardive dyskinesia consequent to phenothiazine treatment. The repetitive and involuntary movements of the mouth, tongue, and jaws are most disconcerting to the normal social partner, and involve an area of the face which is of considerable significance in the nonverbal exchange of smiles, frowns, and the like. Other neurological disorders which elicit overdistorted or distorted production of nonverbal cues are the various choreas, seizure disorders, and spastic diseases.

For many of these diseases there is no effective remediation and the victim must simply learn to live with the problem. Prosthetic devices and physical therapy may enable the individual to establish and maintain a productive and self-sufficient life but the social and interpersonal handicap will persist. It is likely that many of these patients lead comparatively lonely and socially circumscribed lives, acutely aware that their visits to public places such as restaurants and concert halls may elicit discomfort in others. One would predict that these individuals, though otherwise competent, would be especially prone to mental and emotional problems consequent to their social disability.

Several neurological disorders can handicap people in quite a different way: instead of eliciting overproduction and exaggerated responses, these patients are incapable of displaying nonverbal behaviors. In the case of the various paralyses, particularly those involving facial musculature, the normal range of affective expression may be markedly limited so that the requisite expressive cues are absent or damped. A good example of this kind of deficit is the mask of Parkinson's disease. Though the patient may be experiencing the full and rich panoply of emotional response, it fails to register in the shifting pattern of expressive cues observable to social companions. It is clearly unsettling to be engaged in a warm or humorous exchange with a person who shows a blank response to one's initiatives. We have learned to expect smiles and head nods at appropriate points in the conversation, and when they fail to occur, it is disconcerting and jarring. The hemiparalyses of Bell's palsy or of some stroke victims are also obstructive to social communication in that very unusual or grotesque expressions may be emitted as the enervated half of the face responds while the paralyzed half droops expressionlessly.

One would assume that the social effects of paralysis of the expressive musculature may not be as great an impediment to social relationships as the overproductive syndromes. While the viewer senses that something is wrong in the face-to-face exchange with a myasthenia gravis patient, it is nowhere near as intrusive and alarming as the excessive and discoordinated expressions that are sometimes shown by CP victims.

Disorders of Affect

The social consequences of neuromuscular dysfunction occur in individuals who may have perfectly normal capabilities in other respects. They think and feel as keenly as others but cannot produce the visible nuances of behavior which subserve the nonverbal communication function. However, there are other kinds of disorders in which affective expression is entirely intact but the individual suffers from a disease that affects those underlying emotions which are transmitted nonverbally. Subjects who respond inappropriately to environmental situations may display heightened expressions of rage, sadness, or elation which reveal the existence of a serious neurological disorder, for example, Jacksonian seizures, tumors invading the limbic areas, or sequelae of some inflammatory diseases. Overreaction or emotional lability is very alarming to social partners. They neither expect nor welcome episodes of inappropriate weeping or of maudlin affection. Bouts of rage are especially frightening to onlookers who rightfully fear that the individual may do them bodily harm even in the absence of provocation. Patients who consistently manifest excessive and irrational emotional expressiveness may have to be isolated in order to receive psychiatric and medical treatment until the physician is reasonably sure they are not a danger to themselves or to others. These are difficult patients even for the skilled professional to deal with and must be handled with great diplomacy and discretion.

There are, of course, individuals who present the obverse picture: they perform acts of great violence and brutality with no visible signs of affect. They are the most unpredictable and fearful of all because their previous behavior and their present situation do not seem to warrant the extreme behavior which is manifested. These cases are generally seen by the physician only after they have committed some sensational and bizarre act of violence which is quite out of keeping with their reputation as respectable and predictable persons. Even though the press feasts on these lurid cases, they do not represent a very large segment of the neurologically ill and, since they are identified only post hoc, examination generally helps us to understand but not to prevent their crimes against society. One important exception is the case of toxic states which may be induced by phencyclidine,

LSD, alcoholic blackouts, and so on. A program of education and rigorous enforcement of statutes against illegal drugs can preclude some incidents of seemingly random homicide which are occasionally reported to have been perpetrated during hallucinatory or fugue states.

A vital part of the neurological examination is the determination of recent changes in the emotional lability and mood of the patient from reports of the family, close friends, and employer. Atypical irritability, despondency, or euphoria as manifested in disturbed social interactions may be the only premonitory clues that the individual has a serious neurological disorder which demands immediate attention. Affect disorders, whether from neoplasms or infection, will be reflected as subtle changes in the predictability of the patient over time. It is important to pay attention to such changes.

Disorders of Reception

Another kind of impediment to social interaction may occur when a patient is unable to recognize or interpret expressive signals from social partners. In extreme cases the patient may not even be able to recognize faces [3, 12, 27]. As with the other varieties of disorder that we have considered, the recognition deficit can occur in all degrees from the common loss of sensory capability due to aging (hearing loss or visual impairment) to the almost global impairment which may occur with a stroke.

The importance of reception to social functioning is illustrated by the frequent paranoia of the hard-of-hearing. They miss the shadings and content of verbal conversation while they still apprehend the smiles and gazes of companions. It is easy for them to misinterpret the nonverbal cues as indications that others are talking about them and making fun of their infirmities. They miss the point in jokes and sense that they have been the butt of cruel humor. Similar problems affect the visually handicapped who cannot see the smiles and affectionate glances of partners or who fail to detect the expression of annoyance and pique in their fellow workers.

Difficulties of reception impose a burden on social relationships because the critical timing of the exchange may be disturbed and the affective content of the interaction may have to be made more explicit than desired in the verbal productions of partners. Thus, the stroke patient may seem to be childish in his persistent demands for some small personal attention (filing his fingernails) when his wife is pursuing some other task. He fails to see that she is expressing annoyance at the interruption both vocally and facially until she bursts out with some hostile comment that he must just wait until she is finished with what she is doing. The patient is hurt and the wife is both angry and ashamed, all because the husband just could

not pick up the subtle signs that would have indicated an impending out-
burst. It is typical that many of the messages which are exchanged nonverbally are exactly those things that we wish to avoid talking about openly:
messages of love, desire, coldness, or disgust. To take a mundane but important example, we hesitate to tell others about their offensive breath or
personal odors but give them the message via increased social distancing,
head aversion, and expressions of disgust. It is a violation of the social
norm to tell another, even a social intimate, that his presence is offensive in
some very personal way.

Lateralization of Nonverbal Expression
and Recognition

There is a good deal of evidence that the right hemisphere is especially involved in the production and reception of nonverbal communication [39].
Studies of facial recognition clearly demonstrate that patients with right-
hemisphere lesions do particularly poorly on tests of recognition [3, 12,
48]. So while right-hemisphere strokes are spared the aphasias of the left
hemisphere, they still have a difficult time socially because they cannot
receive important nonverbal messages from others.

Buck and Duffy [5] did a study of the facial expressiveness of groups
of aphasic patients, those with right-hemisphere damage, Parkinson's patients, and control subjects with no history of neurological impairment.
Videotapes were made of these subjects while they were viewing a set of
standard pictures which were chosen to evoke different affective expressions. The study results indicated that both the Parkinson's and the right-
hemisphere-damaged groups were deficient in the quality and intensity of
facial expression. The aphasics with left-hemisphere damage were actually
superior to normals in facial expressiveness, a finding interpreted as a possible disinhibition of left-hemisphere influences.

Conclusions

Several implications of neurological disorder and nonverbal behavior
should be of concern to the practicing neurologist. Disturbances of movement and expression are not only important for the differential diagnosis of
a neurological involvement but they also play a major role in the eventual
adjustment of the patient in his community. While it seems patently unfair
that someone who through no fault of his own cannot modulate his expressions in conformity with social demands, it should be recognized that
normal members of society are captives of their early learning and socializa-

tion and find it difficult to overcome their own discomfort and unease with disabled persons. What makes it particularly difficult with the nonverbal behaviors is that they really are a "secret code" in the sense that most individuals, though manifestly following the rules, can neither explicate the rules nor consciously monitor these behaviors. The explicit norm to be helpful and compassionate to the disabled may be contravened by subtle indications of withdrawal and condescension which continually reveal to the patient and his family that he is considered less than an equal. The process of stigmatization which Goffman [18] so cogently described impacts on the patient and his family, souring their human relationships and forcing them into relative isolation. Of course some individuals rise above their disability and perform exceptionally but thousands retreat into their disability and avoid public encounters. For some the disease may even become a crutch to explain away all their other shortcomings so that remediation is actually unwelcome [21].

The neurologist can be helpful to the patient and his family by an understanding and supportive role in difficult times. He should be alert to evidences of emotional disorder as the full social impact of the patient's condition is revealed to the family. He can provide suggestions as to how the disorder might be tempered in public places; for example, it might be expedient to utilize a wheelchair for a palsy patient when traveling to shopping malls or restaurants even though the individual need not use one at home or with close friends. Early arrival and late departure at concerts may minimize unwelcome attention as the patient moves laboriously toward his seat. Practice and deliberate attention to nonverbal cues can help the patient to modulate facial expressions and paralinguistic features of speech. The patient may be supported by new social relationships with other patients who share his kinds of problems, what Goffman calls an association with the "own and the wise."

The task of the neurologist is much more difficult than that of the surgeon, the internist, or the pediatrician. He cannot simply diagnose and attempt to treat a problem but must be concerned with wider aspects of the individual in society. While the hypertensive takes his medication and goes on with his life with his friends and family, the epileptic has trouble getting a job without lying about his condition and always wonders whether others "know about him" or not and what might happen if he has a seizure. The neurologist must be a doctor to the whole person.

References

1. Altmann, S. ed. 1967. *Social communication among primates.* Chicago: Univ. of Chicago Press.

2. Argyle, M., and Cook, M. 1976. *Gaze and mutual gaze.* Cambridge, England: Cambridge Univ. Press.
3. Benton, A., and Van Allen, M. 1968. Impairment in facial recognition in brain-damaged patients. *Cortex* 4:344-358.
4. Brody, E., and Rosvold, H.E. 1952. Influence of prefrontal lobotomy on social interaction in a monkey group. *Psychosom Med* 14:406-415.
5. Buck, R., and Duffy, R. 1979. Nonverbal communication of affect in brain-damaged patients. Prepublication manuscript.
6. Cadell, T., and Cressman, R. 1972. Group social tension as a determinant of alcohol consumption in Macaca mulatta. In *Proceedings of the third congress on experimental medicine and surgery in primates, Lyons, 1972.* Basel: Karger, pp. 250-259.
7. Chevalier-Skolnikoff, S. 1973. Facial expression of emotion in nonhuman primates. In P. Ekman, ed. *Darwin and facial expression: A century of research in review.* New York: Academic Press, pp. 11-89.
8. Cressman, R., and Cadell, T. 1971. Drinking and the social behavior of rhesus monkeys. *Q J Studies Alcohol* 32:764-774.
9. Crowley, T.; Hydinger, M.; Stynes, A.; and Feiger, A. 1975. Motor stimulation and altered social behavior during chronic methadone administration. *Psychopharmacologia* 43:135-144.
10. Crowley, T.; Stynes, A.; Hydinger, M.; and Kaufman, I.C. 1974. Ethanol, methamphetamine, pentobarbital, morphine, and monkey social behavior. *Arch Gen Psychiatry* 31:829-838.
11. Deets, A.; Harlow, H.; Singh, S.; and Blomquist, A. 1970. Effects of bilateral lesions of the frontal granular cortex on the social behavior of rhesus monkeys. *J Comp Physiolog Psychol* 72:452-461.
12. De Renzi, E., and Spinnler, H. 1966. Facial recognition in brain-damaged patients. *Neurology* 16:145-152.
13. Dicks, D.; Myers, R.; and Kling, A. 1969. Uncus and amygdala lesions: Effects on social behavior in the free-ranging rhesus monkey. *Science* 165:69-71.
14. Exline, R. 1971. Visual interaction: The glances of power and preference. In J. Cole, ed. *Nebraska symposium on motivation, 1971.* Lincoln, Neb.: Univ. of Nebraska Press, pp. 163-206.
15. Franzen, E., and Myers, R. 1973. Age effects on social behavior deficits following prefrontal lesions in monkeys. *Brain Res* 54:277-286.
16. Franzen, E., and Myers, R. 1973. Neuronal control of social behavior: Prefrontal and anterior temporal cortex. *Neuropsychologia* 11:141-157.
17. Goffman, E. 1959. *The presentation of self in everyday life.* Garden City, N.Y.: Doubleday and Co.
18. Goffman, E. 1963. *Stigma: Notes on the management of spoiled identity.* Englewood Cliffs, N.J.: Prentice-Hall.

19. Harlow, H.; Rowland, G.; and Griffin, G. 1964. The effect of total social deprivation on the development of monkey behaviors. *Psychiatric research report #19*. Washington, D.C.: American Psychiatric Association.

20. Harlow, H.; Schlitz, K.; and Harlow, M. 1969. Effects of social isolation on the learning performance of rhesus monkeys. In C. Carpenter, ed. *Proceedings of the second international congress of primatology, vol. 1: Behavior*. Basel: Karger, pp. 178-185.

21. Horowitz, M. 1970. *Psychosocial function in epilepsy*. Springfield, Ill.: Charles Thomas.

22. Kjellberg, B., and Randrup, A. 1973. Disruption of social behavior of vervet monkeys (Cercopithecus) by low doses of amphetamines. *Pharmakopsychiatr Neuropsychopharmakol* 6:287-293.

23. Kleck, R. 1966. Emotional arousal in interaction with stigmatized persons. *Psychol Rep* 19:1226.

24. Kleck, R. 1968. Physical stigma and nonverbal cues emitted in face-to-face interaction. *Hum Relations* 21:19-28.

25. Kleck, R.; Buck, P.; Goller, W.; London, R.; Pfeiffer, J.; and Vukcevic, D. 1968. Effect of stigmatizing conditions on the use of personal space. *Psychol Rep* 23:111-118.

26. Kleck, R.; Ono, H.; and Hastorf, A. 1966. The effects of physical deviance upon face-to-face interaction. *Hum Relations* 19:425-436.

27. Levin, H., and Benton, A. 1977. Facial recognition in "pseudoneurological" patients. *J Nerv Ment Dis* 164:135-138.

28. Lorenz, K. 1952. *King solomon's ring*. New York: Crowell-Collier.

29. McKinney, W.; Young, L.; Suomi, S.; and David, J. 1973. Chlorpromazine treatment of disturbed monkeys. *Arch Gen Psychiatry* 29:490-494.

30. Miller, M. 1976. Dorsolateral frontal lobe lesions and behavior in the macaque: Dissociation of threat and aggression. *Physiol Behav* 17:209-213.

31. Miller, R.E.; Caul, W.; and Mirsky, I.A. 1967. Communication of affects between feral and socially isolated monkeys. *J Pers Soc Psychol* 7:231-239.

32. Miller, R.E., and Deets, A. 1976. Delta-9-THC and nonverbal communication in monkeys. *Psychopharmacology* 48:53-58.

33. Miller, R.E.; Levine, J.; and Mirsky, I.A. 1973. Effects of psychoactive drugs on nonverbal communication and group social behavior of monkeys. *J Pers Soc Psychol* 28:396-405.

34. Mitchell, G.; Raymond, E.; Ruppenthal, G.; and Harlow, H. 1966. Long-term effects of total social isolation upon the behavior of rhesus monkeys. *Psychol Rep* 18:567-580.

35. Myers, R., and Swett, C. 1970. Social behavior deficits of free-ranging monkeys after anterior temporal cortex removal: A preliminary report. *Brain Res* 18:551-556.
36. Myers, R.; Swett, C.; and Miller, M. 1973. Loss of social group affinity following prefrontal lesions in free-ranging macaques. *Brain Res* 64:257-269.
37. Richardson, S.; Hastorf, A.; Goodman, N.; and Dornbusch, S. 1961. Cultural uniformity in reaction to physical disabilities. *Am Sociol Rev* 26:241-247.
38. Rosvold, H.E.; Mirsky, A.; and Pribram, K. 1954. Influence of amygdalectomy on social behavior in monkeys. *J Comp Physiol Psychol* 47:173-178.
39. Sackeim, H.; Gur, R.; and Saucy, M. 1978. Emotions are expressed more intensely on the left side of the face. *Science* 202:434-436.
40. Sapir, E. 1927. The status of linguistics as a science. *Language* 5:207-214.
41. Sassenrath, E., and Chapman, L. 1975. Tetrahydrocannabinol-induced manifestations of the "marihuana syndrome" in group-living macaques. *Fed Proc* 34:1660-1670.
42. Sassenrath, E., and Chapman, L. 1976. Primate social behavior as a method of analysis of drug action: Studies with THC in monkeys. *Fed Proc* 35:2238-2244.
43. Schlemmer, R.; Casper, R.; Sieman, F.; Garver, D.; and Davis, J. 1976. Behavioral changes in a juvenile primate social colony with chronic administration of d-amphetamine. *Psychopharmacol Commun* 2:49-59.
44. Suomi, S.; Harlow, H.; and Lewis, J. 1970. Effect of bilateral frontal lobectomy on social preferences of rhesus monkeys. *J Comp Physiol Psychol* 70:448-453.
45. Thompson, C.; Schwartzbaum, J.; and Harlow, H. 1969. Development of social fear after amygdalectomy in infant rhesus monkeys. *Physiol Behav* 4:249-254.
46. Thompson, C., and Towfighi, J. 1976. Social behavior of juvenile rhesus monkeys after amygdalectomy in infancy. *Physiol Behav* 17:831-836.
47. Von Cranach, M., and Vine, I., eds. 1973. *Social communication and movement*. New York: Academic Press.
48. Warrington, E., and James, M. 1957. An experimental investigation of facial recognition in patients with unilateral cerebral lesions. *Cortex* 3:317-326.

Index

Index

About the Contributors

Horacio Fabrega, Jr., M.D., is professor of psychiatry and anthropology at the University of Pittsburgh. He received the M.D. from Columbia University and was trained in psychiatry at Yale University. He was a Research Fellow at the Walter Reed Army Institute and the University of Texas and has been a visiting professor at the University of London, Queen Square.

Gilbert H. Glaser, M.D., Sc.D., is professor and chairman of the Department of Neurology of Yale University School of Medicine. A former president of The American Academy of Neurology, he has contributed more than two hundred scientific articles and three books to the medical literature. He is visiting professor at the Park Hospital for Children, Oxford, England, and has been visiting professor at the Institute of Neurology, National Hospital, Queen Square, London.

Robert E. Miller, Ph.D., is professor of psychiatry (psychology) at the University of Pittsburgh School of Medicine. He received the Ph.D. in psychology from the University of Pittsburgh. He is an authority on nonverbal behavior in man and primates and on the interface of psychiatry, psychology, and movement.

O. Carter Snead III, M.D., is assistant professor of child neurology at the University of Alabama in Birmingham. He received the M.D. from West Virgina University and trained in pediatrics at Duke University. His neurology training was done at Yale University.

Edward M. Stricker, Ph.D., is professor of psychology and biological science at the University of Pittsburgh. He graduated from the University of Chicago and Yale University and has been visiting professor at The Johns Hopkins University School of Medicine. Dr. Stricker has published numerous articles in neural mechanism and the physiology of instinctive behavior.

Michael J. Zigmond, Ph.D., is associate professor of biological sciences and psychology at the University of Pittsburgh. He also is associate director of basic research for the Clinical Research Center for Affective Disorders at the Western Psychiatric Institute and Clinic. Dr. Zigmond received the Ph.D. from the University of Chicago. He has published more than fifty articles and reviews in the scientific literature.

About the Editor

James R. Merikangas, M.D., F.A.C.P., is assistant clinical professor of psychiatry at Yale University School of Medicine and is on the neurology staff of Yale-New Haven Hospital. He is a graduate of The Johns Hopkins University School of Medicine and completed specialty training in both neurology and psychiatry at Yale. He is former chief of electro-encephalography and the Behavioral Neurology Program at the Western Psychiatric Institute and Clinic of the University of Pittsburgh. Dr. Merikangas has published in the areas of EEG, movement disorders, and psychiatry.